The Reconstructed Past

The Reconstructed Past

Reconstructions in the
Public Interpretation of
Archaeology and History

■

Edited by
John H. Jameson Jr.

ALTAMIRA
PRESS

A Division of Rowman & Littlefield Publishers, Inc.
Walnut Creek ■ Lanham ■ New York ■ Oxford

ALTAMIRA PRESS
A Division of Rowman & Littlefield Publishers, Inc.
1630 North Main Street, #367, Walnut Creek, CA 94596
www.altamirapress.com

Rowman & Littlefield Publishers, Inc.
A wholly owned subsidiary of The Rowman & Littlefield Publishing Group, Inc.
4501 Forbes Boulevard, Suite 200, Lanham, MD 20706

PO Box 317, Oxford, OX2 9RU, UK

British Library Cataloguing in Publication Information Available

Library of Congress Cataloging-in-Publication Data

The reconstructed past : reconstructions in the public interpretation of
archaeology and history / edited by John H. Jameson, Jr.
    p. cm.
    Includes bibliographical references and index.
    ISBN 0-7591-0375-5 (cloth : alk. paper)—ISBN 0-7591-0376-3 (pbk. : alk. paper)
    1. Historic sites—Conservation and restoration.   2. Historic sites—Conservation and
restoration—United States.   3. Historic sites—Interpretive programs.   4. Historic sites—
Interpretive programs—United States.   5. Excavations (Archaeology)   6. United
States—Antiquities—Collection and preservation.   7. Historic preservation—United
States.
    I. Jameson, John H.
    CC135.R395   2004
    363.6′9′0973—dc21   2003002645

Printed in the United States of America

♾ ™ The paper used in this publication meets the minimum requirements of American
National Standard for Information Sciences—Permanence of Paper for Printed Library
Materials, ANSI/NISO Z39.48–1992.

The past is such a curious creature,
To look her in the face
A transport may reward us,
or a disgrace.
Unarmed if any meet her,
I charge him, fly!
Her trusty ammunition
might yet reply!

—Emily Dickinson, "The Past."

Contents

PART III. VIRTUAL RECONSTRUCTIONS

PART IV. THE FUTURE OF RECONSTRUCTION

Foreword

Reconstructions have always been the most problematic of the range of physical treatments available to managers of historic sites. Ever popular with the visiting public, they pose a myriad of problems for the historic-site administrator. The best reconstructions evoke a strong sense of the past; the worst evoke a sense of the past that never was. In many instances, without proper on-site explanation, the public is unaware of the difference because buildings are never footnoted in the same way that monographs and articles about the past are. Even the suspecting public has a hard time differentiating between the two, for it takes multiple questions, combined with honest answers and a fair amount of digging, to discern the true relationship between the direct historical evidence and the appearance of the reconstruction. Indeed, all reconstructions look like they represent the past whether they are accurately produced or not. And therein lies the problem: While they claim to represent the past, reconstructions exist on a spectrum that ranges from strong documentary and archaeological evidence to pure fantasy.

The examples in this volume illustrate the variety of reconstructions that exist and the motivations that inspired them. Collectively they serve as markers that permit the inquisitive visitor to discern the relationship to reality represented by a particular reconstruction. The use and avoidance of reconstructions has been evident within the National Park System since it entered the historic preservation field during the early 1930s. With the presence of Colonial Williamsburg looming over the Washington headquarters of the National Park Service (NPS), preservation professionals had to decide early whether the Service would adopt the liberal reconstruction policy of the Rockefeller-inspired vision of Williamsburg or follow a different path. The initial policy statement of the National Park System Advisory Board in 1936 suggested that rather than encouraging the wholesale reconstruction of missing structures, the service should reconstruct only representative structures. Its first venture into the reconstruction business, however, with George Washington's birthplace left a sour taste in the mouths of Director Horace Albright and other agency executives.

The birthplace had been constructed by the Wakefield National Memorial Association in honor of the bicentennial of the president's birth. Based on almost no evidence, the conjectural reconstruction reflected a rectangular brick structure in which the Mount Vernon Ladies' Association believed George surely should have been born. Following the dedication of the house in 1932, the National Park Service almost immediately identified a nearby archaeological site as representing the president's birth site. The good news was that the reconstruction had not been built on the original site thereby saving the archaeological record for future study. The bad news was that the site represented a U-shaped dwelling that was most probably of frame construction. The disparity between the archaeological evidence and the fanciful reconstruction could not have been more striking. Learning early that reconstructions could pose more problems than they solved, the NPS adopted a conservative policy allowing reconstructions only when strict criteria were met.

Over the years, professional discussions about the viability and utility of reconstructions have been lively and have resulted in the development of alternatives to reconstruction in addition to the creation of numerous reconstructions. Notable illustrations of places where the reconstruction opponents carried the day include Franklin Court, where only a stainless steel frame marks the three-dimensional outline of Benjamin Franklin's home in Philadelphia. Fort Bowie in southern Arizona was preserved as a ruin after National Park Service historian, William Brown, argued persuasively that the ruins were far more authentic and compelling than any possible reconstruction. Former chief historian, Robert Utley, argued against the reconstruction of the first Fort Smith in Fort Smith, Arkansas, and the foundations of that structure are all that represent the building today. On the other hand, because of their popularity, proposals for reconstructing buildings generally carry the day as the articles in this volume attest.

Reconstructed buildings do provide a three-dimensional pedagogic environment in which visitors can acquire a heightened sense of the past. But this is true only in those cases where the structure is rebuilt with a minimum of conjecture. Weighing the appearance of the reconstruction against the historical evidence available to guide the reconstruction is no easy task. Yet, until one does that, one cannot judge the educational value of the effort. Does the reconstruction reflect the past or does it merely reflect the aesthetic wishes and biases of the reconstructors? Does the reconstruction look like it did historically, or does it look like the way its proponents wish it had looked in the past? These questions cannot be answered generally. They can only be answered after hard and long examinations of the available evidence, both documentary and archaeological. This book goes a long way in presenting the landscape within which reconstructions exist. The only certainty is that the debates on whether reconstructions aid or interfere with our understanding of history will always be surrounded by complexity and controversy.

Dwight T. Pitcaithley
Chief Historian, National Park Service
January 2003

JOHN H. JAMESON JR. ■

Introduction
Archaeology and Reconstructions

The Reconstructions Dilemma

To reconstruct or not to reconstruct, *that* is the question facing many agencies and site managers worldwide. One of the most controversial topics and challenges in historic site management has rested on this question. In contemplating a particular project, one must ask if the project meets tolerable standards of authenticity, economy, and pragmatism. Where is the line that, when crossed, takes us to unacceptable degrees of conjecture and supposition, to that "slippery path of speculation toward the netherworld of fantasy"? (See chapter 2.) Are we professionally irresponsible and intellectually arrogant in even *contemplating* such efforts? While archaeologists have long pointed out the value of archaeological research in establishing authenticity as a prerequisite to reconstructions and restorations, architects and historians, for the most part, have been slow to recognize this. It is in more recent debates about authenticity that archaeology's role has come to be considered indispensable.

To a modern archaeologist or architectural historian connected to these projects, a potential ethical conflict emerges when on-site reconstructions and restorations contribute to the damage or destruction of the original archaeological record. Another potential ethical issue for archaeologists is that reconstructions can be a catalyst for archaeological investigation and data recovery, giving them jobs. For agencies and site managers, the overriding issues are whether the reconstruction effort is justified in the first place, that is, are we being too speculative and misleading, and has the agency properly evaluated and planned for long-term maintenance costs.

Reconstructions as discussed here consist of measures to preserve any remaining prehistoric or historic materials, features, and spatial relationships, and are based on the accurate duplication of features documented through archaeology and archival research rather than on conjecture or speculation. Depending on the point of reference and experience of the experts involved, reconstructions are sometimes synonymous and functionally overlap with restorations and similar preservation/replication efforts. Predominately in the past, reconstructions have differed from restorations in that they have involved new construction of various components of the cultural landscape.

This volume examines the pros and cons and effectiveness of reconstruction as a public interpretation device and a promotional tool for heritage tourism. The authors present international examples that have been tempered by agency policies, divergent presentation philosophies, and political and economic realities. Many of the articles in this book stem from a 1997 symposium that I organized and chaired for the annual conference of the Society for American Archaeology, in Seattle, Washington.

Perennial Controversy

The reconstruction of historic and archaeological sites and features has long been a contentious subject for many archaeologists and architectural historians in North America. The term "reconstruction" has often carried ambiguous and negative connotations among preservation purists. Many have advocated a strict, conservative approach, emphasizing data and material authenticity. They claim that the public is unnecessarily misled by reconstructions that have not been absolutely verified by archaeological and documentary research. They often find themselves in conflict with a more liberal approach to verification that emphasizes educational and interpretive values.

Despite policies that demand authenticity and thorough documentation, the U.S. National Park Service (NPS), a traditional leader in historic preservation, has sometimes taken an ambivalent stand on using reconstructions as preservation and educational tools (Jameson and Hunt 1999: 35–62). The historical controversy surrounding the concept of reconstruction notwithstanding (see chapter 3), many educational archaeologists, historians, and park interpreters believe that reconstructions that are well planned and do minimal damage to the archaeological resource are useful and justified as public interpretation tools. Reconstructions are important, they say, because they provide a three-dimensional encounter with history to which people can relate and comprehend within their own experience. Reconstructions provide spatial and dimensional reality and intimacy to material culture that cannot be accomplished by storytelling or two-dimensional and small-scale exhibits. The popularity of reconstructions in providing three-dimensional "reality" and scale of physical fabric of historical settings has resulted in a great variety of reconstructions that have simultaneously created interpretive and budgetary challenges to their builders and keepers.

Modern public interpretation programs seek to present a variety of perspectives to multicultural audiences that result in a greater understanding and appreciation of past human behavior and activities. In these settings, archaeologists and interpreters collaborate and use their knowledge and skills to create opportunities for the audience to form intellectual and emotional connections to the meanings and significance of archaeological records and the peoples who created them (NPS 2000a; Jameson 1997: 12–13). As a backdrop to programs and exhibits, reconstructions can facilitate interpretive efforts that seek to form these emotional and intellectual connections. On the negative side, at some sites, there has been a tendency to interpret the reconstructions as "the site" rather than as props. For better or for worse, both the popularity and the controversy of reconstructions will always be with us.

Because contemporary cultural perceptions and norms influence any reconstruction effort, and the complete details about a site can never be recovered, a true replication of the past can never be achieved. However, a number of notable full-scale reconstructions have been carried out internationally for purposes of archaeological experimentation, tourism, and education. An excellent comparative overview of these projects, drawing mostly from European examples, is provided in the 1999 volume *The Constructed Past: Experimental Archaeology, Education and the Public,* edited by Peter Stone and Philippe Planel.

Reconstructions in the United States

The philosophical arguments for and against the practice of reconstructing historical and archaeological sites in the United States are rooted in the early developments of the historic preservation movement. The first wave of preservation sentiment was associated with the rise of public concern in the early and mid-1800s for the preservation of places and sites associated with the American Revolution of 1775–1783. Interest in archaeological conservation per se did not gain impetus until the late 1870s and early 1880s, when reports by the Smithsonian Institution and others raised public awareness of the prehistoric pueblos in the North American Southwest. The public became increasingly alarmed over the widespread looting that was damaging and destroying these magnificent ruins. An increased conservation sentiment at the national level was reflected in the creation, in 1905 and 1916, respectively, of the U.S. Forest Service and the National Park Service. In many instances, these agencies have served as role models for counterpart agencies at the state level. Established within the U.S. Department of the Interior, the NPS was given the mission of preserving "in such manner and by such means as will leave them unimpaired for the enjoyment of future generations" the vanishing natural and cultural heritage sites deemed of national significance. Over the years, as the scope of responsibility of the NPS for preserving and managing cultural sites has evolved and expanded, the role and value of reconstructions as public interpretation tools have been continually debated (see chapter 3; Jameson and Hunt 1999: 35–62).

The opening of Colonial Williamsburg by the Rockefeller Foundation in 1933, coupled with the passage of the Historic Sites Act of 1935, signaled an expanding public interest in historic preservation and enhanced both public and private interest in preserving archaeological sites. At Colonial Williamsburg, a reconstructed historic community of the mid-1770s was based on detailed historical and limited archaeological research. These reconstructions proved to be immensely popular with the public. The reconstruction technique at Colonial Williamsburg involved "re-creating" over four hundred and fifty buildings in an effort to completely restore the town (see chapter 2). This popular, yet conjectural, technique became the standard applied to hundreds of reconstructions in the United States for decades to come. It pervaded and guided the work of the NPS and other federal agencies in scores of New Deal public works projects carried out in the years preceding World War II (see chapter 3; Jameson and Hunt 1999: 38–39).

In the National Park Service, policy statements have historically steered away from reconstruction as a means of interpreting historic sites. However, the actual treatment of historic sites has tended more toward interpretation via reconstruction rather than preservation-in-place.

Reconstructions as interpretive devices were used very early in NPS history. Pipe Spring National Monument, for example, was acquired by the NPS in 1924, with restoration of standing structures and reconstruction of ruins initiated the following year. This was followed in the 1930s with the reconstructions at George Washington Birthplace National Monument and Colonial National Historical Park (see chapter 3; Jameson and Hunt 1999: 41), Morristown National Historic Park in New Jersey, and Ocmulgee National Monument in Georgia (see figure 1; Jameson and Hunt 1999: 45). More conjectural techniques exemplified at Colonial Williamsburg were employed at reconstructions of other eighteenth-century sites such as the fur-trade buildings at Grand Portage National Monument, and a log hospital, earthen fort, and several soldiers' huts at Morristown. A few state-sponsored reconstructions also followed a more conjectural path, such as the eighteenth-century frontier outpost of Fort Loudoun (see chapter 9).

Pre-Columbian Sites

Although much less common than historic period sites, a number of notable attempts at reconstruction and restoration have been made at sites dating before AD 1500. Many of these have been at Southwest pueblo sites and mound sites of the Lower Mississippi Valley and Southeast. Most of the original work at these sites was carried out before 1970 and would not meet the current NPS definition or standards for reconstruction (see chapter 3). In many cases, they are a combination of reconstruction (new materials meant to re-create the appearance of a nonsurviving site or feature) and restoration (re-creation or repair of a surviving site or portion of a site)

Figure 1. 1937 photo of the entrance to the reconstructed prehistoric earthlodge at Ocmulgee National Monument, Georgia. Work was carried out in the 1930s under the Works Progress Administration (WPA) "New Deal" relief program (Fairbanks 1946).

using data from limited archeological work and conjecture. In some cases, where the input and sensitivities of claimant tribal groups are taken into account, the work is more accurately described as preservation-in-place rather than reconstruction or restoration (see chapter 13).

As early as six thousand years ago, when ancient Egyptians were erecting stone pyramids, Native Americans began establishing communities with large arrangements of earthen mounds. The mound building cultural tradition eventually spread into many portions of southeastern North America. Dating from the Mississippian period (ca. A.D. 900–1400), Ocmulgee is an example of one of the few prehistoric mound sites in the NPS and the only one to date with significant attempts at public interpretation. At Ocmulgee, a prehistoric earthlodge was "restored" in 1937 within a concrete and steel protective shell under the direction of an NPS historical architect following careful archaeological excavations and recording (see figures 1, 2, and 3; Fairbanks 1946: 94–108). The earthlodge was a ceremonial earthen structure that stood on the north side of the Mississippian village. It likely served as a meeting place for the town's political and religious leaders. The clay floor is about a thousand years old. Other examples where interpretations have been

Figure 2. 1937 photo of the interior of the reconstructed earthlodge at Ocmulgee National Monument. Note in situ earthen features that have been incorporated into the reconstruction (Fairbanks 1946).

attempted include Cahokia Mounds in Illinois, Moundville in Alabama, Pinson Mounds and Chucalissa in Tennessee, and Etowah Mounds in Georgia (Jameson and Hunt 1999: 44–45).

Prehistoric pueblo sites in the southwestern United States are the architectural remnants of indigenous peoples who occupied stone or adobe community houses in more than eighty villages. Pueblo villages were established in northern and western New Mexico, northeast Arizona, Utah, and Colorado. Also present at many of these sites is archaeological and architectural evidence of earlier (ca. A.D 400–700) pithouses with kivas (underground or partly underground chambers used for ceremonies or councils). The Pueblo cultural tradition, the oldest north of Mexico, continues to be maintained by the present-day Hopi, Zuñi, and Acoma peoples. Aztec Ruins, New Mexico, represents one of the most significant sites affiliated with the Chaco and Mesa Verde Anasazi or Ancestral Pueblo cultures. The monument was established in 1923 and designated a World Heritage Site in 1987. Archaeologist Earl Morris supervised the original total reconstruction in 1934. The Great Kiva at Aztec has recently been restored and re-roofed by NPS. Some of the best-known reconstructions and restorations are at Mesa Verde National Park, Colorado. Established

Figure 3.   Recent photo of the entrance to the reconstructed earthlodge at Ocmulgee National Monument. (Courtesy, National Park Service.)

by Congress on 29 September 1906, Mesa Verde is the first national park set aside to preserve the works of people. UNESCO designated Mesa Verde National Park as a World Heritage Cultural Site in 1978. The pre-Columbian cliff dwellings are the most notable and best preserved in the United States (see figure 4). In 1966, Pithouse C was reconstructed at Step House based on archaeological work at the site from the 1890s, 1920s, and 1960s, and from wood and mud casts observed at other nearby pithouses (see figure 5; Jameson and Hunt 1999: 46–49).

Historic Period Sites

Jamestown, Virginia, site of the first permanent English settlement in North America, is an interesting case in that the overall public presentation covers all aspects of the historical dilemma of whether reconstructions are justified. It is also one of the best examples of public and private interests vying for "a piece of the rock" vis-à-vis one of America's most renowned historic sites. Nearly all of James-town Island containing the original settlement is managed by the National Park Service as part of Colonial National Historical Park.

In the 1930s and 1940s, with the experiences at Colonial Williamsburg (see chapter 2) and other sites such as George Washington's Birthplace (see chapter 3) as backdrops, and following the recommendations of on-site archaeologists such as

Figure 4.   1950s reconstruction of Balcony House cliff dwelling, Mesa Verde
National Park, Colorado. (Courtesy, National Park Service.)

J. C. Harrington, NPS decided that reconstructions at Jamestown were, with minor
exceptions, off limits, with the "preservation purists" winning the day. Beginning
in the 1940s through 1957, the National Park Service did replicate the original brick
foundations of the seventeenth-century settlement above ground to represent and
preserve the archaeological findings beneath them, per the recommendations of Harrington (figure 6). Over time, visitors believed that they were looking at the real
thing (Karen Rehm, personal communication, 2003). Although Colonial National
Historical Park has recently carried out an extensive program of archaeological studies that provides scientific and historical information for interpretive programs and
site protection projects (NPS 2000b), future reconstructions are not planned (Jane
Sundberg, personal communication, 2003).

In the 1950s, for the 350th anniversary of Jamestown, the National Park Service donated land to the Commonwealth of Virginia for the construction of a recre-
ated "James Fort," an Indian village, and full-sized replicas of the original 1607
ships. The Association for the Preservation of Virginia Antiquities (APVA) was
established in the late 1880s to preserve Jamestown as well as other Virginia landmarks. Having received a donation of twenty-two and one-half acres on Jamestown
Island at the site of "Old Towne" in 1893, APVA worked to control the erosional
forces of the James River in addition to preserving the sites of an early church and

Figure 5.   Repair in 1983 of reconstructed pithouse at Step House, Mesa Verde
National Park, Colorado. (Courtesy, National Park Service.)

a series of joined buildings known as the Ludwell Statehouse Group. APVA's extensive archaeological research program in the 1990s, *Jamestown Rediscovery*, resulted
in locating the archaeological remains of the "first fort," other structures, features,
and more than a half million artifacts. As both the NPS and the APVA prepare for
the 400th anniversary of the founding of Jamestown, in 2007, limited reconstruction
is being considered. Presently, however, only segments of the fort have been replicated by APVA. NPS will adhere to its policy of no on-site reconstructions for structures on its portion of the island. Also, in keeping with the 2007 anniversary, NPS
is partnering with the University of Virginia to produce *Virtual Jamestown* that will
include computer-generated models of conjectural reconstructions based on the lat-
est evidence (Karen Rehm, personal communication, 2003).

   For the most part, the triad of management and presentation at Jamestown has
coexisted in relative harmony in a spirit of cooperation and noncompetitiveness.
Thus, through cooperative efforts at federal, state, and private levels, the Jamestown
public presentation, when viewed as a package, satisfies the educational/interpretive
goals of the pro-reconstructionists, while maintaining strict conservation of the original historic fabric.

   In contrast to Jamestown and many other national park areas with limited or
no reconstructions, Fort Vancouver National Historic Site, Washington, is a striking

Figure 6.   Photograph of archaeologist J. C. Harrington during excavations at Jamestown. (Courtesy, National Park Service.)

example of reconstructionist forces winning the day (figures 7 and 8). Fort Vancouver was the administrative headquarters and main supply depot for the Hudson's Bay Company's fur trading operations and the center of political, cultural, and commercial activities in the Pacific Northwest during the first half of the nineteenth century. When American immigrants arrived in what became the Oregon Territory during the 1830s and 1840s, Fort Vancouver provided essential services and supplies to begin the immigrants' new settlements. Armed with thorough documentation of

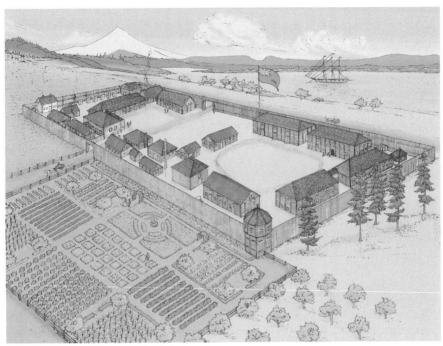

Figure 7. Artist's rendition of 1840s Fort Vancouver, Washington. The National Historic Site is a notable example of a presentation strategy of complete reconstruction of the archaeologically recorded structures.

the architectural and archaeological details of the fort, the NPS has undertaken a program of comprehensive reconstruction. Championed in the 1960s by Congresswoman Julia Butler Hansen, chairman of the House Interior Appropriations Subcommittee, and in response to local sentiments to promote heritage tourism, the NPS has reconstructed the entire stockade, plus many interior buildings such as the bake house, blacksmith shop, an Indian trade shop, and the chief factor's house. Also planned for the future is the restoration of a portion of the employees' village, also known as Kanaka Village, west of the stockade, where the workers of the Hudson's Bay Company and their families lived. All plans for reconstructions and any changes to existing reconstructions are reviewed by the Washington State Historic Preservation Office.

The interpretive staff at Fort Vancouver National Historic Site is currently integrating the input of professional archaeologists, university field schools, and volunteer avocations into the interpretive programs. Improved techniques of archaeological inference are used to explain how decisions are made on the details of the reconstructions. In keeping with modern conservation standards, the program is beginning to push away from complete data recovery prior to reconstruction to

Figure 8. Archaeological test units record the location of a fur store where furs were cleaned and baled for shipment to England. Fort Vancouver National Historic Site, Washington. (Courtesy, National Park Service.)

developing ways to conserve portions of archaeological features that underlie the reconstruction. Also, archaeologists are intensively involved in the site's planning process and work closely with historical architects (NPS 2003).

Since the 1970s, most on-site reconstructions, including Fort Vancouver, have been subjected to higher levels of scrutiny regarding historical and archaeological authenticity and "truth" in public presentations. These projects have required a prerequisite stage of detailed archaeological investigations. Notable examples include Bent's Old Fort National Historic Site (see chapter 12), Ninety-Six National Historic Site in South Carolina (figure 9), Andersonville National Historic Site in Georgia (figure 10; SEAC 2003), Fort Stanwix in New York (figure 11; see chapter 3), and Mission San Luis in Florida (figure 12; Hann and McEwan 1998: 75–81).

Conclusion

In the era of the New Deal of the 1930s, the initial ripples of agency in-house opposition to reconstructions were more than countered by the current of popular and political sentiment resulting from the tremendously popular Colonial Williamsburg.

Figure 9. Detail of reconstructed stockade at Ninety Six National Historic Site, South Carolina. The reconstruction follows the archaeologically recorded 1781 component that was superimposed on an archaeologically recorded 1775 fortification component (Jameson and Hunt 1999: 56–57; photo by John H. Jameson, Jr.).

Throughout the history of the NPS, many opposed to reconstructions in matters of principle have nevertheless given some allowances for coping with the popularity and reality of reconstructions at historic sites and parks. They contend that reconstructed structures need not skew our sense of the past as long as they are presented and understood as one generation's attempt to memorialize the other. Given the historical controversy surrounding the concepts of reconstruction, proponents realize that they must come to terms with the limitations of knowledge obtainable through archaeological and historical research and modern analytical techniques; they know that they can never really know the complete "truth" about a site. Nevertheless, site managers, when deciding to use reconstructions in telling the interpretive story, know they must deliver images and "props" that are both educational and engaging in their effect. These effects should create impressions that enable visitors to make emotional connections to archaeological and historical records that help them to understand and relate to the context, meaning, and significance of the resource.

If we want interpretations that are more effective, we need to reach out to our communication partners—site managers, interpreters, and educators—and arm them with the knowledge and understanding of how archaeology can contribute to people's sense of identity and ultimately improve their lives. In the present-day current of heritage tourism, we can hope that, for the future, only reconstructions that are well thought out and do minimal damage to the archaeological resource will be considered as management and education alternatives.

Figure 10. Reconstructing the archaeologically recorded north gate at Andersonville National Historic Site, Georgia. The reconstructed gate and corners of the prison stockade are important to the public interpretation program because they provide full-scale and realistic imagery and dimensions (Jameson and Hunt 1999: 57–58).

Chapters in This Volume

The chapters in this volume represent an array of philosophies and conceptual approaches, by archaeologists, architectural historians, and site managers, to reconstructions as historic preservation and public interpretation devices. Although most of the contributors would characterize their experiences with reconstructions as positive, we can appreciate that these descriptions are tempered by the realization that authenticity and integrity of information are indispensable ingredients for success and that archaeology plays a vital role.

In chapter 1, Donald Linebaugh describes the pioneering and heroic work of Roland Wells Robbins in carrying the banner in the political and managerial quagmire that surrounded the restoration efforts in the 1940s and 1950s at an important metaphor of Americana: Thoreau's cabin at Walden Pond. Chapter 2, by Marley Brown and Ed Chappell, describes the development of what is arguably the most influential reconstruction and restoration project: Rockefeller's Colonial Williamsburg. Barry Mackintosh explains in chapter 3 how the sites of the National Park Service, despite formal policy statements, were strongly influenced by Colonial Williamsburg and were hardly immune to the politics and controversies that have always

Figure 11. Reconstructed palisades at Fort Stanwix National Monument, New York. (Photo courtesy of Steven Pendery, National Park Service.)

Figure 12. Reconstructed council house and chief's house (background), Mission San Luis de Apalachee State Park, Tallahassee, Florida. (Photo by Seth Johnstone.)

punctuated reconstructions and related restoration efforts. In chapter 4, Esther White gives us a glimpse from Mount Vernon of a common dilemma: How do you know when you have enough evidence to accurately reconstruct a "lost" building, and, at a highly visible site like Mount Vernon, how do you reconcile the sometimes conflicting values surrounding authenticity, evidence, and mission of the museum?

Another group of chapters provides an interesting and imaginative array of case studies relating to experimental archaeology, living history programs, and cultural landscape interpretations. In chapter 5, Harold Mytum describes how Castell Henllys in Wales has succeeded because of its indigenous Celtic associations, where the reconstructions help to bring historic accounts to life and are validated by their location on a real site, fostering national identity through archaeology. In chapter 6, Peter Fowler and Susan Mills describe another experimental, open-air approach at Bede's World near Jarrow in northeast England. Here, the aim has been to provide an interpretive alternative and contrast to those in continental Europe that typically represent the early medieval period with a monastery with its stone-built, plastered walls, richly decorated with stone carvings, paintings on wooden boards, and glass windows. Bede's World involves no on-site reconstructions, but rather a "re-created" open-air landscape illustrating the secular, timber-building tradition of early medieval populations in Britain that was rarely seen in later periods.

Anne Killebrew, in chapter 7, describes the philosophical dilemma surrounding the reconstructions and restorations at the Byzantine village of Qasrin in the central Golan Heights. The lesson learned here is that the archaeologist's most important task in public presentation is to provide data that can be used to illustrate the multivocal and multicultural nature of a shared, rather than a specifically owned, past. In describing the replication efforts at an Iroquoian Longhouse in Ontario, Canada, Ron Williamson in chapter 8 argues that attention to particular details, such as the roofline on a longhouse, is much less important than the preparation of a sound public interpretation program. The replicated structure takes a back seat to the recognition and presentation of the inherent cultural values of such places. Chapter 9, by Joe Distretti and Carl Kuttruff, describes the efforts at the eighteenth-century Fort Loudoun in Tennessee to reconstruct above the waterline of a reservoir as near as possible to the original location of the fort. It is significant that at Fort Loudoun the project archaeologists and historians played a major role in designing and implementing the interpretive program, ensuring a high standard of authentication. In chapter 10, Marion Blockley provides an explanation of the approach to reconstruction/restoration at the World Heritage Site of Ironbridge Gorge, site of some of the earliest activities of the Industrial Revolution.

Four of the chapters focus on what is perhaps the major philosophical dilemma for many reconstruction schemes: whether to expend limited resources on a combined reconstruction, re-creation, restoration effort or to emphasize preservation-in-place. We can see examples of this dilemma playing out in chapter 11 at the mammoth Fortress Louisbourg in Canada, that Bruce Fry describes as a tourist magnet and also "a vast educational tool, evoking some sense of eighteenth-century French colonial lifestyles." Rodd Wheaten in chapter 12 tells how the National Park Service learned some hard lessons and went through some internal soul searching over whether to fully reconstruct, partially reconstruct, or not reconstruct at all at Bent's Old Fort and Fort Union. The questions of what and how to preserve and interpret, and preservation-in-place versus reconstruction are the foci of chapter 13 by Lynn Neal at Homolovi Ruins State Park, Arizona.

Recent advances in computer technology have facilitated an exciting new arena of opportunities for automated, virtual simulations and projections that do not require physical construction. In chapters 14 and 15, we learn about the value and growing potential of computer-generated reconstructions from Karen Brush and Robert Daniels-Dwyer, respectively.

The commentary and conclusions chapter by Vergil Noble points out that, on sites where politics, economics, and educational goals have determined that reconstructions take place, archaeologists who want to have a positive influence in producing accurate educational messages must make a commitment to practice good science, act ethically, and work responsibly with others.

References

APVA (Association for the Preservation of Virginia Antiquities)
  2002   Three Institutions at Jamestown, www.apva.org/tour/three.html [accessed 18 October 2002].

Fairbanks, Charles H.
  1946   The Macon Earth Lodge. *American Antiquity* 12 (2): 94–108.

Hann, John H., and Bonnie G. McEwan
  1998   *The Apalachee Indians of Mission San Luis.* University Press of Florida, Gainesville.

Jameson, John H., Jr.
  1997   Introduction. In *Presenting Archaeology to the Public: Digging for Truths.* AltaMira, Walnut Creek.

Jameson, John H., Jr. and William J. Hunt
  1999   Reconstruction vs. Preservation-in-place in the National Park Service. In *The Constructed Past: Experimental Archaeology, Education and the Public,* ed. Peter G. Stone and Philippe G. Planel, pp. 35–62. Routledge, London.

NPS (National Park Service)
  2000a   *Effective Interpretation of Archeological Resources, The Archeology-Interpretation Shared Competency Course of Study.* Stephen T. Mather Training Center, National Park Service, Harper's Ferry, West Virginia.
  2000b   *Jamestown Archaeological Assessment, 1992–1996.* National Park Service, Colonial National Historical Park, Virginia.

2003   Personal communication, Doug Wilson, Fort Vancouver National Historic Site, Washington.

SEAC (Southeast Archeological Center)
2003   Archeology at Andersonville, www.cr.nps.gov/seac/ [accessed 10 February 2003]. Southeast Archeological Center, National Park Service, Tallahassee, Florida.

Stone, Peter G., and Philippe G. Planel, eds.
1999   *The Constructed Past: Experimental Archaeology, Education and the Public, One World Archaeology 36.* Routledge: London.

PART I

Definitions and History

DONALD W. LINEBAUGH ■

Chapter One

Walden Pond and Beyond
The Restoration Archaeology of Roland Wells Robbins

To reconstruct or not to reconstruct? For Roland Wells Robbins there was never a question. Robbins, a self-educated historical and industrial archaeologist, had a personal stake in restoration and reconstruction archaeology; it was his livelihood. But he also had a philosophical commitment "to make history come alive by digging it up, getting others involved—making something live again in people's imaginations" (Dodson 1985: 116). Rooted in his coming of age during the depression, this philosophy manifested itself in a lifelong commitment to reconstruction and public archaeology. As such, Robbins's projects provide an opportunity to critically examine the many actors in the drama of early reconstruction and restoration projects, and consider issues of internal and external politics, personal convictions, funding pressures, and interpretative differences (Linebaugh 1996). This chapter will explore two of Robbins's reconstruction/restoration projects, the Saugus Iron Works site in Massachusetts, excavated between 1949 and 1953, and the Philipsburg Manor Upper Mills site in New York, excavated between 1956 and 1961.

Roland W. Robbins's career in historical archaeology had its origins in an amalgam of personal experiences and larger social and cultural trends. His family situation, lack of stability in early life, and ordeals during the Great Depression motivated him to seek security and control over his life through hard work and a curiosity about the American past. He probed historical incidents for representations of economic and social stability, literally seeking foundations. Fueled by concerns with rapid growth and industrialization and middle-class anxieties over eastern and southern European immigration, Progressive reformers also pursued the foundations of the country's heritage. The convergent Colonial Revival movement, with its heady blend of nativism, antimodernism, and elitism, likewise represented a longing for stability and roots (Lindgren 1995: 52, 6). The resulting historic preservation movement, engaged in its own search for foundations that increasingly embraced archaeology, championed the protection and preservation of buildings and sites that venerated the American past. Within this framework, Robbins fashioned his career in restoration archaeology as the "pick and shovel historian."

While pursuing his work as a window washer and handyman in and around Concord, Massachusetts, Robbins completed his first research project, an inquiry into the history of Concord's *Minute Man* statue and its sculptor Daniel Chester French (see figure 1.1). Based on the success of this project, he was encouraged by members of the Thoreau Society to locate the exact site of Henry David Thoreau's

Figure 1.1.   Roland and daughter Jean take a break from window washing, October 1942. (Courtesy of the Roland Wells Robbins Collection, the Thoreau Society, Lincoln, MA, and the Thoreau Institute at Walden Woods.)

cabin at Walden Pond. In the fall of 1945, armed with "a pocket compass, a ninety-eight cent G.I trench shovel . . . [and] a couple . . . probing rods," and well aware of the potential that the project held, Robbins began excavation (Robbins 1947: 19). Over the course of the next two years, Robbins located and excavated the cabin's stone chimney foundation, stone corner piers, and root cellar (Linebaugh 1994). The site was eventually commemorated with a monument of stone markers, designed by Boston architect Thomas Mott Shaw, outlining the cabin location, and later by a replica cabin designed by Robbins and based on his archaeological work (figure 1.2). Robbins also sold replica Walden cabin kits and plans during the mid-1960s, noting in the brochure that "if it is your wish to live deliberately to make a place in your life to house your dreams, your privacy, or your own personal life style . . . then the Thoreau-Walden Cabin is your happy answer" (Robbins n.d.). The Walden project resulted in the publication of *Discovery at Walden*, Robbins's lively account of his excavation experiences (Robbins 1947). The book was very well received and along with media coverage of the discovery brought Robbins to the attention of historical societies and house museums across New England.

Building on his discovery at Walden Pond, Robbins was engaged to investigate many important sites that were eventually reconstructed or restored, for instance, the seventeenth-century Saugus Iron Works in Saugus, Massachusetts; the ca. 1627

Figure 1.2. Reconstruction of Thoreau Cabin at Walden Pond, 1989. (Photo by Donald W. Linebaugh.)

John Alden House in Duxbury, Massachusetts; Shadwell—Jefferson's eighteenth-century birthplace—near Charlottesville, Virginia; the seventeenth- to nineteenth-century Philipsburg Manor Upper Mills in North Tarrytown, New York; and the eighteenth-century Hancock-Clarke House in Lexington, Massachusetts. The preservation organizations that managed these sites were increasingly using historical archaeology to reconstruct and restore their properties for public consumption.

Saugus Iron Works

The postwar period, marked by a broadening focus on restoration and reconstruction, was an age of anxiety, "a time when concerns about national security, swift social change, and a profound sense of historical discontinuity troubled people deeply" (Kammen 1991: 537). Historical museums and heritage sites around the country reacted to the growing postwar angst and began to market themselves as sources of patriotic inspiration and keepers of the legends of early America. Many of these organizations sought to educate the public through new research initiatives and revised interpretive displays, while fulfilling their desire to preserve oases of the pastoral, preindustrial past at a time of startling technological and urban change. Other groups "fetishized history," glorifying American exceptionalism and praising technological and industrial progress (Kammen 1991: 538; Wallace 1986b: 150). The Saugus Iron Works reconstruction, for example, was underwritten by the American Iron and Steel Institute as a symbol of the industry's contribution to the past and present growth of the country. In this context, the Saugus project was wedged between the tradition-oriented, antimodern values of the early preservation movement and a burgeoning commercial utilization of the past. This so-called Corporate Roots Movement had its own agenda that was frequently at odds with the goals and desires of preservation professionals (Wallace 1986b: 150). Similarly, the Philipsburg Manor Upper Mills site was funded by John D. Rockefeller, Jr., creating an organization that held to traditional values, and, like many similar institutions, one that subsequently became closely allied with the heritage tourism movement for its survival.

Robbins's excavations at the Saugus Iron Works fit into the restoration tradition typical of most postwar historical archaeology. In a 1975 review of his work, archaeologist Marley Brown (1975: 5) reported that Robbins effectively located and excavated the major industrial components of the Irons Works. His work went beyond the typical levels of restoration archaeology. This is particularly true considering that Robbins lacked any comparative excavation data from other iron works. The project was also multidisciplinary in its structure, drawing, for instance, on the work of a full-time historian, metallurgical experts from the iron industry, and specialists at the Harvard Biological Laboratories and Botany Museum.

Robbins's decisions to excavate at Saugus were based on a dialogue with the documentary evidence and on following features such as the furnace base, anvil bases and hammers, watercourses, and waterwheel pits to determine building locations or activity areas (figure 1.3). Robbins gathered a wide range of documentary sources that "helped him in interpreting his archaeological finds" (Beaudry 1975: n. p.; Robbins 1949: 40, 1950: 40, 1953: 37). He recalled that most of his work at local and regional libraries and research centers was directed at obtaining a "little better idea of what I should look for. . . . I had to learn to identify the iron works buildings, what we should expect to find, what a blast furnace consisted of . . . that sort of thing. I thought that that would be the best information to have if I was going to dig" (Robbins 1948: 4; 1949: 33, 1952: 123). Archaeologist Mary C. Beaudry, who analyzed the use of documentary sources for the project, writes that during the excavations "he did not have the advantage of a full-scale [historical] research report to guide his investigations," or even a complete chain of title for the property (Beaudry 1975: n. p.). "Robbins was able to make fairly accurate statements about the remains he uncovered, based on the small-scale research which he personally conducted," she concluded (Beaudry 1975: n. p.).

Robbins supplemented his documentary research with visits to other iron making sites throughout the New England and mid-Atlantic regions. These opportunities for comparative research were very important in that little descriptive information

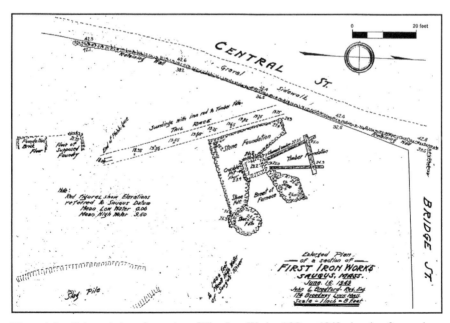

Figure 1.3.   Enlarged plan of a section of First Iron Works, 16 June 1948, showing furnace base and waterwheel tail race. Drawing by John L. Bradford. (Courtesy of the Roland Wells Robbins Collection, the Thoreau Society, Lincoln, MA, and the Thoreau Institute at Walden Woods.)

was available through written sources. The sites that he visited, although often dating to the eighteenth and nineteenth centuries, provided opportunities to visualize the Saugus features because of their extant aboveground ruins (Robbins 1950: 212). Robbins also had the opportunity to study sites and features with historical links to Saugus, such as the furnaces at East Braintree and West Quincy, Massachusetts, where he spent several days probing and testing in an effort to identify common construction features and activity areas.

Robbins excavated by natural strata and utilized very general vertical and horizontal controls within test units and trenches. His plan drawings provide accurate horizontal information on the locations of both features and artifacts. Marley Brown (1975: 3) notes that for plotting features and artifacts, "Robbins resorted to simple triangulation using whatever landmarks were convenient." Robbins carefully recorded field sketches in his notebooks and daily log, while the precise mapping of features, including elevations, was provided by professional surveyors and engineers (Robbins 1949: 25; 1952: 50). He also had a professional photographer record his work with thousands of black-and-white photographs. He personally took thousands of color slides, and shot 16mm movie footage that was eventually used for the production of the "full color" film *The Saugus Ironworks Restoration* (winner of the 1955 Golden Reel Festival's award in history and biography) (Robbins 1949: 24, 31; 1952: 117; First Iron Works Association, Inc. and American Iron and Steel Institute 1955).

Robbins clearly understood soil changes and was able to read this evidence with increasing precision, recognizing fill sequences and features such as structural postholes. He excavated many small trenches and test units to determine the stratigraphy and identify ironwork disturbances and natural soils or subsoils before doing more extensive excavation (Robbins 1950: 113). His field notes for these test units and trenches provide extremely detailed descriptions of the stratigraphy, including soil color, type, and depth, as well as disturbances within the profiles (Robbins 1950: 123, 175, 189). This work assisted in both feature identification and in "restoring the original contours" of the land. Although stone foundations continued to be of primary interest, Robbins identified numerous postholes and intact posts related to iron works buildings (Robbins 1949: 45).

During excavation of trenches, test units, and features, artifacts were recovered primarily by hand sorting. Soil removed from iron works features was also periodically screened for artifacts (Robbins 1949: 28, 35; 1950: 98). Materials such as iron waste, slag, ore, and sands from the casting area were regularly sampled and sent to various metallurgical laboratories for analysis (Robbins 1950: 77, 135, 145, 172). Unusual artifacts thought to be critical for the interpretation of features and iron works buildings, such as the 500-pound forge hammerhead, were piece-plotted through triangulation (Robbins 1950: 138). Robbins was also extremely careful in removing, and precise in recording, large artifacts and features such as the intact waterwheels and wharf sills (Robbins 1951: 69; 1953: 18) (figure 1.4).

Artifacts from the excavation were stored with horizontal and limited vertical

Figure 1.4. Visitors to the Saugus site looking at remains of furnace waterwheel and race-way (Robbins stands in base of wheel pit with remains of original wheel). (Courtesy of the Roland Wells Robbins Collection, the Thoreau Society, Lincoln, MA, and the Thoreau Institute at Walden Woods.)

(feature-related) provenience information. While the artifacts were never systematically analyzed, as typical of many restoration-driven projects during this period, Robbins used the artifacts for feature interpretation and dating. He researched clay tobacco pipes, iron wares and pottery, and also employed the expertise of collectors and professionals, including Smithsonian curator C. Malcolm Watkins (Robbins 1950: 102, 215). Robbins also established an arrangement with Barbara Lawrence and staff at the Harvard Zoological Laboratory to analyze faunal remains (Robbins 1949: 20, 26, 30, 37).

The Saugus site produced thousands of artifacts, and exhibited excellent preservation of metal, wood, and leather. This preservation presented enormous conservation problems that concerned Robbins from the very beginning of the excavations. Robbins contacted several iron conservation specialists, and eventually began a series of experiments with Professor Uhlig of the Massachusetts Institute of Technology (Robbins 1951: 21; 1952: 58; 1953: 38). Even more problematic than metals were wooden artifacts. Robbins voiced his concerns with wood preservation problems in early 1949 and quickly began searching for help with this conservation challenge (Robbins 1949: 28). With the discovery of the waterwheel sections in 1950, he renewed his search for suitable wood treatments, and, in early 1951, Dr. Elso Barghoorn at the Harvard Biological Lab conducted a series of experiments testing possible treatments on samples of iron works wood.

Although Robbins prepared a series of annual reports on his excavations at Saugus, he never wrote his final report on the work because of his abrupt resignation in 1953 (Robbins 1950: 92). The record of his work is thoroughly documented, however, in his detailed daily logs, numerous letter reports on specific features and excavation areas produced for the Reconstruction Committee and architects, and excellent mapping and photographic documentation.

Promoting the Relevance of Archaeology

The restoration goals of the Saugus project clearly drove the overall research, particularly the archaeology. Robbins was responsible for locating and excavating the major iron works structures and restoring the landscape, while the architects were to provide plans for the restoration and supervise the construction (figure 1.5). Brown (1975: 15) suggests that there was "little effective cooperation between the archaeologist, the historian, and the architects." This lack of cooperation was particularly evident between the researchers and the architects, although it is clear that even Robbins and historian E. Neal Hartley did not work as closely as possible. Both Hartley and the Reconstruction Committee often advocated documentary over archaeological evidence, particularly in cases of conflicting data. For instance, Hartley (1957: 176) wrote that "the absence of documentary reference to a second hammer, made the actual use of two hammers [as evidenced by Robbins archaeological data] highly questionable." Brown (1975: 15) noted, "[I]t is obvious that, at least in the case of the refinery forge, archaeological evidence was either entirely ignored or modified in the final design." While this type of situation was not altogether unusual for a restoration-driven project, it concerned Robbins, who strove for thoroughness and accuracy, and it contributed to his eventual resignation.

Robbins was discouraged by what he felt was the architect's lack of interest in and ignorance of the archaeological evidence. Robbins and several other members

Figure 1.5. Saugus furnace during reconstruction, casting bed area under roof to right, June 1952. (Courtesy of the Roland Wells Robbins Collection, the Thoreau Society, Lincoln, MA, and the Thoreau Institute at Walden Woods.)

of the Joint Restoration Committee, including chairman Quincy Bent, were concerned about the quality of architectural work by staff at Perry, Shaw, Hepburn, Kehoe, and Dean. Several years into the project, Robbins recorded that, "[F]or the past 2 years the architects have had the opportunity to study the detail and features of the furnace . . . etc; and yet are confused and ignorant of desirable furnace foundation data . . ." (Robbins 1951: 80).

Later the same year, surveyor John Bradford was asked by architect Harrison Schock to provide his drawings of excavations in the wharf site, but Robbins told Bradford to do "no such thing" (Robbins 1951: 108). Robbins commented, "[M]y experience with Schock proves he has not the ability to understand the details of my business. . . . As such I do not intend to have Schock 'decipher' and interpret something which is still in its preliminary state and very complex" (Robbins 1951: 109).

Robbins was not the only staff member to be irritated by Schock. Joint Restoration Committee chairman Quincy Bent noted, "Mr. Schock's personality leaves much to be desired. He has a rare talent for rubbing people the wrong way, and has clashed on several points with Robbins and Hartley" (Quincy Bent quoted in Harte 1951). In early 1952, Robbins recorded that Schock had not written or phoned to request information since September 1951, adding:

[H]ow can I be refusing him data if he doesn't ask for it. All my work has been with [project manager Conover] Fitch. . . . I have shown the utmost patience with the architects in many respects. . . . Apparently Schock again has his rear in a sling and is going to try and use Robbins as a means of getting out of it (Robbins 1952: 18).

Following a meeting of the Joint Reconstruction Committee in 1952, Robbins reported that both he and Hartley had remained silent about problems with the reconstruction, noting that "this silence was our tribute to Fitch, who is a hellava nice fellow—and not personally responsible for the architects' errors" (Robbins 1952: 23). In mid-1953, committee member and iron works expert Charles R. Harte resigned because of his own frustrations with the reconstruction designs, particularly the forge layout and furnace (Robbins 1953: 77). Problems also existed within the infrastructure of the Joint Reconstruction Committee, particularly the free hand given to chairman Quincy Bent, a retired Bethlehem Steel executive (Carlson 1978: 11). Robbins came into conflict with Bent early in the project, and their disagreements grew as the project evolved.

The First Iron Works Association and the American Iron and Steel Institute's managers pushed Robbins's work and the physical reconstruction as fast as possible (figure 1.6). Funding was not unlimited, and both organizations had their own finite agendas for the finished complex. In large part, these agendas arose out of the

Figure 1.6.   Forge and slitting mill buildings at completed Saugus Iron Works reconstruction, 1989. (Photo by Donald W. Linebaugh.)

increasing use of the past, specifically historic sites, for political and commercial purposes. The application of tradition and nostalgia to marketing, whether for manufacturing, sales, or tourism, grew steadily following World War II. Ties between the past and the present were seen everywhere (figure 1.7).

The American Iron and Steel Institute celebrated the ironwork's legends and traditions and the progress of American industry in the 1955 film, *The Saugus Iron Works Restoration: A Shrine to Pioneers of American Industry* (First Iron Works

Figure 1.7.   Virginia Electric and Power Company ad exploiting the Falling Creek Ironworks site. (Courtesy of Dominion Resources, Inc., Richmond, VA.)

Association, Inc. and American Iron and Steel Institute 1955). The film's message was clear: science and careful research could verify history, and the traditions of the past could successfully be linked to the commercial realities of the present. The past and the present dissolved into one as the movie screen was filled with the image of several colonials sitting in front of the fireplace in the Saugus Ironmaster's House. "Before this very fireplace," the narrator explained, "New England's earliest settlers dreamed of the day that America would meet its own needs for iron" (First Iron Works Association, Inc. and American Iron and Steel Institute 1955).

Cold War Patriotism and Economic Incentives

The Cold War threat of the early 1950s was taken seriously, and the production of materials for the resulting military buildup was extraordinary. The process of selling America's might and strength in the world was in full swing; a link to the past that embraced the tradition of American independence and progress provided an excellent backdrop for this buildup. The use of historic sites and symbols to support democratic beliefs and the war against communism, both in public and private agencies, became quite common (Kammen 1991: 586–87). The themes of progress, patriotism, and national security are echoed throughout the 1955 Saugus film. "The Saugus Ironworks of 1650," the narrator explained, "is a prime example of the industrial pioneering that made America what it is today" (First Iron Works Association, Inc. and American Iron and Steel Institute 1955). "The spirit of Saugus and the skills of Saugus men," he continued, "passed from father to son, from skilled workman to apprentice and helped to win the war of independence" (First Iron Works Association, Inc. and American Iron and Steel Institute 1955). As the film reached the end, the narrator informed the viewer that the ironworks at Saugus is no monument to a dead past, it is a reminder of the great advances which the iron and steel industry has made and will continue to make. Helping to provide the sinews of our national security and the basis for our unmatched standard of living (First Iron Works Association, Inc. and American Iron and Steel Institute 1955).

American industry was actively converting from wartime to civilian production, and progress and technology loomed large in advertising appeals. "The great centers of iron and steel production which serve America today," the narrator explained, "represent the evolution and expansion of the industry from the early days of Saugus. Today, Saugus is not only a shrine but a measure of progress as well" (First Iron Works Association, Inc. and American Iron and Steel Institute 1955).

The messages of a site like Saugus were many, and the potential to use its history and traditions for regional promotion and tourism were also great. "The conversion of historic houses into shrines often had promotional overtones," argues

Wallace (1986a: 175). In 1960, for example, the New York State Joint Legislative Committee on Preservation and Restoration of Historic Sites reported that "tourism has become big business . . . and historic sites more and more are luring the tourist" (Wallace 1986a: 176). Heritage and patriotism became the bywords of travel literature and promotional campaigns run by state and regional economic development committees, and the number of visitors skyrocketed (Wallace 1986a: 176).

According to the author of the 1958 *Yankee Homecoming* tourist guidebook, the primary objective at Saugus was to build as faithful and authentic a reproduction of the original as was humanly possible; the promise of authenticity was important for drawing visitors (Frost 1958: 33). Although Robbins was very proud of his work at Saugus, he was not completely satisfied with the authenticity and accuracy of the finished reconstruction. His experiences at Saugus made him wary of the personalities, power, and influence of outside funding sources and their control of restoration and preservation decisions. Although at times apprehensive of the organizations for which he worked, Robbins did not stop pursuing other similar archaeological projects. To do so would have limited his ability to earn a living at archaeology and would have affected his mission to create tangible reminders of the past. In fact, by the mid-1950s he embraced and encouraged the participation of the commercial world and had formulated his own grand ideas integrating archaeology into popular culture:

> General Mills and similar commercial organizations spend millions annually on the Lone Ranger, Space Cadet, etc. The comic books are turning to stories on American History and Pioneering. And Davy Crockett lives again! I believe that the stuff I uncover can be just as fascinating. The factual material I find may not be good for public consumption, but when it is properly mixed with "legend," it is quite edible. Someday—and I hope that it will be in my day—the commercial organizations will swing to using data based on my kind of work. And when they do they will wonder why they hadn't thought of it earlier! (Robbins 1955)

Although Robbins realized both the educational and economic implications of embracing the past for the general populace, he also personally "thought wistfully about individualism, self-reliance, and other verities associated with the colonial period and the early republic," when faced with "vague though genuinely felt threat[s] to freedom" (Kammen 1991: 537). It was not just the threats of the rapidly changing twentieth-century world that worried Robbins, but the daily personal and economic perils of his chosen career. Robbins did not brood over his anxieties or insecurities—he put them to work with furious determination and energy. At Saugus, he had learned a lot about himself and the evolving worlds of historic preservation and historical and industrial archaeology. Robbins concerns about the quality of the Saugus reconstruction, however, did not stop him from pursuing other similar archaeological projects.

In 1954, he began an excavation project at Shadwell, the birthplace of Thomas Jefferson. Working for the Thomas Jefferson Birthplace Memorial Park Commission, Robbins systematically investigated the site, re-excavating several cellars previously dug by architect Fiske Kimball, and identifying many new features. Although Robbins voiced his concern that adequate information had not been uncovered to support an accurate reconstruction, the commission proceeded to erect a typical period building.

As at Saugus and Shadwell, Robbins continued to labor for preservation organizations that were engaged in developing their properties through historical restoration, reconstruction, or monument building. The often complex and varying goals and objectives of these groups, ranging from educational interpretation to tourism, made planning and implementing the excavations difficult and required Robbins to do far more than excavate. While the smaller and less complicated digs, such as Shadwell and Alden, allowed him to concentrate on the archaeology, the major venture at Philipsburg Manor Upper Mills, like Saugus, required him to wear many hats, and regularly brought him into conflict with museum personnel and their restoration-oriented goals.

Philipsburg Manor Upper Mills

Following his Shadwell project, Robbins advertised his services widely to historical societies, industry, and government agencies, seeking new archaeological challenges. In 1956, he began work at the Philipsburg Manor Upper Mills site in North Tarrytown, New York. At Philipsburg Manor, Robbins was faced with a large seventeenth- to nineteenth-century commercial and industrial site that had been extensively filled and altered during previous restoration activities (figure 1.8). He spent five years removing the previous reconstruction, excavating the original complex of buildings, and observing the administration of a historical site.

John D. Rockefeller, Jr. became involved in the Philipsburg Manor Upper Mills project in 1940, when the Historical Society of the Tarrytowns requested money to turn the Philipse Castle, or Philipsburg Manor house into a "historic shrine" (Kammen 1991: 550). Rockefeller initially donated the money needed to purchase the property, which sat below his Pocantico Hills compound, and to complete repairs to make the house suitable as a headquarters for the society (Hosmer 1981: 70). As the project progressed, Colonial Williamsburg staff members, Edwin Kendrew and Finlay Ferguson, were engaged to record changes made to the house (Hosmer 1981: 70).

The continued lobbying effort of the society's president along with the Colonial Williamsburg architect's report to Rockefeller convinced him to fund a major restoration of Philipse Castle beginning in 1941. Although Colonial Williamsburg's employees provided advice on the project, they were not involved in the day-to-day restoration process. When Colonial Williamsburg staff visited the site in 1942, they were not happy with what they saw, particularly the quality of the archaeology

Figure 1.8.   Log dam cribbing under excavation; Philipse Castle dwelling in background, 1961. (Courtesy of the Roland Wells Robbins Collection, the Thoreau Society, Lincoln, MA, and the Thoreau Institute at Walden Woods.)

(Hosmer 1981: 70). In 1952, the newly formed Sleepy Hollow Restorations (SHR) board brought in several Williamsburg staff members to assist in "increasing the educational merit and significance of these restorations while carrying forward their established traditions" (Dana S. Creel quoted in Kammen 1991: 340). One of their new initiatives, a thorough research program to reevaluate the previous restoration and the site's interpretation, resulted in Robbins's employment as consulting archaeologist (figure 1.9).

Figure 1.9. Dismantling 1940s mill reconstruction at Philipsburg Manor, 1959. (Courtesy of the Roland Wells Robbins Collection, the Thoreau Society, Lincoln, MA, and the Thoreau Institute at Walden Woods.)

Research Methods

Robbins's initial approach to the excavation of the Philipsburg Manor Upper Mills site was one that combined a review of historical research, previous archaeology, and limited field survey. He began his work by reviewing "the early setup by Frederick Philipse and his descendants," particularly the available maps and plats (Robbins 1956: 1). He used plans from the 1940s restoration to identify areas with promising features and those that had been previously disturbed (Robbins 1956: 8). He and the director of research, Robert G. Wheeler, put a great deal of effort into understanding the previous excavation and restoration work (Robbins 1957: 81; 1961: 24). Robbins examined early photos and lithographs of the property to identify the changing physical layout of the mill and manor house complex, and he turned to documentary materials when faced with specific archaeological and interpretive questions (Robbins 1957: 80; 1961: 33; 1959: 48).

A program of historical research was carried out concurrently with the archaeological investigations. The effort, coordinated by Wheeler and a small staff of historians, provided a constant flow of historical documents and information on the configuration of the property (Anonymous 1956). Although it appears that this was shared between Robbins and Wheeler early in the project, the cooperation between the archaeologist and historians apparently deteriorated over time. Five years into the project, Robbins remarked that historian Leo Hershkowitz "was the first historian on the project that had been up to see me and my work" (Robbins 1961: 21). At a later meeting, "Hershkowitz told me that I had done a wonderful job. It made me feel good being in the presence of Wheeler who has never given me a word of appreciation for my work with this Goddam [*sic*] complicated mess" (Robbins 1961: 38).

Although the site was in every sense a "complicated mess," Robbins took a commonsense approach to surveying the property, informed by both the results of the previous archaeological excavations and the ongoing historical research. In contrast to the "shallow" Shadwell and Alden sites, Robbins characterized the Philipsburg Manor Upper Mills project, like Saugus, as a "deep" excavation. In the parlance of academic archaeologists, Robbins was distinguishing between plow zone and deeply buried, stratified sites. He approached each of these site types differently in terms of his excavation methods and became convinced that the "deep" site could only be efficiently approached with the assistance of mechanical equipment. For instance, after establishing the stratigraphic sequences across the site, Robbins had the machine remove the "modern" nineteenth- and twentieth-century soils. He would leave a buffer or interface over the colonial strata or "contact surface" that was then removed by hand troweling and shoveling, and expose features like foundations (Robbins 1962).

His first survey effort at Philipsburg Manor Upper Mills consisted of probe rod testing to relocate several previously identified foundations, and test trenching and "test holes" to identify cultural and natural features, assess the impact of previous archaeology, and establish the stratigraphic sequence (Robbins 1956a: 1–9; 1956b; 1956c; 1956d). This initial three-month survey program was intended to assess the potential for finding significant new information about the early mill and millpond and adjacent manor house, and to establish the value of a complete excavation and restoration of the site (Robbins 1956a: 33).

As he enlarged the excavations in the second and third years, Robbins expanded his system of test trenches, test units, and small "spot checking holes" or shovel tests. He systematically investigated several areas of the property using systematically spaced 2x2-foot test units. This testing method, he said, allowed him to identify foundation or structural features, assess the stratigraphy, and guide his placement and excavation of larger units. Robbins excavated by natural strata and utilized vertical and horizontal controls by laying out a grid system over the entire site and establishing a datum for elevations. Before the fall of 1957, Robbins's survey work consisted primarily of test trenches and units that were recorded in his field notes and plotted on the general plan of the restoration using simple triangulation methods (Robbins 1957: 7, 92). In the fall of 1957, Robbins worked with engineer Hank Fridy to "lay out a master grid" (Robbins 1957: 77). The grid system was used for plotting all features, such as the dock area or later test trenches, and to record individual artifacts (Robbins 1957: 92; 1958: 13, 25, 76; 1960: 67).

Figure 1.10.   Excavation of seventeenth- and eighteenth-century cribbing below original mill, 1960. (Courtesy of the Roland Wells Robbins Collection, the Thoreau Society, Lincoln, MA, and the Thoreau Institute at Walden Woods.)

Robbins identified and recorded these features in plan, as well as in profile. For example, working near the manor house he noted that they had identified "what appeared to be a post mold. . . . The upright was at least 12" thick originally" (Robbins 1960: 64). In addition to his descriptions and drawings, Robbins's photographs of the unit and trench profiles, usually with a stadia rod for scale, provide excellent records of the stratigraphy across the site. In many cases, the individual layers are marked to indicate soil type and description, such as fill, contact surface, or a specific feature. Like Saugus, the work at the Philipsburg Manor Upper Mills project was also meticulously documented with Robbins's color slides and 16-mm film, and project photographer Bill Hennessey's black-and-white photographs.

While the quality of Robbins's vertical information and control over the artifacts is more problematic, he did store them with some level and/or feature data. Although Robbins seemed to confuse the terminology of level and feature, the artifacts were marked and stored with specific horizontal and vertical references that related to the depositional sequences of the site.

The artifacts from Philipsburg Manor Upper Mills were never systematically analyzed as part of Robbins's work, but his staff cataloged the finds and prepared artifact inventories and tables (Robbins 1959: 9; 1960: 40–41, 76, 80). During the excavations, Robbins used artifacts to date the various levels and features, particularly to distinguish between the more modern fills and the seventeenth- and eighteenth-century "contact surfaces" (Robbins 1957: 48). Throughout the fieldwork, he enlisted the help of experts for preliminary identification of the diagnostic artifacts, and had his assistants work on washing and numbering artifacts when no fieldwork was possible (Robbins 1957: 47; 1958: 48–49; 1959: 3, 14; 1960: 20, 52; 1961: 17).

As at Saugus, Robbins also engaged in a range of special studies related to overall site interpretation, including faunal analysis, geo-archaeological work on the peat beds that underlay the pond and their relationship to sea level rise, and tree ring dating. Robbins's use of a faunal analyst to study the bones from several areas on the site is of particular interest, although it was not his first experience with this type of study. Robbins arranged to send the Philipsburg Manor material to Dr. Leon A. Hausman, and over the next several years Hausman provided identification and analysis of faunal remains from several excavation areas on the property (Robbins 1958: 66, 80, 78–85; Hausman 1959). Dr. Hausman also assisted in examination and identification of seed remains removed from several "stratified soils" within the nineteenth-century mill foundation. Robbins also utilized tree ring dating techniques for establishing the original surface contours of the site. He employed tree experts to determine the tree's age, and he used this information to establish the temporal

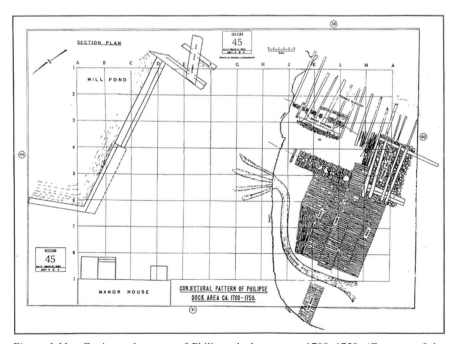

Figure 1.11. Conjectural pattern of Philipse dock area, ca. 1700–1750. (Courtesy of the Roland Wells Robbins Collection, the Thoreau Society, Lincoln, MA, and the Thoreau Institute at Walden Woods.)

position of fill sequences, particularly around the manor house and millpond (Robbins 1958: 33; Fenska 1958). These special studies were important to Robbins, according to his former Philipsburg Manor Upper Mills assistant Susan McKanna (née Colby), because "Robbins wanted people to accept his ideas but understood his limitations, particularly his lack of formal education. He compensated for this through verification with special analysis" (McKanna 1991). Regardless of his motivation for using studies like faunal analysis, they were exceptional in the field of historical archaeology during this period.

Organizational Conflicts

During his five years at Philipsburg Manor Upper Mills, Robbins found himself increasingly at odds with the management of Sleepy Hollow Restorations over the direction of the archaeological investigations. Like his work at Saugus, he quickly discovered that the decision-making process regarding the archaeological work was in the hands of historians and museum professionals who had little experience in or knowledge of the realities of archaeological research. Robbins's dispute with the staff over his vacation was the final skirmish in a conflict that had been brewing for several years.

All went well for the first year or more of fieldwork; however, by the fall of 1958 an incident involving a chapter of Robbins's book *Hidden America* (the first popular volume on historical archaeology) indicated that Robbins's generally positive relationship with the Sleepy Hollow Restorations staff had begun to deteriorate (Robbins and Jones 1959). The board initially insisted that the chapter on the Philipsburg Manor Upper Mills site be removed from the book; however, they eventually compromised and allowed the chapter, but only with complete editorial oversight and final approval of the material on the excavations (Robbins 1958: 45, 67). Upon receiving the edited chapter from the SHR staff, Robbins (1958: 67) exclaimed, "They massacred it! . . . It sounds like a report—and that is what we didn't want it to sound like. They even tried to get Herbie [the backhoe operator] to express himself differently—in academic language! . . . [It] dissolved my friendship with Wheeler."

The chapter was eventually included in the book after several rewrites, but the incident marked a turning point in Robbins's relationship with the SHR staff. He had come to realize that he did not have the freedom over his work that he sought; he was not a coequal professional colleague.

By the end of 1958, Robbins had become familiar with the internal staff tensions and personality problems at SHR. Although he was, by his own admission, no saint, Robbins found that he was increasingly drawn into the internal office politics of the organization. This was particularly disturbing because none of the parties, the board members, director Cater, or research department head Wheeler, had any real

Figure 1.12. Reconstructed mill and dam, restoration of Philipse Castle underway, ca. 1965. (Courtesy of the Roland Wells Robbins Collection, the Thoreau Society, Lincoln, MA, and the Thoreau Institute at Walden Woods.)

appreciation of the demands of his work and its difficulties. Robbins voiced his concerns about the historians' lack of understanding for his work in 1960:

> Bob is never anxious to have us complete anything. He thinks because you know there is something at a certain place, you have all of the answers you need. YET HE WOULD BE THE FIRST TO THROW THE BLAME ON YOU ONCE HE IS TAKEN TO COUNT [*sic*]! . . . I think that in his confusion he has made many promises, which can't be kept, and in his dilemma is cutting many corners to cover him [*sic*] up (Robbins 1960: 81).

Project planning and budgeting was a constant problem for Robbins and the SHR staff due to both the depth and complexity of the features and the lack of communication and understanding between the archaeologist and project sponsors. Try as he might to accurately predict the time and effort involved with various sections of the work, Robbins was frequently surprised by new features, complex stratigraphy, and major weather problems that delayed the excavations (Robbins 1959: 64; 1060: 60, 66, 72, 74–75). These delays, most beyond the control of Robbins or anyone undertaking such a massive project, were a constant source of irritation among Robbins, Wheeler, and the SHR administration.

As the project progressed, another concern of Robbins's was the lack of contact that he had with restoration architects at Perry, Shaw, and Hepburn. After a brief meeting with architects Conover Fitch and Andy Hepburn, Jr., in early 1960, Robbins did not report working with them again until the fall (Robbins 1960: 26). In October 1960, Robbins took Wheeler, Cater, and Andrew Hepburn on a short tour of the excavations. When they returned to the site the next day, however, he was not invited to join them. Although Wheeler told him that they were not "going over details," Robbins was very upset because he perceived that he had been bypassed. He told Wheeler "he [Wheeler] was in no position to explain the details of my work and findings to Hepburn, or to anyone else for that matter" (Robbins 1960: 86). Robbins ended up spending most of the afternoon with Hepburn, who he believed, "wants this job done right—with no short cuts being taken. HURRAH!" It appeared to Robbins that the SHR managers thought that they had all the information they needed about major portions of the log dam and dock sites; however, Hepburn expressed many reservations and posed questions that required additional archaeology before he could "submit any report for restoration" (Robbins 1960: 86–87, 99–100).

During the final year of the project, Robbins's anxiety level increased as pressure mounted to finish the archaeological investigations and begin the restoration (Robbins 1961: 1). Robbins's relationship with Bob Wheeler also continued to disintegrate as the tension increased. For instance, he noted that he was "brought up to date on Bob Wheeler's customary double-talking methods. It's a shame that he is so sick" (Robbins 1961: 15). To Robbins's way of thinking, Wheeler was attempting to wrest control of the archaeological information from him. Wheeler, on the other hand, had been largely responsible for Robbins's position at the restoration and had, in a sense, sponsored him within the organization and community. The relationship between Robbins and Wheeler began with Robbins in the position of expert consulting archaeologist but was later transformed into one in which Robbins was an employee "under Wheeler's department." As their desire to complete the project and finish the restoration grew, the newly organized management team exerted more and more control over Robbins's expanding excavations. Wheeler was increasingly placed in a position of making decisions that directly affected Robbins's work and reduced his autonomy. This was particularly troublesome to Robbins because he knew that Wheeler had little knowledge about archaeological matters.

As the Philipsburg Manor Upper Mills project unfolded, the restoration goals at times stifled Robbins's development of the archaeological research, a situation that ultimately contributed to his early departure. Although the motivations and direction of the restoration staff hindered the needs of the archaeology, the Philipsburg Manor Upper Mills excavations made many positive contributions. Robbins identified the changing layout of the mill complex and manor house over several hundred years, successfully dealt with difficult excavation conditions, experimented with new field techniques and studies, and launched an education program that brought the story and excitement of the work to the public.

Despite Rockefeller's interest and the early "concern for authenticity and substantial attention to public relations," historian Michael Kammen wrote, "Sleepy

Hollow Restorations did not achieve the immediate success that Williamsburg had enjoyed" (Kammen 1991: 550). The archaeology of Philipsburg Manor Upper Mills and conflicts with Roland Robbins were only two of the many concerns of the new staff members, who sought to professionalize the organization, complete the reconstruction project, and attract more visitors. They regularly confronted a range of issues and faced the expectations of both their board of directors and benefactor, John D. Rockefeller, Jr. Archaeological assistant Sue Colby remarked wryly on a Rockefeller visit to the site that "our patron saint, John D., was here on Friday and half of the people here are still cleaning dirt off their foreheads from bending so low—but he seemed to like the place very much and was particularly impressed with the "'dig-it-yourself' pile" (Colby to Ginsburg 1957).

Conclusion

For Robbins, Sue Colby's observation exemplified the social and political circumstances that influenced large-scale multidisciplinary reconstruction and restoration projects. Robbins, an outsider from the beginning, was a keen participant observer of the dynamics of these often multiheaded organizations. He was repeatedly struck by the power of individuals and associations to manipulate and alter restoration projects. Critical theorists point out that this type of personal and organizational politics is detrimental to objective research. In fact, nowhere is this type of influence more damaging than in interdisciplinary projects such as restorations and reconstructions.

The cast of characters that participate in these projects, including the lay public, play out a social and political drama that directly affects the outcome of the project, no matter how professional the group. Is the archaeologist a processualist or post-processualist, humanist or scientist, academician, or CRM consultant? Is the historian from the New Left, social history, or quantitative school? Is the architect an artist or businessman, architectural or art historian? Is the organization private or public, education or entertainment oriented, a profit or nonprofit? How then to cope? The management of interdisciplinary research is no small challenge; however, it can be made easier by a candid appreciation for and understanding of the political and social dynamics of the organization(s) and researchers involved. Good management of these projects also requires a principal investigator who can function as an interdisciplinarian, or, if you will, intellectual ombudsman.

Like practitioners today, Robbins got into conflict and trouble when he tried to do too much, going beyond the original scope of work. Expectations were often unclear on both sides. Historical groups, architects, historians, and administrators were often not aware of what archaeology could actually provide vis-à-vis restoration and reconstruction. Likewise, Robbins was not often privy to the needs and desires of the organizations that employed him. He frequently saw the larger site interpretation as his only goal, and of course he was also influenced by his need to stay employed. Regardless of his relationships with his employers, Robbins always valued the reconstructions at Saugus and Philipsburg Manor because, despite their flaws, they retained the ability "to make history come alive by digging it up, getting others involved, . . . making something live again in people's imaginations" (Dodson 1985: 116). In the final analysis, the restoration archaeology of Roland Robbins and many of his contemporaries can instruct us in understanding the development of past restoration efforts and in crafting new approaches to interdisciplinary restoration and research ventures.

References

Anonymous
   1956   The Philipse Castle Land and Structures. Manuscript prepared by the Research Department, Sleepy Hollow Restorations, Tarrytown, N. Y. The Roland Wells Robbins Collection, the Thoreau Society, Lincoln, MA.

Beaudry, Mary C.
   1975   Archaeology and the Documentary Record. In *An Evaluation of Roland Wells Robbins Archaeology*, edited by Marley R. Brown III, n. p. Saugus Ironworks National Historic Site, Saugus, Mass.

Brown, Marley R., III.
   1975   *An Evaluation of Roland Wells Robbins Archaeology*. Saugus Iron Works National Historic Site, Saugus, Mass.

Carlson, Stephen P.
   1978   *The Saugus Iron Works Restoration: A Tentative History*. Saugus Iron Works National Historic Site, Saugus, Mass.

Colby, Susan
   1957   Correspondence to Carl Ginsberg, October 1957. The Roland Wells Robbins Collection, the Thoreau Society, Lincoln, MA.

Dodson, James
   1985   The Man Who Found Thoreau. *Yankee* 49: 62–65, 116–123.

Fenska, Richard R.
   1958   Letter to Roland W. Robbins, 3 June 1958. Historic Hudson Valley—Archives, Tarrytown, N.Y.

First Iron Works Association, Inc. and American Iron and Steel Institute
   1955   *The Saugus Iron Works Restoration*. 16-mm film. New York, Filmfax Productions.

Frost, Jack [pseudonym?]
   1958   *Yankee Homecoming: Official Sketch Book*. Boston, Yankee Homecoming Council.

Harte, Charles R.
1951   Letter to Roland W. Robbins, 7 August 1951. The Roland Wells Robbins Collection, the Thoreau Society, Lincoln, MA.

Hartley, E. Neal
1957   *Ironworks on the Saugus*. University of Oklahoma Press, Norman.

Hausman, Leon A.
1959   Letter to Roland W. Robbins, 23 January 1959. Historic Hudson Valley—Archives, Tarrytown, N.Y.

Hosmer, Charles B., Jr.
1981   *Preservation Comes of Age: From Williamsburg to the National Trust, 1926–1949*. University Press of Virginia, Charlottesville.

Kammen, Michael
1991   *Mystic Chords of Memory: The Transformation in American Culture*. Alfred A. Knopf, New York.

Lindgren, James M.
1995   *Preserving Historic New England: Preservation, Progressivism, and the Remaking of Memory*. Oxford University Press, New York.

Linebaugh, Donald W.
1994   "The Road to Ruins and Restoration: Roland Wells Robbins and the *Discovery at Walden*." *The Concord Saunterer* 2(1)(Fall 1994):33–64.
1996   The Road to Ruins and Restoration: Roland W. Robbins and the Professionalization of Historical Archaeology. Ph.D. dissertation, American Studies Program, College of William and Mary, Williamsburg, VA.

McKanna (nee Colby), Susan.
1991   Personal communication.

Robbins, Roland Wells
n.d.   The Thoreau-Walden Cabin. Brochure printed by House of Thoreau, Concord, Mass. The Roland Wells Robbins Collection, the Thoreau Society, Lincoln, MA.
1947   *Discovery at Walden*. George R. Barnstead and Son, Stoneham, Mass.
1948–1953   Saugus Ironworks Daily Log, First Iron Works Association, Saugus, Massachusetts." The Roland Wells Robbins Collection, the Thoreau Society, Lincoln, MA.
1955   Letter to Evan Jones, 30 April 1955. The Roland Wells Robbins Collection, the Thoreau Society, Lincoln, MA.
1956a   Daily Log, Philipsburg Manor Upper Mills, Sleepy Hollow Restorations, North Tarrytown, N.Y. The Roland Wells Robbins Collection, the Thoreau Society, Lincoln, MA.
1956b   Bay Trench M3, 10/3/56 to 10/31/56. Field notes. Historic Hudson Valley—Archives, Tarrytown, N.Y.
1956c   2nd Dock Site at Mill (Section thru M3 Trench), 10/5/56. Field notes. Historic Hudson Valley—Archives, Tarrytown, N.Y.
1956d   Bay and River Course Tests (Section-Looking N.W.), 9/13/56. Field notes. Historic Hudson Valley—Archives, Tarrytown, N.Y.

1956e Fieldnotes—Tests near Tree Stump #1, Sheets #1-3, 12/7/56. Historic Hudson Valley—Archives, Tarrytown, N.Y.
1956f River Yard Data on Soil Levels, 12/20/56. Field notes. Historic Hudson Valley—Archives, Tarrytown, N.Y.
1957   Daily Log, Philipsburg Manor Upper Mills, Sleepy Hollow Restorations, North Tarrytown, N. Y. The Roland Wells Robbins Collection, the Thoreau Society, Lincoln, MA.
1958a Daily Log, Philipsburg Manor Upper Mills, Sleepy Hollow Restorations, North Tarrytown, N. Y. The Roland Wells Robbins Collection, the Thoreau Society, Lincoln, MA.
1958b Section 57 Plan Sheet, November 1958, Historic Hudson Valley—Archives, Tarrytown, N.Y.
1959a Daily Log, Philipsburg Manor Upper Mills, Sleepy Hollow Restorations, North Tarrytown, N.Y. The Roland Wells Robbins Collection, the Thoreau Society, Lincoln, MA.
1959b Sections 45 and 51 (Below Utility Lines [M-1-1]), 7/29/59. Field notes. Historic Hudson Valley—Archives, Tarrytown, N.Y.
1960a Daily Log, Philipsburg Manor Upper Mills, Sleepy Hollow Restorations, North Tarrytown, N.Y. The Roland Wells Robbins Collection, the Thoreau Society, Lincoln, MA.
1960b Report of Archaeological Work Conducted for the Sleepy Hollow Restorations During 1959. The Roland Wells Robbins Collection, the Thoreau Society, Lincoln, MA.
1961   Daily Log, Philipsburg Manor Upper Mills, Sleepy Hollow Restorations, North Tarrytown, New York." The Roland Wells Robbins Collection, the Thoreau Society, Lincoln, MA.
1962   Voice of America, Sidney Diamond, moderator, audiotape of 27 June 1962. The Roland Wells Robbins Collection, the Thoreau Society, Lincoln, MA.

Robbins, Roland W., and Evan Jones
1959   *Hidden America*. Alfred A. Knopf, New York.

Robbins, Roland W., and Robert Wheeler
n.d.   Over-All View of 17th Century River-Yard Complex at Philipsburg Manor, Upper Mills. Historic Hudson Valley—Archives, Tarrytown, N.Y.

Robbins, Roland W., and Harvey Zorbaugh
1960   The Empire State. Audio tape of educational television program presented by the Board of Education, Garden City, New York, 24 February 1960. The Roland Wells Robbins Collection, the Thoreau Society, Lincoln, MA.

Wallace, Michael
1986a Reflections on the History of Historic Preservation. In *Presenting the Past: Essays on History and the Public,* edited by Susan Porter Benson, Stephen Brier, and Roy Rosenzweig, pp. 165–202. Temple University Press, Philadelphia.
1986b Visiting the Past: History Museums in the United States. In *Presenting the Past: Essays on History and the Public,* edited by Susan Porter Benson, Stephen Brier, and Roy Rosenzweig, pp. 137–164. Temple University Press, Philadelphia.

MARLEY R. BROWN III AND EDWARD A. CHAPPELL ■

Chapter Two

Archaeological Authenticity and Reconstruction at Colonial Williamsburg

That the ability to reconstruct the past will continue to improve as the "craft" of archaeology matures is widely accepted within the profession, underpinning what is left of the discipline's conservation ethic. This assumption also sustains the "revisionist impulse" at museums like Colonial Williamsburg. The act of "revisionist" reconstruction is a raison d'être for the museum's current archaeological and architectural fieldwork. Recent examples of reconstructions, compared to those from earlier in the organization's history, illustrate the complex relationship between material authenticity, site-specific interpretation, and the larger objectives of educational programming at American historic sites.

In the second edition of his now classic account of the discovery of Wolstenholme Town, retired Colonial Williamsburg archaeologist Ivor Noël Hume articulated what has become a key issue in the debate over site reconstruction based on archaeological evidence—the potential of this interpretive strategy for misleading the public:

> Once we cut boards of undocumented width and secured them with treenails of conjectured sizes, we were sliding down the slippery path of speculation toward the netherworld of fantasy. It is true that few if any restoration or reconstruction projects avoid it, and Williamsburg is certainly no exception. Nevertheless, when presenting a period about whose military domestic architecture we know all too little, the need for integrity is even greater (1991: 336).

Noël Hume's account of his on-site treatment of the discoveries at Martin's Hundred takes great pains to distance the reconstructed wooden "ruins" of Wostenholme Towne, which were intentionally built to resemble a half-built or destroyed shell, from a full-scale, life-size version (figure 2.1). In fact, he had earlier disavowed the idea of any pictorial representation of the discoveries there because, as he

Figure 2.1. The reconstructed wooden "ruins" of Wostenholme Towne. (All figures in chapter 2, courtesy Colonial Williamsburg Foundation.)

had written twelve years earlier (in his first edition of Martin's Hundred), "ideally, reconstructions, be they on the ground or on paper, demand that you know the correct answer to every engineering and architectural question" (1979: 232). But he ultimately relented after acknowledging that archaeologists have an obligation both to keep faith with the past and to inform the public by "putting living flesh back on the bones of history" (op. cit.). In the end, Noël Hume not only endorsed the paintings commissioned by National Geographic, which most certainly left the public with a very detailed idea of what these structures looked like, regardless of their accuracy, but also he created the ruins of the enclosed settlement so that his public could have some understanding of what he had found.

Archaeologists actively engaged in the public interpretation of their research findings are often confronted with the kind of accommodation described by Noël Hume, especially when their work is undertaken for museums located on the actual sites where important historical events took place. Although archaeological sites discovered in these settings could be simply filled in, and their significance communicated through publication, the prospect of reconstruction or some other in situ treatment is commonly considered and the integrity of the archaeologist thereby put at risk. This is especially true when archaeologists work at sites lacking above-ground remains and when these sites are owned or managed by private organizations or public agencies having both stewardship and educational responsibilities. When they are present, upstanding remains or ruins may be sufficiently evocative without

reconstruction, simply needing to be preserved or conserved in a way that differenti-
ates original fabric from restorative material. It was such a site, the temple at Dend-
era, Egypt, that provided inspiration for Noël Hume's "ruins-like" reconstruction of
Wostenholme Towne (1991: 332).

But most North American archaeologists at work on prehistoric and early historic sites located within outdoor museum settings cannot take advantage of above-
ground ruins for their interpretation and for a number of reasons, they find
themselves under increasing pressure to choose full-scale reconstruction. The lack
of visibility of site remains poses an interesting dilemma for those considering
reconstruction as the public education vehicle. Faint building footprints, whether
comprised of post-hole patterns, brick footings, or even root cellar distributions,
present the archaeologist with the opportunity to be very convincing when corrobo-
rative two- and three-dimensional architectural evidence exists, or to be overly speculative and creative when such information cannot be obtained. This spectrum thus
becomes the slippery path to which Noël Hume referred.

This is not the case at other kinds of outdoor museums. Old Sturbridge Village, for example, is presented as an early-nineteenth-century village that never
existed, made up of various buildings brought from elsewhere, a creation much like
many European folk museums (Chappell 1999b). The village that re-creates the life
of the first English settlers of Massachusetts who landed at Plymouth in 1620 is
entirely reconstructed without benefit of direct physical evidence and located several
miles away from where the Pilgrims built their first settlement (Plimoth Plantation
in Plymouth, Massachusetts). Such museums can and do employ the results of
archaeological research, whether it takes place on the sites of the buildings being
moved or at places which might approximate the physical spaces being reconstructed. But as Kenneth Hudson argues in his 1987 book *Museums of Influence*,
there are far fewer open-air museums situated where past historical action occurred,
and none in the world have been so ambitiously developed as what is now known
as the "Historic Area" of Williamsburg, Virginia. Encompassing nearly 175 acres,
Colonial Williamsburg's Historic Area contains over five hundred buildings. Of
these, some eighty-eight contain sufficient early fabric to be considered original.
The remaining buildings have been reconstructed based on both archaeological and
architectural evidence. One of its influences has been, by example, to argue the case
for on-site restoration and reconstruction in favor of the Sturbridge model of assem-
bling parts from here and there.

The scale of what has been built or reworked over the years exceeds the range
of most museums of its kind because of the resources and sustained interest of its
founding benefactor, John D. Rockefeller Jr., and its success in attracting an edu-
cated clientele. As a result, Colonial Williamsburg is an obvious place to explore
the relationship between archaeology and reconstruction. Selected examples from
the history of this project can help clarify the boundaries between the perception of
integrity that prevents archaeologists and their colleagues from having anything to
do with reconstruction and the circumstances that prompt them to traverse that slip-

pery path that leads from the solid ground of reasonable certainty down through speculation to fantasy. At Colonial Williamsburg, the guideposts along this path have increasingly been erected for an explicit pedagogical purpose and philosophy rather than for some measure of certainty regarding the details of past physical environments (Carson 1998; Chappell 1989; 2002).

Reconstruction, Authenticity, and Archaeology

From the very beginning of what was first called the "Williamsburg restoration," there was awareness on the part of both sponsor and hired expertise that integrity should be scrupulously maintained. In 1928, the Advisory Committee of Architects assembled to oversee the project drafted twenty resolutions that were reframed into ten basic principles that came to be known as the Decalogue or the Bible followed by the architects for over half a century of restoration and reconstruction work. The Decalogue and its companion "Principles Underlying Garden Restoration" prepared by the Landscape Architects Advisory Committee in 1929 were recently merged to become "Guidelines for Architectural and Landscape Preservation." Among its chief provisions are:

> that the structures important to the recreation of the historic environment shall be preserved, restored, and/or reconstructed through thorough and intensive scholarly research, with a minimum of conjecture; that where feasible, features of the eighteenth-century urban landscape of Williamsburg, including streets, gardens, topography, greens, fences, and other physical evidence of life in the capital, shall be preserved; and that no structure shall be erected in the Historic Area for which no physical evidence exists, except where research strongly suggests that such a structure might typically have existed on that site in the eighteenth-century and enough evidence exists for an historically-acceptable design.

The above, written in 1990, indicates that the pursuit of veracity—trying to get the picture right—has remained an essential concern for the research staff at Colonial Williamsburg for seventy-five years. These guidelines also imply a different set of criteria for establishing integrity from that followed by Noël Hume in his interpretation of Wostenholme Towne. In fact, a review of the history of the Williamsburg restoration makes it clear that early architectural reconstructions, even when they took advantage of a destroyed building's very footprints, did not require the presence or acquiescence of professional archaeologists. Williamsburg's creators were able to do quite well without the services of what most readers would consider a professional archaeologist until 1957 (Noël Hume 1978: 23–24). From the point of view of the original team of researchers, the absence of a member trained in the then-current techniques of archaeological excavation and recording had no apparent impact on their assessment of how well they were doing.

So perhaps Noël Hume has conceived the range from uncertainty to fantasy somewhat too narrowly, inasmuch as even those reconstructions fully informed by the most sophisticated field archaeology involve, of necessity, some speculation. The amount of speculation, as well as the degree, to which archaeology contributes to the overall design, can vary tremendously depending on the subject, on the nature of the research techniques available, and on the quality of companion source material, whether it be documents or surviving architectural fabric. More important, the act of reconstruction also depends on the epistemological premises and pedagogical aspirations of the participating scholars and upon the ideological perspectives and political motives of the sponsoring organizations, acknowledged or otherwise (Chappell 1989; 2002).

In terms of epistemology, the critical assumption that certain of the vanished buildings and landscapes of Williamsburg can be rediscovered and brought back with some credence has always guided scholars employed at Colonial Williamsburg, and it does so today. No matter what their disciplinary orientation or professional training, the individuals responsible for building and landscape reconstruction at Williamsburg shared in what can be called, to use the current terminology, a "mitigated objectivism" or "guarded objectivity" (Hodder 1999: 23–24; 159–161). The principals of the restoration have always acknowledged in some way that their efforts inevitably reflected their own time, but they have held out for the capacity to discover substantial fragments of past physical reality and create plausible three-dimensional portraits of it. At the same time, every generation of researchers at Colonial Williamsburg has pursued what David Lowenthal called "the rectified past" (1985: 328).

Now, as in the past, Williamsburg's scholars view themselves as better able to document past physical environments and bring them back through restoration and reconstruction than were their predecessors. Recently, the alleged naiveté of this epistemological stance, one described as a progressive "mimetic realism," has brought foundation researchers some partly deserved criticism at the hands of ethnographers of the heritage industry (Gable and Handler 1996; Handler and Gable 1997: 70–71). But in reality, just as they are becoming more aware of the influence of present-day concerns on their work, most archaeologists and architectural historians have gotten better at recognizing critical aspects of the past. Technical advances in both archaeology and architectural history have been accompanied by a reaffirmation within both disciplines that it is, indeed, possible to recover significant "objective" data about past physical conditions, from the character of architectural remains to the structure of the surrounding landscape (Brown 1999; Hodder 1999).

At various stages of reconstruction, those involved in the restoration of Williamsburg have differed in their respective degree of commitment to educational values as well as in their relative appreciation of and reliance on various avenues of research, including archaeology. A compelling case has been made for the fact that the architects who supervised the bulk of restoration and reconstruction until the early 1960s were more concerned about getting it right and making it aesthetically successful than they were about teaching the public (Lounsbury 1990: 373–389;

Chappell 2002). These same men were willing to pursue their projects without input from professional archaeology, in large part because of pragmatic considerations. But as pressure to complete major reconstruction projects waned, archaeology was able to gain a foothold. Only in the last three decades, however, has the clear link between pedagogical purpose and archaeological research been established. As interpretive planning has become more strategic and comprehensive in nature, the specific objectives of excavation have broadened. The stronger the educational motive for undertaking a particular restoration or reconstruction, the greater the potential reliance on archaeological excavation. At the same time, the stronger the educational mandate has been for individual projects, the greater the risk that individual proponents of projects are willing to take—risks of a kind that Noël Hume was unwilling to take in his treatment of Wostenholme Towne.

Commitment to educational objectives or pedagogical principles can lead to reconstructions with less extensive physical evidence, a circumstance anticipated and validated by the aforementioned guidelines. Wording to the effect that buildings can be brought back as long as they are known to have once existed and there is adequate "historically reliable" information upon which to base their design permits the reconstruction of structures needed to complete a more fully representative presentation of eighteenth-century Williamsburg. The fact that there may be only indirect physical evidence upon which to base these reconstructions can be outweighed by the need to include them in order to tell a more broadly truthful story. So, when considering reconstruction as the interpretive vehicle for archaeological discoveries, it goes too far to say that the public educational end always justifies the means, but a clear and uncompromising pedagogical objective can be thoughtfully balanced against the amount of explicit evidence available (Chappell 1999).

In the Beginning: Building the Palace

Although they may not have employed recovery techniques that had long been accepted by the professional archaeologists of the day, the architects who oversaw the first major reconstruction within Williamsburg, the 1706–1781 Governor's Palace (figure 2.2), well understood the value of a carefully exposed building footprint. They also appreciated the potential contribution of artifacts recovered from the dirt to characterize architectural detail, of both a structural and a finish nature. Excavation was undertaken here prior to reconstruction, then, and the resulting evidence proved to be essential to the final design, even though the building's exterior appearance depended primarily on information garnered from other sources. Two Revolutionary-era governors occupied the site after the last royal governor, the Earl of Dunmore, beat a hasty retreat to British gunboats anchored offshore in 1775. Fortunately for the museum, the second of these governors was Thomas Jefferson, an obsessive note-taker and inveterate remodeler, even as British forces threatened the town and

Figure 2.2. Governor's Palace at Colonial Williamsburg.

his own safety. Jefferson sketched a measured plan of the existing Palace, as well as drawing several schemes for changing it—the only plans of the building and its courtyard that survived into the twentieth century. Happily, an earlier three-dimensional view of the Palace also survived, a copper engraving plate probably intended for a now-lost history of Virginia by William Byrd II (Pritchard and Sites 1993).

Excavation thus played a collaborative role in the Palace reconstruction. It provided an explicit horizontal outline for the house, ancillary buildings, courtyard, and garden walls, a framework onto which evidence from Jefferson's plans and the so-called Bodleian Plate could be usefully placed. It also contributed a handful of architectural details, like a collapsed pier showing the variety of first-floor brickwork, remains of stone-paved cellars, and decorative carved marble elements from two Palace mantels. While the modern architects' plans would have suffered tremendously without the elevation information on the Bodleian Plate, the foundations and remains of landscape features provided the most explicit grounding for the arrangement of the site.

Bits and pieces of written evidence were also brought to bear on the re-creation. Of these, the only rich resource was a group of detailed inventories of the building's contents, listed room by room, after the death of Dunmore's predecessor, Lord Botetourt (Hood 1992). The Botetourt inventories provided essential evidence for how the spaces functioned as well as how they were furnished. The 1930s planners used the Botetourt inventories selectively, choosing to represent some of the spaces as Botetourt and his staff used them, and others as the architects and curators imagined they were used by earlier administrations. The inventories were weighed more critically in 1980, when the foundation revised the appearance of the Palace to reflect Botetourt's time there. The site shifted from illustrating eighteenth-century British taste transferred virtually intact to America to a portrayal of late-colonial governance as expressed in the physical accommodations for the last royal governors. Interestingly, a current interpretive focus on Williamsburg in the months before the American Revolution has moved the spoken presentation to Dunmore's occupancy and left the Botetourt scene somewhat bereft. This mismatch of storyline and furnished building underscores the point that reconstruction should not be so fickle as to respond solely to educational initiatives of the moment.

While excavation provided concrete evidence for how the Palace site evolved over three-quarters of the eighteenth century, the crude extraction and analytical methods of the 1920s and 1930s left very limited evidence for precisely how the landscape was transformed and various sections of the estate were used. The process of reconstruction left the archaeological record far less intact than the documentary one, and less accessible to reevaluation and use by later generations of museum planners. Still, a limited excavation inside the Palace cellar in 1994, during installation of a new air-conditioning system, revealed artifactual and archaeobotanical evidence that an important modification in the plan of the governor's residence was accomplished earlier than had been assumed, and was probably planned and executed by the Virginia leadership before the arrival of their generation's best-known designer, Lt. Governor Alexander Spotswood (Smith 1999).

Rediscovering Peyton Randolph's Backyard

Archaeology as a professional discipline has played a more substantial and complex role in the restorations and reconstructions undertaken by Colonial Williamsburg since Ivor Noël Hume's creation of the Department of Archaeology in the early 1960s. Although it took Noël Hume some years to implement fully a stratigraphic approach to excavation, his work at such sites as Anthony Hay's cabinet shop and Henry Wetherburn's tavern was fundamental to the nature of subsequently reconstructed and restored buildings and landscape features. His findings in the yard and around the lost outbuildings of Wetherburn's Tavern make the reconstructed Wetherburn work yard the most compelling yet accomplished by the Foundation. These and other projects set the basic standard for the approach taken to uncovering what remained of Peyton Randolph's elaborate domestic complex two blocks from the Palace (figures 2.3 and 2.4). Governor Francis Nicholson conceived Williamsburg (and Annapolis, which he also designed) as an intensely occupied metropolis, with houses and shops filling the street frontages of relatively narrow lots. Both capitals prospered in the eighteenth century, but they resembled towns more than cities, with

Figure 2.3. Peyton Randolph house and out buildings in 2000.

Figure 2.4. Peyton Randolph's backyard during excavation.

detached buildings lining the streets and smaller ancillary structures trailing behind them.

Rich residents of both towns assembled multiple lots and created townsteads in neighborhoods beyond the commercial and residential cores. One of these Williamsburg citizens was Sir John Randolph, clerk and later speaker of the House of Burgesses, who in 1723 purchased a house and tenements built six years earlier by William Robertson, long-time clerk of the Governor's Council. Randolph created a more substantial service yard, remodeling one of the tenements as a kitchen for his household's use and building a smokehouse and dairy, while leaving some of the other buildings in place (Edwards 1988; Graham 1985).

Sir John Randolph died in 1737, and in little more than a decade his wife Susannah and younger son Peyton extended the old family house and transformed the rear yard, increasing space for domestic work at the expense of moving most, if not all, tenants off the property. They first enlarged the kitchen; then Peyton Randolph demolished most of it to build a new two-story kitchen, laundry, and quarter. He had the big kitchen connected to the house by a covered passage, built additional structures for preparing and storing meat and grain, and added or remodeled two small dairies.

Peyton Randolph's successful political career is well documented, and a probate inventory taken after his death in 1775 is informative about how the property functioned on the eve of the Revolution. But what is known about the evolution of the site comes almost entirely from physical evidence, above and below ground. Indeed, there are no early descriptions or illustrations of the property, and no documentation for dates of construction. The house survives relatively intact, and architectural investigation has provided most of its specific history. Not a single outbuilding remains, and the complex story of how they were built, altered, and lost is the result of crude excavation in 1938 and 1954, and detailed stratigraphic reinvestigation between 1978 and 2000.

Reconstruction of the buildings that existed there late in Peyton Randolph's life is now almost complete. It may be fairly described as the culmination of the Foundation's growing technical ability to combine clues resulting from excavation in the ground and from the careful examination and interpretation of surviving architectural fabric, explicated by intensive study of contemporary work buildings and elite houses in the region. The overriding objective of this project is not to showcase these investigations, interesting as they are to visitors, but to use the various outbuildings, along with the house, to teach about the development of family life— both elite European American and largely enslaved African American—at the end of the colonial era. By re-creating the full spectrum of spaces in which race relations played out on the property, the Foundation can present a more compelling story than it could do with only the owner's house, where the design and use of each room reinforced the owner's perception of status and appropriate deference.

Lively museum programs at Williamsburg and elsewhere have demonstrated that stage sets, old or new, are very useful in developing discourse about life in the past. Perceptions of living conditions are far richer if the settings can be seen, smelled, and felt. Along with the evocative character of surviving and reconstituted landscapes come some dangers, however. Among these is the possibility that some aspects of past conditions will be grossly misrepresented and that the degree of veracity—or authenticity—is overstated. Museums have long erred in emphasizing what they believe is accurate, realistic, authentic, in favor of an honest expression of what's relatively secure and what's largely hypothetical. Explaining the research and design process draws museum-goers into thinking about historical interpretation in favor of absorbing unqualified presentations of how the past is perceived. Archaeology, whether done in the dirt or among the surviving elements of extant buildings, has strong power to engage people in such a deconstructive discourse. The Peyton Randolph project has provided an important opportunity to explain these processes as well as present their results.

Toward Socially Engaged Reconstruction: The Carter's Grove Quarter

Carter's Grove provides a more graphic example of this process. In a survey of Carter's Grove in 1970–1971, archaeologist William Kelso, working under Noël Hume's direction, encountered a series of pits in an area west of the mansion house. At the time, they were interpreted as tanning pits. Some years later, Kelso's discovery of many such pits in a context that could be reliably identified as a slave quarter at nearby Kingsmill plantation, led to a revision of the tanning pit attribution—they became identified as root cellars. After more than a decade, the decision was made to reconstruct slave quarters at Carter's Grove based on the spatial distribution of these pits and the careful survey of slave quarters, both those surviving on the ground and those revealed in subsequent excavation at other Chesapeake plantations (figure 2.5).

The act of revision that led to the "archaeological authentication" of slave quarters in a specific area at Carter's Grove is not terribly problematic, inasmuch as root cellars have since been found on countless slave quarter sites. But the contents of these cellars and their role in interpreting the daily lives of the slaves who resided in the quarters continue to attract controversy and new interpretation. Historical archaeologists are now actively debating the broader implications of such discoveries, notably the ideological implications of the consumer participation model being used by some to account for slave possessions as well as the pits' implications for the changing nature of social relations among slaves (Epperson 1990; Neiman 2000). Many archaeologists would much rather emphasize the processes by which slaves resisted their owners than speak to how they may have selectively imitated their masters' lifestyles. Such issues must be acknowledged in the interpretive process. The point is that archaeology has been fundamental in developing the Carter's

Figure 2.5.   Slave quarter at Carter's Grove.

Grove quarter; it has provided identity for a previously unknown site. The fact that this identity required discoveries at other sites in order to be recognized underscores the invaluable contribution that historical archaeology can provide when it is treated as a cumulative body of knowledge rather than viewed as a unique site-specific source for reconstruction.

   Likewise, details for the reconstruction of houses, gardens, and agricultural buildings were based on archaeological and documentary research and on architectural fieldwork at many comparable sites. Much of the detail is clearly hypothetical. It is intended to raise questions about the nature of material life in the eighteenth-century Chesapeake as well as to offer an array of possible answers. The Carter's Grove pits provided explicit locations for long-lost buildings, and they afforded a dramatic visual contrast between the slaves' houses and the home of their master several hundred yards away. But archaeological investigation did more than provide defensible architectural footprints and plausible choices for furnishing the reconstructions. It began to raise issues about the role of material possessions in an unexpected and controversial part of the American experience.

   Although the case of the Carter's Grove slave quarter is exceptional in one regard—it is the first such reconstruction of precisely its kind—the pedagogical purpose is little different from that which has motivated the reconstruction of Peyton Randolph's outbuildings. Whether in the quarters at Carter's Grove, or the newly reconstructed kitchen spaces behind the Peyton Randolph house, the objective is to expose as many of Williamsburg's nearly million visitors a year to essential interpretive topics like race relations and slavery delivered in what Kenneth Hudson described as "a clear and uncompromising manner." It is such larger educational opportunities that motivate the decision to reconstruct at Colonial Williamsburg, not merely the scholarly and financial ability to accomplish such projects. The temptation to put, in Noël Hume's words, "living flesh back on the bones of history" is always there. But without an overriding educational purpose, Colonial Williamsburg could easily become the consumer-driven historical theme park that many people now mistakenly assume it to be.

The Future of Reconstruction at Colonial Williamsburg

With such strong educational purpose in evidence, the opportunities for archaeologists and their colleagues at Colonial Williamsburg to participate in large-scale reconstruction are likely to continue. The price is generally not small. One development officer at Colonial Williamsburg recently used the term sticker shock to describe donor reaction to the cost of reconstructing the eighteenth-century Peyton Randolph work buildings, because of the extent of specialized labor involved in using preindustrial construction techniques as part of public programs. There is no question that larger and more complex projects, no matter how well justified pedagogically, may be slow to develop, though ultimately they will. During the last five years, Colonial Williamsburg archaeologists and architectural historians have collaborated on two ambitious research projects, one concerned with a mid-eighteenth-century coffeehouse and the other with Williamsburg's third colonial-era theater, known as the Hallam-Douglass Playhouse. These two properties are clearly useful to a full understanding of the public society that emerged in colonial Virginia in the decades leading to the Revolution. On a practical level, their reconstruction would more accurately represent the scale of development on the eastern end of Williamsburg's Historic Area. Nonetheless, the cost of their full reconstruction could defer them as far as another generation.

In the meanwhile, their design and interpretation can take advantage of a very different approach to three-dimensional representation, that of virtual reconstruction using digital imagery. Archaeologists have used computerized graphics even before the personal computer (PC) made an appearance in the early 1980s, but refinements in software in the last few years have made it possible to bring great visual scope and detail to computer renderings of subjects such as buildings and landscapes. Many archaeologists and architectural historians have taken advantage of these advances in their attempts to satisfy public interest in the results of archaeological excavation. Virtual reconstruction, like the National Geographic–sponsored paintings of Wolstenholme Towne, permits a visiting public to conceptualize past physical settings, and, unlike the paintings, they can be readily taken apart and made anew. In this way, they are superior to both traditional artwork and certainly the full-scale reconstruction. Every reconstructed outdoor museum has buildings that the current generation of curators would like to adjust or obliterate. In some situations, as at Plimoth Plantation, every generation seems to get their chance at revision. At others, what was wrought fifty years ago still stands regardless of current perspectives because of the cost of redesign and replacement.

In this regard, Williamsburg occupies a fortunate position. Almost seventy-five years of restorations and reconstructions have resulted in certain buildings and landscapes that, when evaluated from the perspective of modern archaeology and architectural history, would fail many of the criteria that Noël Hume worried about in his conception of a site treatment for Wostenholme Town. Structures, large and small, were erected on foundations that were not fully understood with the aid of stratigraphic analysis. Often, small structures like privies were erected where no foundations were ever present. Gardens were designed despite absence of on-site physical evidence. But Colonial Williamsburg has never ceased the process of research and reconstruction, thereby enabling its staff of archaeologists and architectural historians to improve their skills at documenting the full range of earlier physical environments, from individual structural components and general interior architectural finishes to large landscape arrangements. This improved capability is fact, not ideology. Dendrochronology, phytolith identification, and specialized materials analysis bring greater clarity to site investigations, however fragmentary the remains. But if it were not for the adoption of a serious and well-considered educational philosophy, one noticeably more critical in the past decade, improved reading of the ground and surviving architectural fabric would simply be, to use a term that James Deetz often employed, but so much "sterile methodological virtuosity."

The lesson that Williamsburg's experience has for those who would advocate reconstruction as a major interpretive strategy within public historical archaeology today must come down to this obvious point: Without a commitment to addressing the most consequential issues that historical research can identify, no matter how controversial the issues are, there is little to be gained by the simple act of showing visitors the approximate shape and scale of a building or landscape from the past. Even if the reconstruction is extremely faithful to known evidence, the site can just as easily become a warehouse for high-style English antiques as it can an engaging and informative museum building. Though the antiques are few, the same can be said, of course, for the reconstructed quarters at Carter's Grove. The act of building these structures may have been, at the time, usefully innovative and even daring. But if they are used simply as a place where visitors can absorb an oversimplified or narrow glimpse of how slaves appear to have lived, the intention and effort that contributed to their reconstruction is entirely undermined. Archaeologists must therefore find their integrity not only in the details, which they and their architectural historian colleagues are now extremely adept at discovering. They must find this quality in the relationship between reconstruction (and reconstructions) and the experiences of history that they can engender on the part of the visiting public.

In short, "archaeological authenticity" in the context of architectural reconstructions does not guarantee archaeological integrity. Those critical site visitors who have been to the Martin's Hundred–related exhibits will have seen this point vividly made. There, the normal route taken by the public is through an indoor museum that leads to a tunnel, out of which the ruins of Wostenholme Towne emerge. These ruins are, quite literally, created in the visitor's mind by an artist's image of the burning settlement, shown on a video screen in the museum's last exhibition case. They were reproduced in situ outside the museum, not to maintain an archaeologist's architectural integrity, but to add dramatic emphasis to an already sensationalized account of the 1622 "Massacre," during which essentially innocent English colonists were murdered by their Indian neighbors. Noël Hume's version of these events is propelled through the use of several speculative exhibit-case reconstructions, the most provocative of which is a plastic skull with a metal instrument embedded in the forehead. This combination of objects is fabricated and is based on no spatially related physical evidence found at the site. Yet, Noël Hume did not present the manner of "the Massacre Victim's" death as a challenge to the archaeologist's integrity in the same way he believed that a less than fully accurate architectural reconstruction would be. The implication is that an archaeologist's creative license with manner of death represents a less weighty issue than inferring some details of early-seventeenth-century woodwork.

The adjectives *appalling* and *outrageous* have been used to describe this treatment of the Powhatan Indians in the indoor archaeological reconstructions of Martin's Hundred (Singleton 1993: 527). The relevance of the fixation on the massacre here is the attention it draws to the true context for gauging integrity within archaeology today, the "slippery path" that archaeologists must walk, the one that leads from speculation to "the netherworld of fantasy" in an increasingly consumer-driven public archaeology. This is a public archaeology all too ready to pander rather than enlighten, to titillate through artifactual trivia at the expense of more substantial treatments of complex historical subjects like the seventeenth-century interaction of European settlers and the native peoples of the Chesapeake. How these subjects are handled is an important measure of the success of on-site archaeological interpretation, and, sadly, the pressure to sensationalize archaeological discoveries has never been greater.

Issues surrounding the proper role of storytelling in archaeology are quite topical, as they should be at a time when archaeologists are searching for better ways to communicate with the public. When done thoughtfully, reconstructions can provide a powerful platform for public interpretation, especially at significant historic sites like Carter's Grove. But they must be motivated by appropriately weighty and meaningful educational programs. Since they require fidelity to detail, take time, and cost real money, reconstructions, by their very nature, may well be a most effective means of counteracting the present flirtation with the Barnumesque impulse.

There are diverse media available to those who seek to tell engaging stories based on the discoveries of archaeology. Many of these media are especially vulnerable to the turn toward sensationalism, notably in the popular press and the cable television industry. Fortunately, the lurid details contained in a magazine piece or even an "educational" video shown on cable can soon be forgotten or, better yet, revised by a subsequent production. Reconstructions and the often permanent archaeological exhibits they foster can be much more problematic because of their considerably longer shelf life. One has reason to hope that future reconstructions based on archaeological research at America's historic sites will be guided by well-considered educational objectives and carefully produced interpretive programs as well as by the growing technical expertise of historical archaeologists and architectural historians.

References

Brown, Marley R.
    1999   The Practice of American Historical Archaeology: A Williamsburg Perspective. In *Old and New Worlds*, edited by Geoff Egan and R. L. Michael, pp. 23–32, Oxbow Books, Oxford.

Carson, Cary
    1998   Colonial Williamsburg and the Practice of Interpretive Planning in American History Museums. *Public Historian* 20:11–51.

Chappell, Edward
    1989   Social Responsibility and the American History Museum *Winterthur Portfolio* 24: 247–265.
    1999a   Museums and American Slavery. In *I, Too, Am America: Studies in African American Archaeology*, edited by Theresa Singleton, pp. 240–258, University Press of Virginia, Charlottesville.
    1999b   Open-Air Museums: Architectural History for the Masses. *Journal of the Society of Architectural Historians* 58: 334–341.
    2002   The Museum and the Joy Ride: Williamsburg Landscapes and the Specter of Theme Parks. In *Theme Park Landscapes: Antecedents and Variations*, edited by Terence Young and Robert Riley, pp. 119–156, Dumbarton Oaks, Washington, D.C.

Edwards, Andrew C., Linda K. Derry, and Roy A. Jackson.
    1988   *A View from the Top: Archaeological Investigations of Peyton Randolph's Urban Plantation*. The Colonial Williamsburg Foundation, Williamsburg, Virginia.

Epperson, Terrance W.
    1994   Race and Discipline of the Plantation. *Historical Archaeology* 24(4):29–30.

Gable, Eric, and Richard Handler
    1996   After Authenticity at an American Heritage Site. *American Anthropologist* 98: 568–578.

Graham, William
1985   *Building an Image: An Architectural Report on the Peyton Randolph Site.* The Colonial Williamsburg Foundation, Williamsburg, Virginia.

Handler, Richard, and Eric Gable
1997   *The New History in an Old Museum: Creating the Past at Colonial Williamsburg.* Duke University Press, Durham, N.C.

Hodder, Ian
1999   *The Archaeological Process: An Introduction.* Blackwell, Oxford.

Hood, Graham
1991   *The Governor's Palace in Williamsburg: A Cultural Study.* Colonial Williamsburg Foundation, Williamsburg, Virginia.

Hudson, Charles
1987   *Museums of Influence.* Cambridge University Press, Cambridge.

Lounsbury, Carl R.
1990   Beaux-Arts Ideals and Colonial Reality: The Reconstruction of Williamsburg's Capitol, 1928–1934. *Journal of the Society of Architectural Historians* 49(4):373–389.

Lowenthal, David
1985   *The Past Is a Foreign Country.* Cambridge University Press, Cambridge.

Neiman, Fraser D.
1998   Sub-Floor Pits and Slavery in 18th and Early 19th-century Virginia. Paper presented at the Annual Meeting of the Society for Historical Archaeology, Atlanta, Georgia.

Noël Hume, Ivor
1978   Material Culture with Dirt on It: A Virginia Perspective. In *Material Culture and the Study of American Life,* edited by Ian M. G. Quimby, pp. 22–41, Norton, New York.
1979   *Martin's Hundred.* Alfred Knopf, New York. 1991. *Martin's Hundred,* 2nd ed. University Press of Virginia, Charlottesville.

Pritchard, Margaret B., and Virginia L. Sites
1993   *William Byrd II and His Lost History: Engravings of the Americas.* Colonial Williamsburg Foundation, Williamsburg, Virginia.

Singleton, Theresa A.
1993   Musuem Exhibit Review of Carter's Grove: The Winthrop Rockefeller Archaeology Museum, Wolstenholme Towne, the Slave Quarter, and the Mansion (Colonial Williamsburg). *American Anthropologist* 95(2): 525–528.

Smith, Frederick H.
1993   *Excavations in the Governor's Palace Cellar.* Colonial Williamsburg Foundation, Williamsburg, Virginia.

BARRY MACKINTOSH ■

Chapter Three

National Park Service Reconstruction Policy and Practice

Reconstruction, the replication of vanished historic structures, has been a mixed blessing to National Park Service archaeology and archaeologists. It has employed numerous archaeologists in efforts to expose building foundations and other remains and provide vital evidence of the structures and their contents. At the same time, it has damaged and destroyed archaeological resources and their potential to yield further data as the state of the art advances.

Not only for its archaeological impact, reconstruction has stirred more controversy than any other NPS cultural resource management activity. In no other realm have outside pressures been more keenly felt, nor has practice diverged more obviously from policy. Typically, local community interests, aided by their elected representatives and often abetted by park staff members, have favored reconstruction projects in parks; cultural resource professionals in Washington, citing policies they have forged, have resisted; and management decision-makers have come down on whichever side they think more likely to serve the interests of the public and the NPS.

Antireconstructionists have sometimes gone so far as to claim that reconstruction is none of the service's business. The NPS is a preservation organization, they argue, and reconstruction is not preservation but the creation of new structures simulating old ones. But the NPS is also charged with interpreting the past to the public, and reconstructions—like them or not—are unquestionably means to this end. The Historic Sites Act of 1935, still a fundamental legal authority for cultural resource preservation and interpretation in the parks, expressly authorizes the NPS to "restore, *reconstruct*, rehabilitate, preserve, and maintain historic or prehistoric sites, buildings, objects, and properties of national historical or archaeological significance and where deemed desirable establish and maintain museums in connection therewith" (emphasis added) (U.S. Government Printing Office n.d.).

The Historic Sites Act was intended to sanction and support the greatly expanded historic preservation program on which the NPS had lately embarked. That program was inevitably influenced by Colonial Williamsburg, the nation's foremost preservation project of the time, which embraced reconstruction on a grand scale. At George Washington Birthplace National Monument, which the NPS acquired in 1930, the service completed a rendition of the long-vanished house in which the first president was born. At Colonial National Monument, another 1930 acquisition, the NPS reconstructed key earthworks on the Yorktown battlefield. At Morristown National Historical Park, established in 1933, the Civilian Conservation Corps (CCC) reproduced typical Revolutionary War soldiers' huts. Even before the remains of Hopewell Furnace became a national historic site in 1938, the NPS employed the CCC to reconstruct several features of that Pennsylvania iron-making complex.

Some of these reconstructions, initiated by outside parties or driven by demands for Great Depression relief projects, were less well conceived and executed than they might have been. The Washington's birthplace project, sponsored by a well-connected private association, proceeded with little evidence of the original house and less regard for what evidence existed. The resulting "memorial mansion," as it was euphemistically called, barely resembled the birth house and was soon determined to be on the wrong site. The original house foundations, which archaeologists discovered nearby, fortuitously escaped destruction (Hosmer 1981: 478–493). This and other early reconstruction experiences led NPS officials to take a more cautious stance by the mid-1930s.

At a 1936 meeting of the Advisory Board on National Parks, Historic Sites, Buildings, and Monuments (created by the Historic Sites Act), NPS chief historian Verne E. Chatelain argued for interpretive alternatives to reconstruction at sites lacking physical remains. Reconstruction could entail an unwarranted focus on one time period at the expense of others, he felt: "Certainly if at Jamestown Island we were to attempt to restore the first Jamestown condition, we must neglect a later Jamestown condition, which is just as important historically." He also noted the impact on archaeological remains: "Otherwise intelligent people . . . seem not to see that in taking steps to effect the restoration of certain historic sites, they are making a decision which may mean the destruction of all the record of a certain period of history, irreplaceable in nature for all time to come" (NPS 1936).

Advisory board member Fiske Kimball, a noted architectural historian and restorationist, took a more positive view of reconstruction. Mentioning Jamestown, where only subsurface foundations remained of the early houses, he declared "as far as practical, we should rebuild destroyed buildings on important historic sites. Even the ruins are more interesting, when used in a restoration." Alfred V. Kidder, the archaeologist on the board, posed the alternative of preserving building foundations as ruins and reconstructing the buildings nearby for "museum purposes" (NPS 1936).

A committee including Kimball and Kidder formed to draft an NPS policy on "preservation, repair, restoration, and reconstruction of historical structures." The resulting statement, formally adopted by the NPS in 1937, observed that "the motives governing these activities are several, often conflicting: aesthetic, archaeological and scientific, and educational." Reconstruction prompted by educational motives could mean the destruction of archaeological evidence. "It is well to bear in mind the saying: 'Better preserve than repair, better repair than restore, better restore than construct,'" the statement declared. But it was not dogmatic; because each of the motives had value, "the ultimate guide must be the tact and judgment of the men in charge." Overall, the statement was less restrictive of reconstruction than later partisans quoting only the "better preserve than repair" maxim would have it.

Most NPS preservation professionals remained unenthusiastic about reconstruction, none more so than consulting architect Albert H. Good. His eloquence on the subject in *Park and Recreation Structures*, published by the NPS in 1938, is worth quoting at length:

> The curse of most historical restorations, reconstructions, or re-creations is an almost irresistible urge to gild the lily. Why persons charged with bringing authenticity to something out of the past feel licensed to indulge their personal tastes and fancies in the direction of improving on known historical or structural fact is not understandable, but it is almost always the rule. As an instance, the chimney on a pioneer cabin was typically a strictly practical affair, utilizing no more materials than were needed to encase the flues, and, if it were on the exterior of the cabin, resulted in something probably ungainly and spindling in appearance by today's standards. The current fashionable silhouette in chimneys is something very much more stocky and ample. The result? Present day reconstructions of the pioneer's cabin generally are garnished with chimneys proportioned to the tastes of today, and the gaunt and gawky utilitarian aspect of the frontier type is completely missed. . . .
>
> Whenever it is proposed to restore or reconstruct anything with pretensions to historical value, there should always be on hand a stubborn horse-sensible codger, skeptical enough to ask "Why?" and too smart-headed to mistake mere enthusiasm and sentiment for a right answer. He should be crowned with laurel forthwith, enthroned as chairman of the project, and charged to ask "Why?" at half-hour intervals until the proposal is tabled or the keys to the finished project are turned over to the Park Authority. . . .
>
> Chairman Smart knows that misguided efforts in so-called restoration have forever lost to us much that was authentic, if crumbling. He is aware that the faint shadow of the genuine often makes more intelligent appeal to the imagination than the crass and visionary replica. He recognizes that for a group to materialize largely out of thin air its arbitrary conception of what is fitting and proper is to trespass the right and privilege of the individual to re-create vanished or near-vanished things within his own imagination (NPS 1938).

The most notable reconstruction controversy of the late 1930s involved the McLean house at Appomattox Court House, where Robert E. Lee had surrendered to Ulysses S. Grant in 1865. In this case, there was good evidence of the building's location and appearance; many of its dismantled bricks even remained on site. In 1939, Superintendent Branch Spalding, a former NPS historian, joined local interests in urging reconstruction of the house and other missing buildings to better interpret the community during the Civil War. Chief Historian Ronald F. Lee disagreed; he preferred to display the foundations and interpret the house through drawings, photographs, and "possibly a model of the building exhibited in a museum on the area." But in what colleagues later called "the second defeat of Lee at Appomattox," he yielded to strong local opinion, and the NPS reconstructed the McLean house after World War II. Later it rebuilt the nearby courthouse to serve as the park's visitor center and museum, an "adaptive reconstruction" obviating a modern facility intruding on the historic landscape.

Many antireconstructionists now concede the appropriateness and effectiveness of the work at Appomattox. Part of the reason for this may be that the reconstructed buildings do not stand alone but fill key gaps in a larger historic complex, like the reconstructed Capitol and Governor's Palace at Williamsburg. Considering Appomattox as a cultural landscape, what has been done is not reconstruction but restoration (defined in part as the replacement of missing elements). Despite the several rebuilt components, Appomattox visitors still find themselves in authentic surroundings.

Not so at Fort Caroline, perhaps the most egregious reconstruction in the national park system after Washington's birthplace. Fort Caroline National Memorial in Jacksonville, Florida, contains no trace of the short-lived sixteenth-century French settlement it commemorates. Even the site of the earth and timber fort was lost to the St. Johns River at least a century ago, displacing any archaeological remains. This did not dampen the local congressman's desire to reconstruct the fort, and the NPS capitulated to his persistence in 1963–1964. The modern Fort Caroline, executed on riverbank fill, reflected major compromises with the sketchy data available on its predecessor. It was significantly smaller and contained none of the buildings known to have been present. The difficulty of maintaining an earthen parapet prompted the substitution of cinderblock, plainly visible despite efforts to cultivate a grassy veneer from sod layered between the blocks. The result was so obviously counterfeit that no one could mistake it for the original—perhaps its only virtue.

Several other forts became objects of reconstruction activity in the following years. Fort Vancouver National Historic Site in Washington lay in the district of the chairman of the House of Representatives subcommittee responsible for NPS appropriations. When she became interested in rebuilding the nineteenth-century post, the NPS was not about to resist. Archaeological remains permitted much better results than the Fort Caroline rendition, but as in virtually all reconstructions, gaps in the physical and documentary records had to be filled by conjecture.

The congressman from the Kansas district containing Fort Scott also exerted influence as a member of the House subcommittee on parks. From 1965 to 1978, when he finally succeeded in bringing the fort under NPS administration, he obtained appropriations to reconstruct several buildings there. NPS professionals had little enthusiasm for Fort Scott, whose significance they judged marginal, and for the reconstructions, some based on inadequate data.

After extensive archaeological and documentary research yielding relatively good data, the NPS also reconstructed, between 1974 and 1976, Fort Stanwix in Rome, New York, and Bent's Old Fort in southeastern Colorado. These large-scale projects were embraced more willingly by the NPS, but again owed much to public and political intervention.

The reconstruction of Fort Stanwix, which had figured in the Revolutionary War, was one of several such projects undertaken for the American Revolution Bicentennial. At the bicentennial's centerpiece, Independence National Historical Park in Philadelphia, two houses were among the bygone buildings slated for replication. One was the Graff house, where Thomas Jefferson boarded while drafting the Declaration of Independence in 1776. Reasonably good evidence permitted a reasonably close copy. But the $1.4 million project was not completed without controversy. Outside proponents overwhelmed NPS professionals who deemed the house insufficiently important to warrant such attention. Whereupon the *Philadelphia Inquirer*'s architecture critic, Thomas Hine, charged the NPS with misplaced priorities in a piece provocatively titled "We're Building Lies about the City's Past" (Mattes 1989: 53–56, 83–88).

The other house proposed for reconstruction was that of Benjamin Franklin, Philadelphia's most famous citizen. Here the outcome was different. Despite significant archaeological and documentary evidence and advocacy by several NPS professionals, senior NPS professionals and managers concluded that data were inadequate to rebuild Franklin's house with the accuracy befitting its importance. Instead, some of its subsurface remains were left exposed, its plan was outlined on the ground, and an open steel framework was erected above to delineate the standing structure. This "ghost reconstruction" was widely applauded as a creative solution to the problem of physically portraying a structure on which detailed information is lacking.

Local interests championed the reconstruction of two more western forts in the mid-1970s. At Fort Smith National Historic Site, Arkansas, archaeologists and historians unearthed evidence of the long-gone first fort, but by professional consensus the data were insufficient to reconstruct. Unpersuaded, the reconstruction proponents enlisted their congressional representatives to bring further pressure on the NPS. Robert M. Utley, NPS assistant director for park historic preservation and a noted western historian, vigorously defended the service's position at a local public meeting in 1976, proclaiming that the extent of conjecture required would "perpetrate a fraud on the American public." Arkansas's congressional delegation declined to pursue the matter, and the NPS was able to stand firm (*Arkansas Gazette* 1976).

Utley and his successor, F. Ross Holland, Jr., took a similar stand against the reconstruction of Fort Union Trading Post in western North Dakota. By the middle of the next decade, however, several factors conspired to tip the balance the other way: the availability of good archaeological and documentary evidence, the effective support of Superintendent Paul Hedren and professionals and managers in the NPS regional office overseeing Fort Union Trading Post National Historic Site, and the persistence of North Dakota's congressional delegation (see chapter 12; Jameson and Hunt 1999:35–62; Matzko 2001). During the late 1980s, the NPS excavated and reconstructed most of Fort Union—one of the largest such projects the service has ever undertaken and the last of its kind at this writing. NPS chief historian Edwin C. Bearss, not always a reconstruction proponent, termed the results "a masterpiece" making the park "a world-class educational site." Even Utley, who had become increasingly opposed to reconstruction on principle, confessed to finding the rebuilt fort an impressive and effective interpretive exhibit after visiting it in his retirement.

All this reconstruction activity proceeded despite NPS policies generally intended to discourage it. After the advisory board statement adopted in 1937, the service made no significant restatement of historic structure treatment policy for thirty years. Its 1968 Administrative Policies for Historical Areas of the National Park System, in effect during most of the bicentennial planning period, declared that reconstruction should be authorized only under the following conditions:

(a) All or almost all traces of a structure have disappeared and its recreation is essential for public understanding and appreciation of the historical associations for which the park was established.

(b) Sufficient historical, archeological, and architectural data exist to permit an accurate reproduction.

(c) The structure can be erected on the original site or in a setting appropriate to the significance of the area, as in a pioneer community or living farm, where exact sites of structures may not be identifiable through research.

The last provision reflected the contemporary popularity of "living historical farms" and other re-created settings for "living history," strongly promoted by NPS director George B. Hartzog, Jr., in the late 1960s and early 1970s. At Lincoln Boyhood National Memorial, Booker T. Washington National Monument, Cumberland Gap National Historical Park, George Washington Memorial Parkway, and elsewhere, park staff members erected log cabins and other structures depicting early farms and settlements in "appropriate" settings with little concern for specific antecedents. (A fine stone chimney on the rude log cabin at George Washington Memorial Parkway's Turkey Run Farm perfectly illustrated Albert Good's old complaint about re-created pioneer chimneys and was much deplored by NPS historical architects.)

During the 1970s, more pressures for questionable reconstructions and growing preservation demands posed by the genuine historic resources in its custody moved the NPS to an increasingly restrictive reconstruction posture. "[W]e are programming millions of dollars in historical reconstructions—of earthworks, of living farms, of pioneer villages—which are of doubtful justification when measured by the administrative policies and which will have to be maintained by the same costly techniques that apply to the genuine article," said Director Ronald H. Walker to his regional directors in a 1973 memorandum prepared by Robert Utley. "Meanwhile, many of our historic houses, old forts, and other structures stand in urgent need of treatment." Another Walker memorandum to the field soon afterward, also drafted by Utley, again discouraged reconstructions less on their merits—which could always be debated—than because they were expensive and took resources better devoted to preservation: "Too frequently . . . the treatment of fragile and deteriorating original fabric commands lower priority than less pressing needs, such as reconstruction of vanished historic structures [and] creation of 'typical' buildings reflective of past ways of life."

The service's next general policy compilation, its "Management Policies of 1975," expressly disallowed the "typical" constructions that had been countenanced at "living history" sites and for the first time reflected concern about the impact of reconstruction on archaeological remains. A reconstruction should now meet four requirements:

1. There are no significant preservable remains that would be obliterated by reconstruction.
2. Historical, archeological, and architectural data are sufficient to permit an accurate reproduction with a minimum of conjecture.
3. The structure can be erected on the original site.
4. All prudent and feasible alternatives to reconstruction have been considered, and it is demonstrated that reconstruction is the only alternative that permits and is essential to public understanding and appreciation of the historical or cultural association for which the park was established.

The archaeological preservation requirement clearly and reasonably placed preservation above interpretation. It said that authentic cultural resources, even those below ground, should not be sacrificed to what are in essence interpretive exhibits. At the same time, the original site requirement, commonly entailing disturbance if not destruction of archaeological remains, was retained and made absolute. How to explain this apparent inconsistency?

During the Fort Union Trading Post reconstruction planning, reconstruction on a nearby site was considered so that the significant archaeological remains of the original fort might be preserved in situ, as Alfred Kidder had recommended in the advisory board's 1936 policy discussion. But the original site rule carried the day. Even before it became so expressly mandated, the NPS never reconstructed a building off the original site when that site was known and available. The materials might be new, but if the reconstruction is on the original site one can at least feel that he or she is "there," in the exact same place where whatever is being commemorated happened. Accuracy of site or place has been deemed at least as important as accuracy of design and materials in conveying a sense of the past through reconstructions.

So, because archaeological preservation and original location were both important, both were required to reconstruct. A not-unintended consequence was to make reconstruction very difficult—at least in theory. The requirement that reconstruction be essential to public understanding of the cultural association for which a park was established was meant to be even harder to meet. There should be few if any historical parks so lacking in resources or integrity that no other interpretive media—models, diagrams, films, or other graphic devices—can convey their past appearance and significance to the public. The cultural resource professionals responsible for this policy language customarily derided reconstruction proposals as affronts to the service's interpreters, who surely possessed the imagination and talent to interpret missing structures without rebuilding them. The interpreters did not always agree, however. And because those who championed their mission were often in charge, not only in the NPS but in Congress, reconstructions like Fort Union Trading Post were proposed, approved, funded, and executed without strict regard for the letter or spirit of the policies.

William Penn Mott, Jr., who became NPS director in 1985, was particularly interested in interpretation. From his perspective, cultural resource management was worthwhile primarily as it served the greater goal of public education and enjoyment. Unlike the preservation professionals who disdained reconstructions as fakes and "expensive life-size toys" whose inauthenticity could never be redeemed by accuracy, Mott saw them as valid educational media in many instances where significant original structures had vanished. Visiting Pecos National Monument in New Mexico, he proposed rebuilding a portion of the historic pueblo. Visiting Andersonville National Historic Site in Georgia, he advocated reconstructing parts of the Civil War prison stockade. NPS preservation professionals successfully discouraged the former project, which would have been very costly and destructive of archaeological remains, but they assisted in accomplishing the latter.

At Mott's instruction, the reconstruction requirements in the 1988 edition of the NPS's "Management Policies" were eased somewhat. A missing structure could now be reconstructed if

(1) reconstruction is essential to public understanding of the cultural associations of a park established for that purpose, (2) sufficient data exist to permit reconstruction on the original site with minimal conjecture, and (3) significant archaeological resources will be preserved in situ or their research values will be realized through data recovery.

The previous prohibition of "typical" structures was retained, but language emphasizing that preservation should always receive first consideration over restoration and reconstruction was dropped.

The only real difference beyond tone in the 1988 policies was the allowance for archaeological data recovery in lieu of resource preservation in situ. While this gave belated sanction to the Fort Union Trading Post work already underway, it had no further practical effect because the NPS undertook no further reconstructions in the next decade.

In 1998, when the NPS next began to revise the "Management Policies,"

Chief Historian Dwight T. Pitcaithley proposed a return to more hortatory language and stringent requirements for cultural resource treatment in general and reconstruction in particular. As published in 2001, however, the policies still allow reconstruction to disturb or destroy significant archaeological resources, provided their data are recovered.

Not that more stringent policies would matter a great deal. By its nature, policy is subject to the discretion of agency managers. Their commitment to it will inevitably vary with the public and political pressures attendant on a public agency. With strong civic and congressional support, the Fort Union Trading Post reconstruction proceeded despite the policies in effect at its inception. So will the next reconstruction project enjoying similar support.

An earlier version of this chapter appeared in CRM Bulletin 13, no. 1 (1990).

References

Arkansas Gazette
    1976   "Reconstruction of Fort Smith Would Be Fraud, Official Says." *Arkansas Gazette*, 30 August 1976, p. 1A.

Hosmer, Charles B., Jr.
    1981   *Preservation Comes of Age: From Williamsburg to the National Trust, 1926–1949*, pp. 478–493. University Press of Virginia, Charlottesville.

Jameson, John H., Jr., and William J. Hunt
    1999   Reconstruction vs. Preservation-in-Place in the National Park Service. In *The Constructed Past: Experimental Archaeology, Education, and the Public*, edited by Peter G. Stone and Philippe G. Planel, pp. 35–62, Routledge, London.

NPS (National Park Service)
    n.d.   Fort Caroline National Memorial file, NPS National Register, History, and Education (NRHE) files; author's personal observations during tenure at Fort Caroline.
    n.d.   Fort Scott National Historic Site file, NPS National Register, History, and Education (NRHE) files, Washington, D.C
    1936   Advisory Board minutes, 7–9 May, National Register, History, and Education (NRHE) files, Washington, D. C.
    1938   *Park and Recreation Structures*, pp. 186–187, Washington, D.C.
    1968   *Administrative Policies for Historical Areas of the National Park System*, p. 23, Washington, D.C.
    1973   Memorandum, Walker to Regional Directors, 18 December 1973, author's files.
    1974   Memorandum, Walker to Deputy Director, Associate Directors, Regional Directors et al., 21 February 1974.
    1975   Management Policies, chap. 5, pp. 16–17.
    1988   Management Policies, chap. 5, p. 7.
    1989   Landmarks of Liberty: A Report on the American Revolution Bicentennial

Development Program of the National Park Service, unpublished NPS report, pp. 53–56, 79–83.

1991 Fort Union Trading Post National Historic Site file, NPS National Register, History, and Education (NRHE) files; memorandum, Bearss to Associate Director, Cultural Resources, 31 July 1991.

2001 Management Policies, par. 5.3.5.4.4.

Mattes, Merrill J.
1976 *Philadelphia Inquirer*, 29 February, p. 9.
1977 [Bent's Old Fort] From Ruin to Reconstruction, 1920–1976. *The Colorado Magazine* 54(4): 57–101.

Matzko, John
2001 *Reconstructing Fort Union*. University of Nebraska Press, Lincoln.

Merritt, Jane T.
1993 The Administrative History of Fort Vancouver National Historic Site. Fort Vancouver National Historic Site file, NPS National Register, History, and Education (NRHE) files, unpublished report.

Sellers, Richard, and Dwight Pitcaithley.
1979 "Reconstructions-Expensive, Life-Size Toys?" *CRM Bulletin* 2(4): 6–8.

U.S. Government Printing Office
n.d. Public Law 74-292, U.S. Statutes at Large 49: 666. Washington, D.C.

Utley, Robert
1998 Personal communication, 17 April 1998.

PART II

Measuring Effectiveness for Interpretation and Site Management

ESTHER C. WHITE ■

Chapter Four

Reconstruction Dilemmas at George Washington's Blacksmith Shop

To reconstruct or not to reconstruct is one of the most interesting questions involving the stewardship of historic properties. Given the power that reconstructed buildings have on influencing our perceptions of the past, how do you know when you have enough evidence to accurately reconstruct a lost building? At Mount Vernon, the home of George Washington, the rules of evidence are exacerbated by the decision to return the plantation's built environment to 1799. Reconstructionists not only need to provide a complete description of how a building probably looked but also to prove that it was in existence in 1799, the year of Washington's death. At Mount Vernon, the reconstuctionists have waged a half-century campaign to bring about the rebirth of Washington's blacksmith shop.

Anchoring the north and south axis of the manicured lawns of Washington's home were two post-in-ground buildings, one dedicated to agriculture, the other to industry. These utilitarian structures disappeared long before the Mount Vernon Ladies' Association (MVLA) purchased the property in 1858. Although vanished, these buildings were not forgotten; their presence and function, a stercorary, or repository for dung, to the south, and a blacksmith shop to the north, were recorded on the Vaughan Plan, drawn by a visitor to the plantation in 1787 (figure 4.1). George Washington, victorious general and first president, was also a farmer and businessman, facets of his life the MVLA is committed to interpreting. In order to fulfill the vision of commemorating George Washington through the comprehensive restoration of his plantation, the stercorary was rebuilt in 2001; the blacksmith shop will be reconstructed within the next ten years.

The blacksmith shop reconstruction will be only the fourth reconstructed building placed within the historic core of the plantation since the establishment of the MVLA. Mount Vernon, with fifteen buildings dating from the eighteenth century, is one of the most complete plantations, retaining mansion, outbuildings, and landscape features. The decision to rebuild the blacksmith shop was not taken lightly; four separate archaeological investigations, untold hours of archival research, and

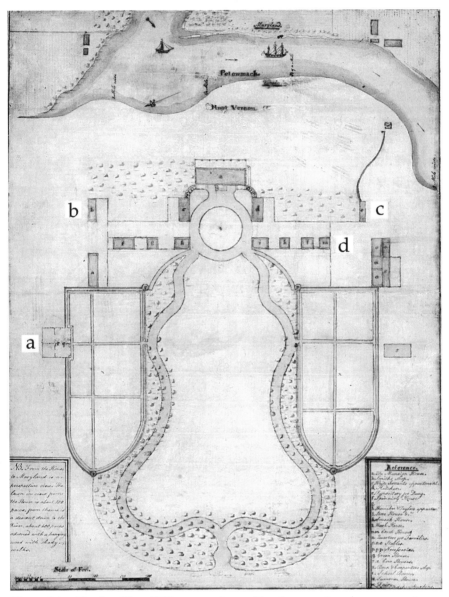

Figure 4.1. Vaughan Plan, 1787; a. greenhouse (the slave quarter wings were not constructed until 1792); b. blacksmith shop; c. repository for dung; d. coach house. (All figures in this chapter, courtesy Mount Vernon Ladies Association.)

countless debates for more than fifty years, focusing on authenticity, evidence, and the mission of the museum, occurred before the MVLA agreed that a blacksmith shop reconstruction was in the best interest of the historic house museum.

Policy for Reconstructions

Founded in 1853, the Ladies' Association purchased Mount Vernon from the Washington family in 1858. Their act saved the core of George Washington's eighteenth-century plantation home from development or destruction. The Ladies' rescue, however, formally opened the doors of Mount Vernon to tourists. These visitors, and the Ladies' desire to save the property, demanded a restoration of Washington's home, which at times was aggressive in nature. Upon her retirement in 1874, the founder of the MVLA, Ann Pamela Cunningham, challenged future generations of the plantation's stewards:

> Ladies, the home of Washington is in your charge—see to it that you keep it the home of Washington! Let no irreverent hand change it; let no vandal hands desecrate it with the fingers of "progress"! Those who go to the home in which he lived and died wish to see in what he lived and died. Let one spot, in this grand country of ours, be saved from change. Upon you rests this duty (Johnson 1991: 52).

This brief statement forms the basis of the restoration and reconstruction policy still guiding Mount Vernon. Through the years, her vision was interpreted as a justification to restore and present Mount Vernon as it appeared in 1799, the year of Washington's death. A surviving probate inventory from 1799 provides documentary details to guide decisions, further reinforcing the mandate to interpret this year.

Reconstruction, the replacement of a structure that no longer exists, has a limited presence at the plantation, due in part to the survival of so many structures original to Washington's tenure. There are nevertheless, a number of major buildings, as well as numerous ephemeral utilitarian buildings, which did not survive the nineteenth century, and Miss Cunningham's statement provides an intellectual challenge with which to weigh the merits of proposed reconstructions.

Three reconstructed buildings are present at Mount Vernon: the coach house, the greenhouse / slave quarter, and the stercorary. In these cases, the levels of evidence guiding the reconstructions were extremely detailed. Having burned in 1853, the coach house was rebuilt on its original foundations at the foot of the south lane in 1893. The southern terminus of nine outbuildings, the coach house probably looked very similar to the surviving eight. Since less than forty years separated its destruction with rebuilding, individuals remembered the original building, providing many details of its appearance.

In 1952, the greenhouse / slave quarter, a building originally completed in 1792, was reconstructed upon its original foundations. The eighteenth-century brick building succumbed to fire in 1835, although one brick wall survived and was incorporated into the new building. Two earlier greenhouses preceded the 1952 greenhouse / slave quarter reconstruction although not on the exact footprint. An 1869 greenhouse was replaced during the 1890s by a greenhouse with quarters for ladies in the wings. This building sought to evoke Washington's, although it was clearly not of his construction. An insurance document, discovered in the 1930s, contained a detailed drawing of Washington's structure. This provided the MVLA with the evidence to replicate the eighteenth-century building.

The stercorary, rebuilt in 2001, incorporates the eighteenth-century cobblestone floor and sections of brickwork revealed by extensive archaeological excavations. Although the exact date and cause of the building's demise is unknown, the investigation proved that it survived into the nineteenth century, fulfilling the 1799 test. Documentary research discovered a drawing of a stercorary published in 1807, which provided missing structural details. In these cases, the detailed evidence, as well as the undisputed existence of the buildings during the critical year of 1799, made reconstruction a straightforward decision.

The Debate on Reconstructing the Blacksmith Shop

The blacksmith shop, on the other hand, is not so simple a candidate for reconstruction. That Mount Vernon supported a blacksmith operation is not disputed; plantation ledgers survive providing extremely detailed records of the location and activities in the shop. Documentary records also identify the blacksmiths, both free and enslaved, who worked in the shop. There was disagreement about the 1799 location of the shop and its appearance. This lack of evidence caused debate among Mount Vernon staff for more than half a century and touched on many of the issues facing the managers of historic properties that look to physical reconstruction as a method of augmenting their programs. These issues include how much evidence is needed to warrant building a modern structure in the midst of authentic ones, the ethics of replacing a historic structure, albeit not of the chosen period, with a modern building, and decisions about what types of activities historic house museums should interpret.

In 1931, Morley Williams, a landscape architect at Harvard University, began a study of Virginia plantations. Williams's research, both archaeological and documentary, focused primarily on Mount Vernon's landscape and evolution, culminating in a staff position as director of research and restoration in 1937. Williams's first report to Council, the MVLA's annual board meeting, stated this newly created department "would be prepared to supervise restorations, supervise them as to authenticity, as to techniques," as well as gather information about the plantation (Williams 1937: 50).

Williams used the Vaughan Plan, to identify nonextant structures for archaeological investigation. Vaughan's plan illustrates a blacksmith shop on the corner of the north lane, and Mount Vernon's director, Colonel Harrison Dodge, confirmed the position for Williams. Dodge related, "it was undoubtedly there because the ground was full of black trash" (Williams 1937: 53).

Williams's archaeological excavation of the site discovered no structural foundation, causing him to surmise wooden posts had rotted. He did discover evidence of a forge foundation constructed of brick. His site map shows postholes forming a yard on the southern side of the hypothesized shop (figure 4.2). It also clearly illustrates one dilemma of putting the blacksmith shop back; there is a brick icehouse on the southwest corner of the shop.

Williams's accompanying report to Council addressed the icehouse. He assumed the icehouse was original to George Washington, but through his research found it first appeared on a mid-nineteenth-century plan, did not contain eighteenth-century brick, and states "there is other evidence which proves very definitely that the ice house could not have been there in Washington's time." He disregards it with a final "so much for that ice house" (Williams 1937: 53–54). But it is just that icehouse which would cause controversy in the ensuing years.

In the post–World War II period, Mount Vernon's successful reconstruction of the greenhouse / slave quarters generated momentum for an expanded restoration program supervised by Williams's successor, Walter Macomber. A restoration architect, trained during the initial re-creation of Colonial Williamsburg, Macomber conducted additional excavations at the blacksmith shop site. The 1955 dig once again uncovered the forge foundation and many ferrous artifacts, but no recommendation about a proposed reconstruction could be made due to "insufficient evidence" (MVLA 1955: 91).

Nine years later, in 1964, the MVLA purchased two early views of Mount Vernon. One of these, *A View of Mount Vernon from the North East*, attributed to Edward Savage and painted in 1792, shows a grey smudge behind a tree in the north grove (figures 4.3 and 4.4). This provided the evidence for a blacksmith shop the proponents for the reconstruction sought. The regent, president of the MVLA, Mrs. Beirne, announced the call for more research on the blacksmith shop in her 1965 report (MVLA 1965: 7).

She, and presumably other Ladies, viewed the blacksmith shop as "the one missing edifice in this otherwise complete plantation." The regent furthermore stated that policy was "to construct only on physical evidence" as at the greenhouse (MVLA 1965: 7). The result of her suggestion was a motion by the Buildings Committee to undertake documentary and physical research on the blacksmith shop

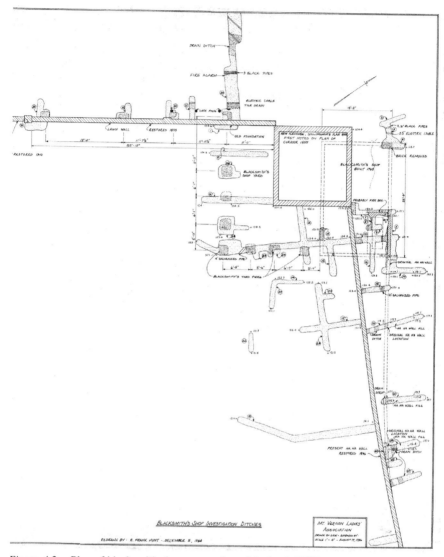

Figure 4.2. Plan of blacksmith shop excavations (Morley J. Williams, 1936).

(MVLA 1965: 32). This investigation continued for the next four years. The site was excavated again in 1968 and a thorough review of the documentary sources conducted.

Documentary references in the plantation work reports record the structure was constructed prior to 1765. A 1786 reference records carpenters repairing the

Figure 4.3.   View of Mount Vernon from the Northeast, 1792 (attributed to Edward Savage).

roof of the shop, which measured 16 feet long. The final reference to the structure was a 1798 farm report documenting a slave working in the smith's shop. Blacksmithing tools are listed on Washington's probate inventory, but a structure for blacksmithing is not specifically named. This evidence unfortunately does not specifically mention a blacksmith shop in 1799, the year of Washington's death.

Because the final reference to the shop itself was the 1798 account, the icehouse, so easily dismissed by Morley Williams as not eighteenth-century / George Washington-related, suddenly became the focus of attention during the 1960s study. Benson Lossing visited Mount Vernon in 1858 and published a drawing of the icehouse, writing that George Washington built it after his retirement from the presidency. He also mentioned that he observed someone working in "the shop near the conservatory" placing the mid-nineteenth-century shop elsewhere (Lossing 1991).

The antireconstruction faction, led by Director Wall, seized upon Lossing's account. This group focused primarily on the lack of evidence for the physical appearance of the blacksmith shop, using the debate about its location as the final punch to stop the building of this structure. As additional evidence against this location of the smithy in 1799, they pointed to the absence of the smith's shop on two insurance policies taken by Washington's heir, Bushrod Washington, in 1803 and 1805. These same policies had proved instrumental in providing the necessary evidence to support the greenhouse / slave quarter reconstruction and the absence of the blacksmith shop proved George Washington abandoned the north lane smithy

Figure 4.4.   Detail of *View of Mount Vernon from the Northeast*, 1792, showing the blacksmith shop (attributed to Edward Savage).

before his death. As early as 10 March 1966, Mr. Wall outlined his position in a memorandum to the Regent, stating: "the evidence is inconclusive; the record is incomplete" (Wall 1966: 4).

The pro-reconstructionists, led by the regent and Mr. Macomber, responded with their own list of positive points. Chief among these was the 1792 painting, which they felt provided ample evidence for a reconstruction. They interpreted the gray paint as a simple wooden shed building with a window. They countered that the inventory, insurance policies, and other documents had numerous known omissions, especially of utilitarian structures, which explained the missing blacksmith shop (Beirne 1966).

The two sides continued to revise their arguments, in general rephrasing their initial views. Mr. Wall presented his views in a position paper that questioned whether the exhibition area should continue to be interpreted to 1799. Mr. Wall succinctly challenged the ethics of destroying a historic structure to build a modern facsimile, no matter how authentic. Wall viewed a reconstruction as "diminishing the integrity of a remarkable group of buildings by intruding an imagined structure." He belied his personal agenda at the close of the paper, however, when he categorized the blacksmith shop as "noisy, dirty, smoky" with "no proper place so near the master's residence, within the formal enclosed area." Wall's discussion focused on how Washington, during his final years, expanded and refined his plantation core. Wall felt Washington would have moved his blacksmith shop farther from his mansion, and he constructed an icehouse at the same spot, since it would be "unobjectionable aesthetically." He stated his position most strongly in closing: "[A] reconstruction, even though we might have data comparable with what we had for the Greenhouse, would have no place in the formal area unless and until it could be established that George Washington did not fulfill his expressed intention of establishing a new icehouse and that the blacksmith shop still stood opposite the Spinning House on December 14, 1799" (Wall 1969).

During Council in 1969, the Building Committee heard from Mr. Wall and Mr. Macomber regarding the blacksmith shop. The Ladies tabled the decision concerning the reconstruction (MVLA 1969: 45). Finally, during the 1974 Council, Walter Macomber forced the blacksmith shop issue, providing the Buildings Committee a plan for reconstructing a "proposed building simple, 12' x 16' . . . built of old material at a cost of approximately $2,500.00" (figure 4.5; MVLA 1974: 46–47). The matter was again tabled and when the building committee met in 1975, the minutes state they still hoped to see a reconstruction, although new evidence was not discovered (MVLA 1975: 42). It was too late for Mr. Macomber, who resigned soon after the 1974 meeting, clearly tired of waiting for the elusive evidence that would provide the necessary proof to rebuild.

Recent Archaeological Investigations

When the MVLA contracted with the Virginia Research Center for Archaeology (VRCA) in 1984 to conduct a survey and assessment of the estate, the blacksmith shop was one of the primary sites the organization sought to explore. These excavations, completed by Mount Vernon's own research archaeological department created in 1987, generated results that were not very different from the interpretations of the 1930s investigation by Morley Williams. The brick forge was uncovered for

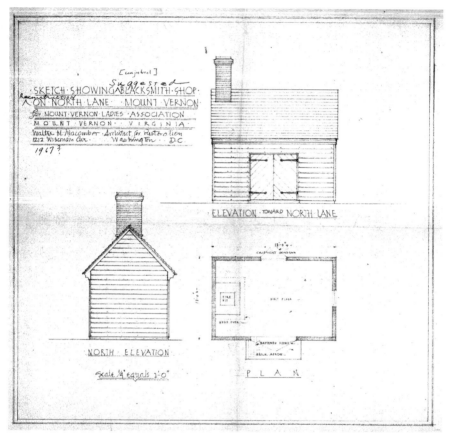

Figure 4.5.   Drawing of the blacksmith shop (by Walter Macomber, 1974?).

the fourth time, and numerous artifacts were discovered (figure 4.6). Significantly, the most recent excavation identified the postholes for the two extant corners of the building, providing a dimension of 18 feet. Based upon this measurement it is now hypothesized the building measured 18 x 24 feet (figure 4.7).

The most recent archaeological excavations provided the evidence that allowed MVLA's archaeology committee to finally decide the fate of the blacksmith shop. In 1990, they made three recommendations to the board: the significance of the blacksmith shop as part of the plantation economy calls for interpretation; the reconstruction will not be undertaken immediately, but when the north lane area is changed the reconstruction should be considered (MVLA 1990). Soon after these recommendations were passed, an exhibit about the blacksmith shop opened on the estate accompanied by a drawing of the proposed reconstruction (figure 4.8).

Figure 4.6. The blacksmith shop's forge, 1987.

Conclusion: The Role of Reconstructions at Mount Vernon

Inclusion of the reconstruction of the blacksmith shop within Mount Vernon's Master Plan indicates not only the MVLA's continued commitment to these recommendations but the dedication of the Association to a vision of a complete eighteenth-century plantation. This vision, to interpret all aspects of Washington's farming enterprise, began in earnest with the 1996 opening of the George Washington Pioneer Farm exhibit, a six-acre re-creation of a sixteen-sided treading barn and associated farmyard and fields, originally located on an outlying farm, not now part of the historic museum. In 2002, Mount Vernon opened a working restoration of Washington's reconstructed 1770 gristmill, located on nearby Dogue Creek. This mill and adjacent whiskey distillery currently being researched are places where Washington's entrepreneurial achievement is explored. The recent reconstruction of the post-in-ground stercorary illustrates the dedication of the MVLA to interpret more than just the refined aspects of plantation life. With the rebuilding of the blacksmith shop, the association will continue this mission. These buildings, at the junctions of the lanes and Ha-Ha walls, within view of George Washington's mansion, represent the reality of eighteenth-century Mount Vernon. Difficult as it might be for the twenty-

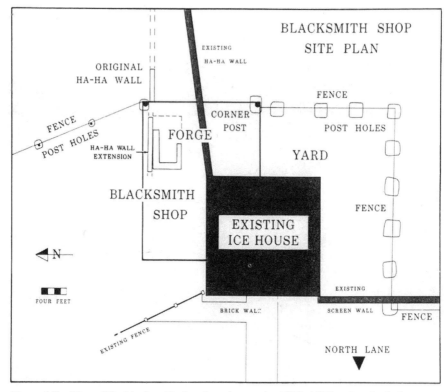

Figure 4.7.   Plan of the blacksmith shop based upon the 1984–1987 archaeological excavation.

first century visitor to grasp, graciousness and refinement *were* just a few short steps from the utilitarian workings of a thriving plantation.

References

Beirne, R.
   1966   The Mount Vernon Blacksmith Shop. On file, Mount Vernon Ladies' Associa-
           tion, Mount Vernon, Virginia.

Johnson, Gerald W.
   1991   Mount Vernon: The Story of a Shrine. Mount Vernon, Virginia: The Mount
           Vernon Ladies' Association, Mount Vernon, Virginia.

Lossing, Benson
   1991   *George Washington's Mount Vernon: Or Mount Vernon and Its Associations,
           Historical, Biographical, and Pictorial.* Gramercy Press, New York.

Figure 4.8. Drawing of the blacksmith shop, 1995.

Mount Vernon Ladies' Association
  1955   Minutes of Council. On file, Mount Vernon Ladies' Association, Mount Vernon, Virginia.
  1965   Minutes of Council. On file, Mount Vernon Ladies' Association, Mount Vernon, Virginia.
  1969   Minutes of Council. On file, Mount Vernon Ladies' Association, Mount Vernon, Virginia.
  1974   Minutes of Council. On file, Mount Vernon Ladies' Association, Mount Vernon, Virginia.
  1975   Minutes of Council. On file, Mount Vernon Ladies' Association, Mount Vernon, Virginia.
  1990   Minutes of Council. On file, Mount Vernon Ladies' Association, Mount Vernon, Virginia.

Wall, Charles Cecil
  1966   Memorandum to the Regent, 10 March. On file, Mount Vernon Ladies' Association, Mount Vernon, Virginia.
  1969   Ice House and Blacksmith Shop: A Summation. On file, Mount Vernon Ladies' Association, Mount Vernon, Virginia.

Williams, Morley J.
  1937   Research and Restoration Department Annual Report. On file, Mount Vernon Ladies' Association, Mount Vernon, Virginia.

Chapter Five

Reconstruction Policy and Purpose at Castell Henllys Iron Age Fort

The reconstruction of Iron Age houses, mainly in timber but also in stone, has been undertaken in Britain for over thirty years. The earliest examples were erected in the context of buildings history, providing a prehistoric dimension through reconstruction to medieval and later buildings that had been moved from their original sites and rebuilt in outdoor museums. In such a situation all the structures were away from their original contexts; the Iron Age houses were different only because they contained no original elements but were totally reconstructed. These houses were based not on generic Iron Age house plans, but on specific examples of excavated remains, though not considering siting or micro topography. This pattern of rebuilding is still popular, and it can be seen for example in the most recent case at St. Fagan's Folk Life Museum at Cardiff.

Experimental reconstruction of Iron Age houses subsequently moved to a more scientific base at Butser Ancient Farm, although a public element was rapidly added to aid finances. Butser is an attempt to replicate a "typical" farm landscape of the British Iron Age, circa 300 BC, an open air laboratory where research into the Iron Age and Roman periods goes on using the methods and materials available for the times. A wide range of houses was reconstructed based on regional Wessex examples. Some ancillary activities were undertaken, and Butser is famous for its crop growing and storage experiments with their consistent unexpectedly high yields (Reynolds 1999).

Some later reconstructions have merely copied the earlier ones, no longer returning to any primary archaeological data, but taking the reconstructed formula and applying it with more or less rigor. This has often been the case either on small-scale projects with limited funds, or commercial enterprises where cost cutting and speed in setting up the enterprise were paramount concerns. In some cases, houses have been reconstructed at a reduced scale, which rapidly leads to perceptions of small people in the past. The smaller scale can be more effective with children, but it is still often misleading.

Castell Henllys is unique in Britain in that reconstructions have taken place on the Iron Age site, and indeed on the exact locations of the buildings. The particular archaeological evidence has been considered within the context of the location within the site, and this was essential with one roundhouse for the understanding of the construction methods employed by the original builders.

When the public access and interpretation of Castell Henllys was initiated, only Butser and some buildings museums had reconstructed Iron Age houses. The then owner of the site, Hugh Foster, an entrepreneur with experience in tourist attractions, wished to create an Iron Age theme experience, but on an original site and with some authenticity. On his death, the site was obtained by Dyfed County Council and placed under the management of the Pembrokeshire Coast National Park, which now owns the site. The balance between these two management regimes, the ongoing archaeological excavations, the tourist and educational visitors, and various constituencies within the local population provide dynamics that are of considerable interest. They highlight the political and cultural roles of heritage interpretation, their fluidity, and their potency.

It is possible to discern within Pembrokeshire the major historical developments within Wales, represented by monuments today. Most that survive relate to periods of external domination, first by the Romans, then the Normans, and later English lords. Though dramatic, the forts, castles, and abbey ruins do not necessarily conjure up and celebrate a culturally appropriate past. In contrast, the excavations and reconstructions at the native fort of Castell Henllys offer the opportunity to explore an indigenous Welsh culture prior to any domination. The attraction of this Golden Age is considerable, whatever the archaeological remains may actually suggest. The romance of the Celtic free spirit was much appreciated by Hugh Foster, and though toned down in some elements of the National Park display, is still clearly there (and allows the public to develop this themselves). This Celtic spirit is in the schools program, and it is very much present in the recreation groups who use the site.

Reconstruction of buildings and other features was undertaken under both private and public management, and these reconstructions included experimental elements (Gilchrist and Mytum 1986; Mytum 1986; 1991b; 1999; 2003).

The Foster Reconstructions

Hugh Foster, an entrepreneurial accountant, purchased Castell Henllys in 1980. He had failed to negotiate the rights to an Asterix theme site, and so he had turned from fiction to reality and an actual Iron Age earthwork fort to form the focus of a tourist attraction. Castell Henllys was a scheduled ancient monument, and thus protected from unlicensed disturbance. After consultation with Cadw, the body responsible for giving scheduled monument consent in Wales, I was approached to carry out excavations in advance of development on the site. The most obvious development, indeed, was the reconstruction of buildings.

The research aims were simply to evaluate the extent and nature of any Iron Age remains; the only published description of the site claimed that it was unfinished (RCAHMW 1925, 259). Trial trenching demonstrated a long and complex sequence of occupation with many defensive changes. By the end of the summer 1981 season, the first roundhouse plan was uncovered, and plans for reconstruction could proceed.

The excavated evidence, combined with principles of mechanics and parallels with other timber buildings both from experimental archaeology and ethnography, allowed reasoned inferences to be drawn on the form of the original building. Foster had become involved with the Friends of Butser, and so he was aware of the reconstructions there. He briefly employed Reynolds as a consultant, which influenced the design of the first house to be reconstructed, and meant that it was very much within the Butser mould. The roundhouse form was one commonly found in Britain—that of a double ring, the inner posts supporting the roof and the outer ring being the wall line itself. The reconstruction produced valuable information regarding the resources of material and people necessary for such a construction (Mytum 1986). The doorposts were larger than all the others, though there was no porch. As excavation proceeded, it became clear that this is the only certain double ring roundhouse on the site, so other reconstructions have been on different structural principles.

Foster was content that archaeologically derived information was used in the reconstruction of the roundhouses, but within the enclosed space, most internal details could not be confirmed by archaeology. The spit and hearth were archaeologically attested, and ovens adjacent to hearths were known at some sites, but as for other features, excavation could not offer much detail. Here, Foster's interpretation took over and the sort of past he wished to create became more obvious. In contrast to the Butser houses, which are kept minimally furnished because of lack of evidence for anything specific, Foster wished the houses to have a lived-in look. Souvenirs from the Mediterranean and handcrafted objects, often of considerable crudity, were placed in the houses. He also commissioned replicas of varying quality, and had furs, skins, and textiles draped around. Benches, a bed, and a loom were provided.

Foster also had clothing made which he wore on site; he would often be working on some craft project and talk to visitors, or just sit in the roundhouse and engage them in conversation. Through this means he would often obtain ideas based on secondhand ethnography and anecdote that he incorporated into his verbal interpretations or implemented in terms of roundhouse furnishing and layout.

Events such as feasts were laid on at which soups were prepared in a large replica cauldron, and lamb roasted on a spit in the house or outside it. At the Celtic festival of Lughnasa, which conveniently fell in the middle of the tourist season, he would have a day of activities to attract larger crowds. The reconstructions provided a focus for all activities, and they gave a sense of place that was enhanced by the

Figure 5.1.   Reconstructed roundhouses at Castell Henllys. (All figures in chapter 5, courtesy of Harold Mytum.)

surrounding landscape. Modern activity was placed in a suspension, a mixture of re-created ancient and clearly twentieth-century elements. This was indicated even by the name of the house—the Prince William roundhouse, as it was conceived at the same time as the prince (son of the Prince and Princess of Wales) and was born at the same time, also.

Following the first reconstruction, excavations continued and a smaller round-house foundation gully was excavated. There was less detail regarding this building, but enough to provide some information on form. Reynolds was not employed on this building, which had no internal supports, and it was built with a lower pitch roof.

A third roundhouse was later constructed, using labor in part derived from Earthwatch volunteers. Foster named this the Earthwatch house. Though having no internal posts, the building was similar in size to the first roundhouse, but it employed the structural principles of the second. This led to practical and design problems with the roof. The only timbers available in a straight and thin enough form were larch (not available in the Iron Age), which is a very flexible wood. One, or probably two, internal ring beams should have been part of the roof design to give some rigidity, but they were left out, thus making the roof flexible. This led to bowing and bending in strong winds, though no structural weakness per se. The

Figure 5.2. Roundhouse interior.

most fascinating feature of this roundhouse, however, is the way in which micro topography and construction worked hand in hand on this site. Most roundhouses in Britain have relatively shallow foundation gullies for post and wattle walls. The main strength comes from the circular plan of the structure and, it is proposed, a wall plate on top of the wall where there is not an inner ring of posts. This round-house was built on a considerable slope. Other Iron Age houses, at Castell Henllys and elsewhere, were placed on a sloping site by cutting a scoop into the ground to make a horizontal surface onto which the normal structural principles could then apply. This is not the solution taken for this house. Instead, the house had a wall plate that was horizontal, and the wall varied in height round the building's circumference. Thus the downhill side of the house had a much higher wall than the uphill.

To provide structural stability, the downhill wall had much deeper foundations than the uphill, making the below ground archaeology very different from that of a normal roundhouse.

It was only during consideration of the reconstruction, and the process of rebuilding in situ, that the full implications of building on that particular site led to this unique archaeological manifestation of the roundhouse. Rebuilding elsewhere may have taken into account all the recorded levels and replicated them, but only if their full significance had already been appreciated. Moreover, having reconstructed the house on its original site, in its original topographical setting, communication to the present day public of the decision-making processes in the Iron Age is much easier. A reconstruction elsewhere, even on an appropriate piece of ground, would not have the contextual information of its location on the site, proximity to other buildings, and relationship to the wider landscape that this reconstruction can bring. It is this level of in situ authenticity, even if details of the reconstruction itself are incorrect, that gives the place a special value to local and visiting public. This is neither a dry, dead real site that has been excavated, revealing incomprehensible scatters of small holes and trenches, nor is it some theme park or museum of artificially assembled structures from a range of locations, often far from the place where they now stand. These reconstructions are threads that link the past, knowable though archaeological excavation, of an actual Iron Age, Celtic site to the present where people can experience with all their senses and soul something of how that past may have been. We have to be careful to make clear what assumptions have been made, but the general perceptions of bulk and the form of the buildings we can be confident of. Detail is less certain, but the public can more easily appreciate the uncertainty there.

Foster's concern was to make the area with reconstructions look busy, and so even where reconstruction could not in any way be accurately postulated, but groups of postholes suggested some structure had been present, he wished to build something. This led to the erection of a scruffy looking "goat hut" (with posts not nearly as large as those used in the Iron Age), and a rectangular building he termed "the smithy" because an adjacent pit may have had a craft function. The reconstructed building was rectangular, though the postholes implied no clear shape, and rectangular buildings of this type are unknown from the British Iron Age. These buildings were not based on any particular rationale apart from what Foster desired in terms of usable space, making use of local materials, and with a finish (bark still on timbers, reed thatch) to match the roundhouse style.

The emphasis of Foster's overall site interpretation was on the dramatic facets of the Iron Age. The Butser project emphasized agriculture and domestic stability, so Foster stressed the mystical and military. This led to two aspects of reconstruction not seen at other locations with Iron Age houses. The defensive emphasis was achieved by the erection of some scruffy-looking palisade on top of the northern, most impressive earthworks. These were first built up with spoil from the excavations so that the actual archaeological deposits would not be damaged by this reconstruction and they were closer to their original size. The reconstruction was along the line of an original palisade, but not so well made as the original would have been, and the timbers were probably too tall. Military life was also emphasized on display panels at the site's defenses, and replica weapons were on display in the roundhouses.

A natural spring to the northwest of the fort on the slopes of the promontory was linked to Celtic religion and the ritual significance of water. This was developed under the park management, but other elements were later swept aside. One of these was a spiral mystic maze of quartz blocks laid out between the roundhouses, inserting ritual within the domestic elements. A replica human skull was placed in one of the roundhouses, linking both military and ritual.

The End of an Era

Hugh Foster died from a heart attack in 1991 and the site was put up for sale. Despite some national media attention there was no immediate sale. The Welsh archaeological community was concerned that all the research and reconstruction work could be undone, but Cadw would not intervene. Moreover, the local people felt that their past might be appropriated and the site returned to farmland or turned into an unsympathetic theme park. Local elected councillors were lobbied, and they argued for the purchase of the site by the Dyfed County Council, to be managed by the Pembrokeshire Coast National Park. The local populace were concerned that their Celtic past was under threat.

The Celtic identity, the concept of a Welsh heritage prior to English influence, is important in this case and is in great part due to in situ reconstruction giving form to that past. Dominated politically and culturally by the English, the Welsh have suffered discrimination against their culture and language even into recent times. This negotiation can be identified archaeologically in the use of language on gravestones (Mytum 1994). Welsh indigenous culture now has a new confidence, however, with teaching through the medium of Welsh in many schools, and some mass media being in Welsh. In the context of this developing cultural awareness, a site providing strong images of an indigenous "pristine" Celtic community was particularly potent. This is evident in that Welsh language media (newspapers, radio, and television) have been far more interested in reporting the results of the excavations and reconstructions than the equivalent English language media.

This Celtic factor was also an important one in the formation of professional archaeological opinion. Although there is an academic debate regarding the association of Celtic with Iron Age, no Welsh Iron Age site is displayed to visitors, even though many lie on public footpaths. Within the national Welsh context, Castell Henllys could begin to redress a presentational imbalance, an imbalance of particular importance given the emotional link of the nation with that period and its Celtic associations.

The Pembrokeshire Coast National Park Interpretation

The National Park, based in an English-speaking southern part of Pembrokeshire (often called "little England beyond Wales") and largely staffed by English speakers, acquired Castell Henllys under political pressure. It was able to turn this to its local political advantage by showing commitment to Welsh speaking north Pembrokeshire. When funds from the British government were made available as compensation for job losses following military cutbacks in the area, investment took place at the site to promote tourism and education. The park employed a full-time manager who lived above the shop next to the site, and designed and erected permanent display panels placed around the site, though not in the area of reconstruction. The ambience of past in the present was retained there; the threads from the Iron Age to the present were not to be cut. With their bilingual text and a range of line drawings, the panels and the self-guided trail leaflet are informative and authoritative. The links with the local environment and resources, and the Iron Age/Celtic associations are prominent.

One reconstruction, only just begun by Hugh Foster but completed by the Park, needs to be mentioned. Besides roundhouses, most Iron Age sites in Britain produce evidence for four-post structures, generally interpreted as granaries with raised floors. Although some reconstructions had been attempted at Butser, they had not been serious attempts to assess their form and function. Reynolds had considered, given the limited archaeological evidence, that almost anything could be built on four substantial posts. This is indeed true, but this reconstruction attempted to build something in the form of a granary, as far as possible retaining the vernacular tradition postulated within the roundhouse reconstructions. Thus, the structure placed on the raised platform was circular (not square as other reconstructions had assumed). This has been a successful reconstruction, and plans are under way to test storage of grain within it. It provides a contrasting structural type for the visitor, and is again built in the original postholes as excavated.

The roundhouses have been maintained, and where necessary re-thatched by the Park. Some of the posts in the internal ring of the first roundhouse have been replaced because their bases have rotted. What are considered more appropriate artifacts have been placed in the structures, and walls whitewashed to make the interiors lighter. New doors, more substantial in form, have been placed on all the buildings, in part in recognition of Iron Age craft skills, in part for security reasons. The smithy and goat hut, despite their lack of authenticity, have been maintained.

The scruffy palisades have been removed, though as yet nothing has been put in place. There are medium-term plans to apply for lottery funding to reconstruct one of the complex dry stone–walled phases of the gateway; this would be the first such reconstruction in Britain.

The mystic maze of quartz blocks has been dismantled and cleared from the site, though the spring has been enhanced by the placing of wooden idols there, and the children tie pieces of cloth to the surrounding branches, as was done until relatively recent times at holy wells. Indeed, the effectiveness of this simulation is such that some of the "New Age" travellers who have settled in the area use the spring as a real spiritual place, and they have placed offerings there. In addition, various Iron Age/Celtic recreation groups use the site, carrying out activities with varying degrees of accuracy and skill. Some individuals in these groups are only interested in experimenting to discover about the past, but many are more emotionally involved, feeling a link with this Celtic past, finding a place in the present through their escape at weekends into this romanticized barbarism. Reconstructions on the actual site of an ancient settlement give particular value to the experience of living and sleeping at Castell Henllys, over some of the other reconstruction sites that travellers also visit. The potency of the place can be indicated through the ceremony of a "wedding" which took place at the site one evening in August 1996 between two members of one of the recreation groups. Castell Henllys is now creating its own subcultures, working within or beyond the strict control of archaeologists, Park site management, or planning authorities.

The educational uses of Castell Henllys were also realized by the Park with the construction of an innovative and well-equipped education center in the valley immediately below the fort, and the employment of education staff. The National Curriculum for Wales includes within its history syllabus a section on the Celtic origins of the Welsh. This reflects the developing sense of national identity within Wales (the English curriculum starts with the Romans and has no prehistory in it at all). Three themes were specified within Key Stage 2, Study Unit 2, which are Iron Age/Celtic, and all of these can be successfully considered at Castell Henllys: tribes, hill forts and chieftains in England and Wales; farming and daily life; Celtic religion: the Druid, myths and legends (Welsh Office 1991, 21; Mytum 2000).

Role-playing and empathy are important in the teaching of history at Key Stage 2. For the children, therefore, the mystical and military aspects beloved by Foster inspire imagination. The children explore and re-create pasts, aided by professional actors and educators in costume. This may not seem very innovative in the United States, but it is unusual in Britain, particularly for remote periods. For the children, they go from the education center through a wooden maze on the ground (a reflection of Foster's on-site maze) across a stream via a wooden bridge, and so are transported back into the past. From then on, going up the hill to the site and during their time there, they imagine they are in the Iron Age. They are Celts, their ancestors. About half the schools experience Castell Henllys through the medium of Welsh.

Figure 5.3.   A public program at Castell Henllys.

Conclusion: The Value of Reconstructions at Castell Henllys

Castell Henllys was saved by local political pressure and can be used in the National Curriculum syllabus because of the in situ reconstructions. The excavated site on its own would not have attracted public concern. Its indigenous, Celtic, Welsh associations, made alive by reconstruction but validated by their location on a real site, were crucial for its survival. This power of national identity can be seen in other Welsh archaeological initiatives. Medieval castles built by the Welsh, such as Dolforwyn (Butler 1990) and Dryslwyn (Caple 1990) have been excavated, consolidated, and will be opened to the public by Cadw; Clwyd County Council has already done this at Caergwle (Manley 1994). In all cases there has been no overt reconstruction because the consolidated remains are impressive enough, but it is the castles of the Welsh princes that now attract new funding, not the English castles such as Caernarvon which, though more impressive, are reminders of English repression.

Castell Henllys is thus part of a wider trend, but the castles of the Welsh princes still were small copies of the English structures. The fort at Castell Henllys, though part of a wider Iron Age cultural tradition, is not tainted by English domination (England was at this stage all Celtic or at least not English!). It can stand proudly for a heritage largely invisible today. The Iron Age farmstead at the National Museum of Wales, St. Fagan's Folk Life Museum, is the only other Celtic facility with external reconstruction available for school visits (Mytum 2000), although a commercial site, Celtica, in north Wales, uses internal high-tech display methods to emphasize Welsh identity and links with a rather mythical past.

Castell Henllys is still unique in being the only Iron Age, Celtic site available for educational use and public display. It has been saved by its power to evoke cultural roots and traditions, and a sense of identity in a people regaining confidence in and command of their cultural lives. It needs to be understood in terms of context with regard to the on-site reconstructions, and in context with regard to its various roles today. The threads linking past and present are nowhere more visible than at Castell Henllys.

References

Anonymous
  1994   A Hand-Made Link to the Iron Age. *The Architects' Journal,* 6 July, 29–39.

Butler, L. A. S.
  1990   Excavations at Dolforwyn Castle, Powys, 1986–90. *Archaeology in Wales 30,* 19–20.

Caple, C.
  1990   The Castle and Lifestyle of a 13th-Century Independent Welsh Lord; Excavations at Dryslwyn Castle 1980–1988. *Chateau Gaillard* 14, 47–59.

Davis, P. R.
  1987   *Carew Castle.* Pembrokeshire Coast National Park Authority, Haverfordwest.

DCCED
  1993   *Pathways to the Past. The Celts at Castell Henllys.* Dyfed County Council Education Department and Pembrokeshire Coast National Park Authority, Haverfordwest.

Gilchrist, R., and H. C. Mytum
  1986   Experimental Archaeology and Burnt Animal Bone from Archaeological Sites. *Circaea* 4(1): 29–38.

Manley, J.
  1994   Caergwle Castle, Clwyd. *Medieval Archaeology* 38.

Mytum, H. C.
  1985   Excavation, Reconstruction and Display: Some Issues in the Presentation of Archaeology to the Public. *CBA Group 4 Forum 1984–1985,* 17–24.
  1986   The Reconstruction of an Iron Age Roundhouse at Castell Henllys, Dyfed. *Bulletin of the Board of Celtic Studies* 33: 283–290.
  1988   *Castell Henllys. A Visitor's Guide.* Department of Archaeology, University of York.

1991a Excavation at the Iron Age Fort of Castell Henllys, 1981–1989. *Archaeology in Wales* 29: 6–10.

1991b Castell Henllys: Iron Age Fort. *Fortress* 9 (May): 3–11.

Mytum, H.

1994 Language as Symbol in Churchyard Monuments: The Use of Welsh in Nineteenth- and Twentieth-Century Pembrokeshire. *World Archaeology* 26(2): 252–267.

1999 Pembrokeshire's Pasts. Natives, Invaders and Welsh Archaeology: the Castell Henllys Experience. In *The Constructed Past: Experimental Archaeology, Education and the Public*, edited by P. G. Stone and P. G. Planel, pp. 181–193, Routledge, New York.

2000 Archaeology and History for Welsh Primary Classes. *Antiquity* 74: 165–171.

2003 Evoking Time and Place in Reconstruction and Display: The Case of Celtic Identity and Iron Age Art. In *Ancient Muses. Archaeology and the Arts*, edited by J. H. Jameson Jr., J. E. Ehrenhard, and C. A. Finn, pp. 92–108, University of Alabama Press, Tuscaloosa.

RCAHMW

1925 *An Inventory of the Ancient Monuments in Wales 7. County of Pembroke.* HMSO, London.

Reynolds, P.

1999 Butser Ancient Farm, Hampshire, UK. In *The Constructed Past: Experimental Archaeology, Education and the Public*, edited by P. G. Stone and P. G. Planel, pp. 124–135, Routledge, New York.

Welsh Office

1991 *History in the National Curriculum (Wales).* HMSO, London.

Chapter Six

Bede's World, A Late-Twentieth-Century Creation of an Early Medieval Landscape

The Venerable Bede was a monk famous in his own time, thirteen hundred years ago. He spent the whole of his life, from boyhood, in the twin monastery of Wearmouth-Jarrow in northern England, living after his thirteenth year in the early medieval monastery at Jarrow, not far from the mouth of the River Tyne. His contemporary influence as a devout man of God and a scholar was considerable throughout Europe, and his prodigious literary output has continued to excite Christians, theologians, philosophers, and historians ever since. Essentially, through the output of the monastic scriptorium, he made available to his contemporaries in early medieval Europe much learning from the late Classical and Early Christian world of the Mediterranean as translations and commentaries, adding original works from his own creative mind and research. Among the last were hagiography and history books, notably his life of St. Cuthbert, a founding father of Christianity in the emergent Anglo-Saxon kingdom of Northumbria in the seventh century AD, and his *Ecclesiastical History of the English People*. This study remains one of the key sources of early history in Britain, and he was a pioneer of modern history.

St. Paul's Church now stands on the site of Bede's monastery. Indeed, it incorporates as its chancel the surviving late-seventh-century chapel in which Bede worshipped; and its nave, an impressive Victorian rebuild, is standing on the same location as a larger monastic church from which fine Anglo-Saxon sculpture was rescued. That sculpture is now displayed in its north aisle. Following archaeological excavations in the 1960s and 1970s, it was possible to indicate for future visitors the layout of much of the Bedan monastery (figure 6.1) and its medieval successor (ruins of which still stand) by using differently colored stones to mark in the grass the positions of various buildings and lines of walls (figure 6.3). Of even greater consequence was the conversion of a nearby house, Jarrow Hall, into a museum to display the material from the excavation and to explore the concept of early Northumbria and its "Golden Age" in the decades either side of AD 700. Northumbria

Figure 6.1. St. Paul's Church, Jarrow, from the bridge over the River Don to its southeast, showing the position of the Bedan and medieval monasteries on the same site and the late-seventh-century chapel forming its chancel. (All figures in chapter 6, courtesy of Peter Fowler.)

was the first of the major early Anglo-Saxon kingdoms that led, two hundred years later, to the emergence of an identifiable "England."

By 1990, Jarrow Hall was ready for major refurbishment; it stood at the core of a complex of new museum buildings, planned to open for the millennium. This ambition was fired by the appropriateness of thus honoring Bede, for it was he who introduced into the developing Christian culture of early medieval Europe the concept of measuring time from the year of Jesus' birth. The neoclassical courtyard and atrium (figure 6.2) echo the architectural ideas brought back from the Roman world to Wearmouth and Jarrow in the late seventh century AD. Meanwhile, major works have changed the local environs, and they now include an "Anglo-Saxon landscape" (figure 6.3).

Gyrwe

Pronounced "Jeerwe," *Gyrwe* is the Old English name from which the modern "Jarrow" derives. We have transposed it to our modern early medieval creation, a land-

Figure 6.2.   Courtyard and entrance to the new museum building, Bede's World, Jarrow.

scape with buildings akin to that which Bede might well have looked out on from his monastic window.

The area covers some twelve acres (ca. five hectares) immediately north of the new museum. It lies on a low, clay plateau above the junction of two rivers, the Tyne to the north and, now in a modern cut which we have enhanced, the Don to the east (figure 6.3). The Don formerly emptied across an extensive area of mud flats farther east, a tidal zone stretching round to the southeast and thus defining part of the original context of the Bedan monastery. West of the monastery, however, and north to Jarrow Hall, the land rises to the local plateau of our Anglo-Saxon farm (figure 6.4). It is likely that this area lay on part of the estate given by the king in AD 681 to support the new monastery, an estate which was probably based on the coastal plateau between the Rivers Tyne and Wear. We have to remember that, to achieve its primary function, a monastery had to feed a number of economically nonproductive mouths, so an agricultural estate to produce both food and rent was essential. One of the farms on the Monkwearmouth / Jarrow estate could well have lain in the area of our Gyrwe, though archaeological investigations before our own development did not recognize evidence of that period.

Satisfactory though it is to think that we may be laboring on land worked by Bede's contemporaries, the thought is not fundamental to our purpose. The important point is not the exact location, but the historical appropriateness of the activity.

Figure 6.3.   Aerial photograph on 8 August 1994, of Bede's World, Jarrow, from the south, with the bridge center bottom, St. Paul's Church and monastic sites by the River Don in the foreground, Jarrow Hall in the center, Phase 1 of the new museum building under construction and, beyond, the seventh-century landscape of Gyrwe as physically completed in 1993. Both banks of the River Don on the right have been landscaped, and the river's profile adjusted, to provide mudflats at low tide to encourage wading birds. The River Tyne is in the background.

Our Approach

"Appropriateness" is all; we often use the word "honesty" in that context. By that, we mean that everything we do at and with *Gyrwe* must have its academic reference point, preferably among primary evidence. That could be a definition basic to

Figure 6.4. Aerial photograph on 6 August 1995, of Gyrwe, showing significant development in the year since the stage shown in figure 6.3. New "Anglo-Saxon" fields with wickerwork fences are appearing along the river, respecting the straight length of "Roman" canalized stream and overlying the fragmentary, rectilinear pattern of "prehistoric" fields. The "prehistoric" burial mound is bottom left and the bow-sided framework of Thirlings Hall, with building materials alongside, is lower center. Phase 2 of the new museum, with exhibition and meeting rooms, now occupies the builders' site, top center.

"authenticity;" so, since in addition to being authentic in that sense, we are also running *Gyrwe* as a public demonstration of an early medieval farm, our invocation of honesty comes in with the need to interpret so that others may become involved. We do not, therefore, display and use a particular type of plough as "Anglo-Saxon," for example. We do say that we do not know what type of cultivating implement was used by workers on the Bedan monastic farm but that, for various reasons which we explain, it is likely to have been from the range of implements which the visitor can see lying at the field edge. Meanwhile, since we have to plough in order to "work" our farm, in practice we might well use two or three examples on the same day, demonstrating their considerable differences in use (figure 6.10).

Similarly, we do not pretend that our numerous animals are exact replicas or descendants of Anglo-Saxon animals when such is not the case. Rather, we are honest, seeking to explain the difference between physical similarity and genetic difference. Our oxen, for example, are Dexter cattle, because genuine strains of Anglo-Saxon oxen no longer exist; but Dexters, properly castrated, grow to about the right size for early medieval draught cattle, as can be demonstrated by comparing them with data from animal bone reports from archaeological excavation of Anglo-Saxon sites. Our sheep, on the other hand, not only look right but, to varying degrees, are genetically authentic in that they are the descendants of unimproved flocks which survived in remote places like islands in the Hebrides and the Irish Sea, beyond the reach of the improving farmers of the eighteenth and nineteenth centuries. Genuine, genetically early medieval pigs are, in contrast, unobtainable, but they were so important to economy and society thirteen hundred years ago that the animal simply has to be represented. What people see is a physical approximation to what would have been on the monastic farm of Bede's day or running wild in Northumbrian woods. The image is so different from what people are used to when they think of present-day "pig" that the point is made, reinforced by a short explanatory panel in our characteristic style on the side of their sty (figure 6.5 and 6.6).

So, overall, our concept is to be honest for its own sake and also, in pursuing honesty, to use the many opportunities created to engage our visitors in what we are trying to do intellectually as well as physically. That is, by referencing everything, we introduce concepts such as primary evidence and secondary sources, the idea that few things are "right" in an absolutist sense, and that historical or archaeological "accuracy" is usually a matter of taking a balanced judgment from incomplete, sometimes conflicting, evidence. That may sound somewhat forbidding for what is meant to be a "popular" visitor destination, so we would stress that none of this is too overt, even though it is very much in our minds.

We nevertheless hope people can simply come and enjoy an afternoon out by seeing an "old tyme farm" with its rather quaint animals and reconstructed thatched buildings. There is nothing to stop anyone experiencing this part of Bede's World, any more than you need to know about early Northumbrian history before visiting the new museum display indoors, or about the Christian liturgy to gain something from the experience of visiting St. Paul's Church. Our visitors are quietly offered the chance to participate, if they so wish, in the process of scholarship itself. Bede's World's mission is, after all, educational rather than merely entertainment for its own sake, though we hope people enjoy what we have to offer. We set out to be a bit different from competing experiences in other museums, at outdoor experiences, and less cerebral theme parks. While our "reconstructions" can be taken at face

Figure 6.5. Semi-wild pigs representing Anglo-Saxon stock at Gyrwe, on 1 December 1997.

value, we encourage people, from schoolchildren onward, to engage with them in more of an intellectual context, too.

As it happens, we are not very keen on the word "reconstruction." Our landscape is a creation, a composite not based on any particular prototype and therefore not a "reconstruction" in the sense of accurately building again something that once existed. Furthermore, since we do not know how our early medieval timber buildings were originally constructed, our efforts can hardly be *re*-constructions. We constructed the experimental buildings partly to try to find out how they might or might not have been built in the first place. But we have also put up other buildings for statutory and practical reasons; those we make appropriate in appearance, so as not to spoil the overall impression of our landscape, but they are neither "authentic" nor experimental. We draw the distinctions honestly.

Fields and Landscape

The area that was to become *Gyrwe* was occupied by several large petrol storage tanks until the mid-1980s; it had previously enjoyed various uses, some industrial, some horticultural. Such was the disturbance to and pollution of the soil that much of it had to be removed by machine and replaced before a new landscape could

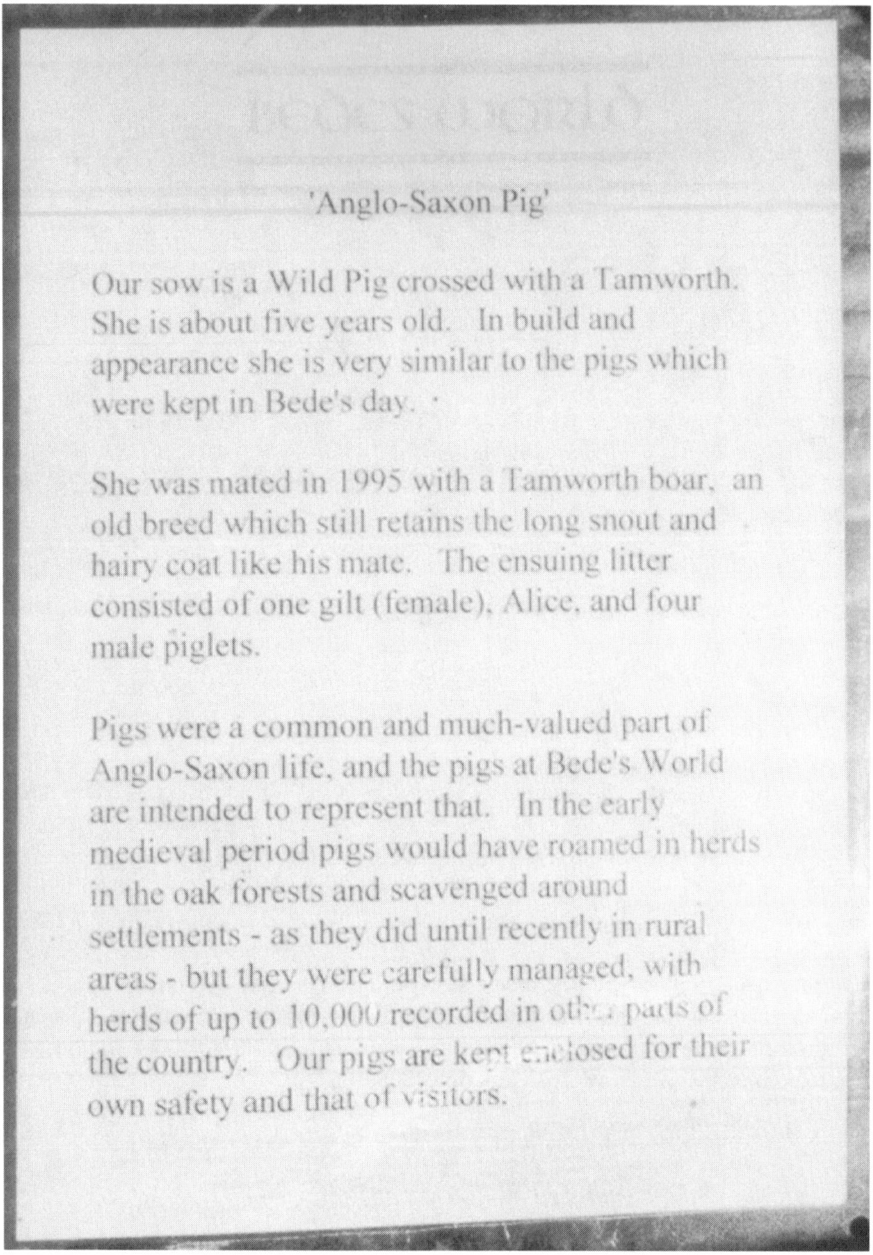

'Anglo-Saxon Pig'

Our sow is a Wild Pig crossed with a Tamworth.
She is about five years old. In build and
appearance she is very similar to the pigs which
were kept in Bede's day. ·

She was mated in 1995 with a Tamworth boar, an
old breed which still retains the long snout and
hairy coat like his mate. The ensuing litter
consisted of one gilt (female), Alice, and four
male piglets.

Pigs were a common and much-valued part of
Anglo-Saxon life, and the pigs at Bede's World
are intended to represent that. In the early
medieval period pigs would have roamed in herds
in the oak forests and scavenged around
settlements - as they did until recently in rural
areas - but they were carefully managed, with
herds of up to 10,000 recorded in other parts of
the country. Our pigs are kept enclosed for their
own safety and that of visitors.

Figure 6.6. The changeable information panel on the wickerwork fence of the pigsty in
1990s Bede's World house-style, explaining and not pretending.

emerge in accord with our vision. The money for this work was entirely nonarchaeological: it was public money, available for the clearance of postindustrial dereliction and the formation of a newly landscaped and more pleasant riverside. Landscaping was going to be carried out anyway, and our intervention scarcely made any difference to what the machines actually did; they had to scrape and shovel and mould hundreds of thousands of tons of debris and soil around these twelve acres to some sort of plan in any case. We merely provided *our* plan to the civil engineers, and interceded sometimes with the machine drivers (figure 6.7). As a result, their efforts fashioned an elongated, shallow bowl falling slightly northward (figures 6.3 and 6.4). It contained a pond fed by a stream, and represented in our eyes a valley. Its rounded, northern end was designed to accommodate our experimental buildings, but no particular layout was in mind initially for the buildings as an *ensemble,* for

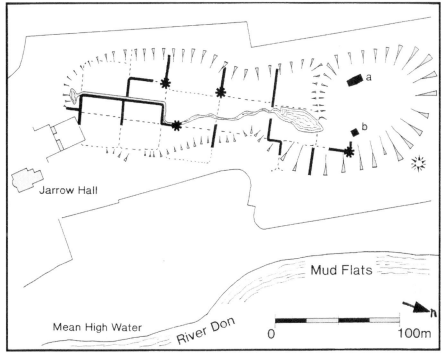

Figure 6.7.   Simplified plan of Gyrwe, the "Anglo-Saxon" landscape at Bede's World created in the 1990s. The solid lines mark banks forming the boundaries of "prehistoric" fields built into this landscape as relict features; the broken lines indicate the overall pattern of which they could have been fragmentary remains in an actual seventh-century landscape. The cogwheel symbols indicate the positions of semi-mature oak trees planted on "old" banks. The Thirlings Hall and the Grubenhaus (sunken floored building), constructed 1995–1997, are marked by "a" and "b," respectively.

we intended to experiment in the construction of individual buildings, not create a fantasy village. This simple physical topography resulting from this considerable use of energy was of itself hardly meaningful, yet the machines produced a new landscape shaped in accord with an intellectual concept rather than solely with a landscape architect's physical design.

Our concept was deeply rooted in the ideas of landscape archaeology. Normally, the landscape archaeologist surveys his or her chosen area, discovering and recording what is there and, as a step in trying to understand what has happened there, dividing the components of the record into different periods or layers in the landscape. Mechanistically, he or she may be able to peel off in the mind and on the map the later materials, working backward toward some theoretical virgin stretch of countryside untouched by human agency. More creative and realistic is the intellectual approach that works forward with the flow of time and follows the processes of landscape formation, recognizing that, at any one time, landscape is itself a composite. This is, after all, one of the main generalizations to emerge from recent research into the landscapes of early England and their workings, at local level as single estates, and as components of much larger and scattered estates (Hooke 1985, 1997).

In physically creating a landscape of ca. AD 700 in 1991–1992, we built into it elements known both locally and elsewhere and likely to have been included in what would already have been an ancient landscape at Jarrow in the time of Bede. Conceptually, had Bede been a field archaeologist, he would have expected to find on the Northumbrian coastal plain in AD 700 pre-Roman burial mounds, fields, and possibly traces of settlements and tracks, and remains of Roman occupation and activity. So we invented in our minds and then drew out on paper what we thought, with some justification, might have been the sort of archaeological landscape—a relict landscape—into which the new monastery and its farms were inserted in the later seventh century. We then created it on the ground (figure 6.4).

Of course it included a Bronze Age round barrow on the local skyline (figure 6.8), and of course traces remained of cultivation in an area occupied and farmed in the last centuries BC and early centuries AD. In fact, the realization of our plan looked almost eerily too convincing from the air (figure 6.4). In real history, such farming may well have been intensified during the Roman centuries, not least with military garrisons to be fed locally, so our landscape included not just remains of early enclosed, small fields but also adjustments to them. In the southern part of the valley, we deliberately made the stream run straight between rather larger, more rectilinear fields, representing the sort of changes that could well have occurred on farmlands of the coastal plain in, say, the second and third centuries AD. The basic evidence for these archaeological features were the authors' own knowledge of landscapes with time depth in Northumberland and elsewhere, and published plans of premedieval field systems from the region (Gates 1982, 1983).

We emphasize, however, that we set out to incorporate an idea rather than copy or reconstruct any particular example. Neither our "early" nor "Roman" fields are

Figure 6.8. The "prehistoric burial mound" on the local skyline, as seen on 1 December 1997, from the southern gable end of the Thirlings Hall at Bede's World.

therefore exactly the same as the two field systems in figures 6.9a and 6.9b, for example, but our earthworks represent that type of evidence fairly accurately and also incorporate the concept of succession. The concept is reinforced when people see present-day "real" activity on the same area, representing early medieval farming in a third arrangement of fields over "Roman" and "prehistoric" ones. For serious educational purposes, it is but a short demonstrative step from the concept of "succession" to that of "landscape stratification."

Every landscape accretes stories about it as well as new features to it, so here we also suggested that the prehistoric barrow could have been used for a beacon to guide boats on the Tyne in Roman times. Interestingly, illustrating our point that landscape features acquire stories and a life of their own, it has already appeared in others' writings as "Fowler's Tump" and "Signal Hill." The mound might too have been the site of the first wooden cross in this landscape, two generations before Bede. Such imaginings refer to more circumstantial evidence such as well-attested folklore about burial mounds and Bede's reportage of Pope Gregory's instruction to Augustine to go out and take Christian worship to pagan shrines. Casual visitors need not of course know any of this and will certainly not have it thrust upon them; they will at best see some humps and bumps in the ground and may not even wonder what they are.

For us, however, our modern simulacrum—not a reconstruction—of a thirteen-hundred-year-old landscape importantly recognizes that it was already an old land-

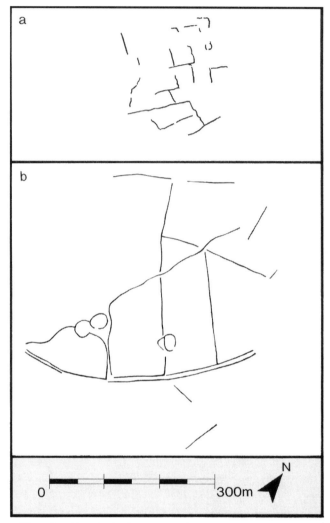

Figure 6.9a. Plan of prehistoric field system, Todlaw Pike, Northumberland (after Gates 1983, figure 16).

Figure 6.9b. Plan of Roman field system, Colberry Hill, Humbleton, Northumberland (after Gates 1982, figure 4).

scape for those who saw it thirteen hundred years ago. We suspect that they would have seen things and known it was an ancestral landscape. It was already a populated place, with a history and spirits and ghosts, a powerful story with which to stimulate the imaginations of our visitors looking at a landscape which, nevertheless, we are at pains to stress we created in the early 1990s. But in that creation, for better or for worse, we built into that landscape a capacity to be more than just a physical artifice.

It is more than that anyway for, theoretical concepts apart, we also try to farm our twelve acres as a working agricultural landscape. Ours is very definitely not a static model; nor is it just a stage set. It is, of course, too small to support a whole farm in the sense of being a freestanding, economically viable unit, but we nevertheless not only keep real animals—with everything that alone entails—but manage the landscape in a realistic, agricultural way as may well have been the case around AD 700 (Fowler 1997). For example, we rotate our cereal and grass crops around the available arable land, and we spread the fertilizing benefits of sheep-grazing carefully over the land. All the time, we are conscious of both the generalities and the detail now available for the early medieval period from environmental research (Rackham 1994; van der Veen 1992).

Our major failures so far are twofold. Our landscape depended critically on being clothed with appropriate vegetation. The sides of the valley were meant to be covered with trees and bushes, giving the impression that the fields below had been cleared from woodland; but many of the ten thousand trees we planted have not taken and, even if they have not died, not one has grown as it should. A combination of overconsolidated slopes, lack of nourishment in reconstituted soils, and unfavorable weather—too dry and too cold for long periods in 1992–1996—has meant that our valley slopes remain grassy rather than leafy to the eye. So far, vegetation on them has not begun to mitigate skyscapes dominated by petrol storage tanks to the west and the highest electricity pylon in the country on the east. The disappointment is all the greater because we so carefully planted only species known to have been native to the Northumbrian landscape of Bede's time—hardy deciduous trees like oak, beech, ash, and hawthorn. We are now replanting, but meanwhile have lost five precious years during which our woodland should have begun to provide an appropriate backcloth to the farmed landscape below it.

The other failure so far simply reflects inadequate resources. We have not yet been able to start serious experimental work on our farm with respect to cultivating techniques, crop-growing, and cereal yields. We want to follow in the footsteps of the pioneers in Denmark (Lerche 1994) and at Butser, Hampshire (Reynolds 1979), contributing our data from a different geology and climate at a slightly different latitude and longitude. But we have had such difficulties with soil and weather, as well as too few willing hands, that so far we have not been able to begin a properly controlled and monitored experimental program.

Such observations and measurements that we have produced suggest that, with various "primitive" cereals to hand, an autumn sowing of spelt is well worthwhile and that a spring sowing before April is a waste of time. Conversely, in 1997, after a very wet summer, we were able to harvest emmer, spelt, and einkorn well into an "Indian summer" in early October. Overall, we have learned that to sow broadcast is to throw the grains away, implying that we have not yet learned how to do it properly here rather than that early medieval farmers did not do it. More positively, we have also learned that taking the extra trouble to plant in rows infinitely improves the chances of a successful crop, provided you have the person-power to hoe the weeds between the rows during the early weeks of plant growth. Such are but snippets of information, however, not the result of proper experimentation. We are planning that our second five years on the farm will overcome these difficulties in wood and field.

"Anglo-Saxon" Buildings

The decision to construct timber buildings grew out of the same fundamental aim of showing secular life in Bede's time. It was considered important to provide for visitors a contrast with the Continental environment of the early medieval monastery, with its stone-built, plastered walls, richly decorated with stone carvings, paintings on wooden boards, and glass windows (figure 6.1). Our historical justification was, of course, that while it is stone-rich ecclesiastical centers and their many fine artistic products that catch the attention of scholar and tourist alike, the majority of people in the early medieval secular world lived in timber buildings. Such were of various sizes, shapes, and designs, and perhaps also elaborately decorated, but they have not survived. Nor has the tradition of timber building itself, already old in the seventh century, survived in Northumbria.

For our experimental program, we decided to select our buildings from settlement sites which had been excavated in the area formerly comprising Northumbria in its heyday, that is, the land between the Firth of Forth to the north and the Humber estuary to the south (see generally, Rahtz 1976, and Powlesland 1997). Only the tools and techniques known to have been used at the time would be employed to build them (figure 6.10). This would obviously have a considerable impact on the construction time-scale. In keeping with the intention of founding our work on sound academic principles, a workshop was held in May 1993 at Bede's World to discuss the experiment. Among those present were archaeologists involved in the excavation of early medieval settlement sites and the most experienced builder of "Anglo-Saxon timber buildings" in the country (whose expertise was subsequently made available to us on-site).

The buildings were selected to demonstrate variety of scale, construction technique, and type. At first they were chosen from just three sites: the seventh-century royal residence of Yeavering1, northwest of Wooler in north Northumberland (Hope-Taylor 1977); the single phase, later mid-seventh century settlement of Thirlings, a few kilometers to the northeast of Yeavering (O'Brien and Miket 1991); and the

Figure 6.10.   Wooden tools of the general sort which might have been in use on the monastic estate in the eighth century and which are used in farming at Gyrwe in the late twentieth century: a hay fork, a spade, an ox-yoke, and a flail.

largely unexplored site of New Bewick in the same area (Gates and O'Brien 1988)(figures 6.11 and 6.12). New Bewick was the only excavated example of a *grubenhaus* (sunken-featured building) in Bernicia, the northern province of Nor-thumbria throughout the sixth to eighth centuries. Published evidence suggested we should choose from a wider range of sites, including the early medieval monastic site at Hartlepool, County Durham (Daniels 1988, 158–210), the monastic site of Whithorn in southwest Scotland (Hill 1997), and the large planned settlement of West Heslerton in North Yorkshire (Powlesland 1997).

We decided that it was important to begin the experiment with a relatively small structure on which construction techniques could be learned without delaying too long the addition of a striking vertical element to the farm landscape. Building A from Thirlings was chosen. It was quite large, about 40 ft. × 20 ft. (12m × 6m), possibly the main hall in the settlement where everyone gathered for feasting and meetings. The building as excavated had a foundation trench some 2 ft. 9 ins. deep (about .80 m) in which stains of the post and panel positions had survived and from which it was possible to suggest the type of wall construction. The ground plan was used to prepare working drawings, including elevations and an axonometric view. The 1 ft. (.30 m) diameters of the timbers were based on those of the stains in the

Figure 6.11.   The cluster of timber buildings at the north end of Gyrwe, Bede's World, on 1 December 1997, with the two completed experimental buildings (Thirlings, a seventh-century hall, "a" on figure 6.7 and Grubenhaus, "b" on figure 6.7) on the left and a nonexperimental shed covering a bread-making oven to the right.

foundation trench. The length of timbers was calculated on the basis that the height of the walls would be about 6 ft. (2 m) above ground level. All of the other calculations were made by working out what was most likely from the ground plan.

In reality, of course, we cannot achieve a true reconstruction because we can never be sure how such a building "worked," let alone what it looked like. What we can show empirically are some versions that are unlikely to have been constructed on practical grounds and others which could have been used. We cannot, and do not, say "this is how it was." As in similar experiments elsewhere, we can narrow the band of probability. In practice, of course, especially when building in and for the public gaze, the building must be able to stand up and withstand the most severe weather conditions.

Before the work began, we had to find a constructor willing and able to tackle it as we intended. We were fortunate in finding a man with experience of traditional boat building where adzes (arguably one of the early medieval carpenter's most important tools) were still used. In due course, he was able to train an unemployed joiner who was employed as our assistant constructor after his training. Though those two have done the bulk of the timberwork, principally preparing the timbers for use, they were also able to train a volunteer who helped them part-time and has now become extremely proficient. Many people have, of course, been involved in

Figure 6.12. View northwestward from the edge of the pond at Gyrwe with, in the foreground, the "monastic cell" based on evidence excavated at Hartlepool, County Durham, and the southern gable of Thirlings Hall.

the construction, digging the foundation trenches, helping to raise the gable uprights and the ridgepoles, thatch the building, make the wattle panels, daub and lime-wash them; but it is the timber preparation that takes time.

The foundation trench was actually excavated by hand, as we intended to adhere rigidly to the principle of replicating all original techniques. Unlike the original builders at Thirlings, however, who were digging trenches in light sands and gravels, our volunteers were hacking their way through heavy, clayey, reclaimed soil, containing a variety of foreign bodies—bricks, pipes, even twisted wire cable. The posts were nevertheless placed exactly as in the original trenches. The trench was back-filled as soon as the posts were in place; the posts were then held together by fitting the wall plates. The plan indicates that the building was based on a two-square module, but in practice was somewhat irregular, with unevenly spaced posts, two opposing doorways of different widths and one end narrower than the other. This last factor necessitated the use of a two-piece ridgepole, resulting in a roof that slopes down considerably at one end. A professional thatcher was employed to thatch this asymmetrical structure; while doing so, he trained a member of staff to thatch.

The paneling in the gaps between the timber uprights of the walls was woven but not daubed until the roof had been thatched; daubing then proved an illuminating experience, begun at the end of March 1997 and completed in May. Various proportions of clay, straw, and water were tried and recorded. Even with the best mixture, there was substantial shrinkage and cracking which fluctuated according to the weather conditions. The solution was to allow the mixture to dry out, then fill cracks and gaps repeatedly until the shrinkage ceased. Different lime-wash recipes were also tried. The linseed oil added to provide a waterproofing element caused the lime-wash to slide off the previous coat; a small amount of boiled linseed oil in the mixture seemed to work best. Even so, on an extremely wet day in June, with rain lashing against the north gable wall, the lime-wash and the daub began to soften, bubble, and disintegrate. It seems likely that maintaining the lime-washed daub in a sound condition was an annual task on these buildings.

Thirlings Building A, as built 1994–1997, has consumed about 30 tons of green, fifty–sixty-year-old oak of the correct diameter for the main structural timbers; substantial quantities of willow, hazel, and birch for the wattle paneling (though small and otherwise waste pieces unsuitable for fencing can be utilized for this); about 25 tons of local boulder clay, straw, and water for the daub; slaked lime, water, brick-dust (for coloring) and boiled linseed oil (waterproofing) for the lime-wash. For the roof, seventy ash poles from Suffolk were interwoven with hazel rods from Cumbria; and eighteen hundred bundles of reed from Tayside in eastern Scotland were used for thatch. In his *Ecclesiastical History* (Colgrave and Mynors 1969, 111.25), Bede mentions a church on Lindisfarne being thatched "after the Scots manner." One hundred and twenty-five bundles of sedge from Cambridgeshire were used to provide a finish to the ridge.

During the three years our small team took to construct Thirlings A, its members were also acquiring the skills needed to create such timber buildings, structures which in the seventh century were the products of tradition and experience. We have certainly made mistakes and have doubtless done and not done things out of sheer ignorance of what was perfectly obvious to a seventh-century craftsman. We also learned another important lesson by constructing such a building. The estate-workers then would have worked in teams, and the timber preparation would have been carried out off-site, probably where the timber was felled, especially if it was growing some distance away from the construction site. In other words, the building would have been prefabricated and would have arrived at *Gyrwe* as a kit ready to assemble. As it was, we innocently wasted a lot of energy transporting bark and unwanted wood on the tree trunks and branches brought from an upcountry estate some fifty miles (80 kms) away. It possessed the only managed woodland that could meet our need. We also learned that there are no longer areas of hazel, willow, and ash coppice in the region capable of providing large quantities of timber to "traditional" specifications.

The importance of that lesson was emphasized by the relatively small resource consumption and ease of construction of our first *grubenhaus*. The archaeological evidence for the New Bewick example (Gates and O'Brien 1988) consisted essentially of a central posthole at each end of a pit about 15½ ft. × 13 ft. × 1½ ft.

deep (4.7m × 3.9m. × 0.5m) (Gates and O'Brien, 1988, 5–8). These features were replicated to these dimensions at *Gyrwe*. The poor quality soil necessitated the use of a wattled revetment in the pit. The roof, for which we had no direct evidence, was constructed with a ridgepole and rafters of ash interwoven with hazel, supporting heather thatch. Heather was probably a popular roofing material in moorland areas, where it can occasionally be found on buildings today; it has proved to be an excellent, waterproof material. The roof sits on the ground around the pit. The gable walls were constructed of horizontal oak planking with half-lapped joints, the planks pegged on to a triangular frame. The door was made of vertical planks and fitted, in the absence of any surviving evidence, with a sliding lock mechanism. Sockets in the frame were lubricated with beeswax, enabling the pivots of this heavy door to rotate easily. No metal was used in the construction of the building.

This *grubenhaus* was left with a sunken floor, accessed by an improbable flight of wooden steps fitted with handrails to satisfy modern regulations for visitors. The structure is, to use a phrase beloved of real estate agents, "deceptively spacious" and can accommodate no less than twenty adults. It seems likely that such buildings were used, as has been noted elsewhere (Rahtz, 1976, 70–81), for a variety of purposes, including storage, weaving, and other crafts, and perhaps even as more than adequate sleeping accommodation. Merely by putting one up we may have stumbled on its "secret"—it is cheap and quick to build, requiring no great skill, especially in comparison to a framed building like Thirlings Hall; and, once up, it can then be used in all sorts of ways. We wonder whether the many agonized archaeological debates about "What was a *grubenhaus* for?" may well be missing the point, for it is the ease of erection and the functional nonspecificity of its design rather than any one specialist function which surely made it so popular a structure.

The hall is now partly furnished and is used by the museum's education service for exploring Anglo-Saxon life and skills, as well as providing a source of information for students and, indeed, all our visitors. It is also in demand by living history groups. The *grubenhaus* is fitted out as a weaving shed with a warp-weighted loom. Plans for building the next two structures are in hand and, in the meantime, we have not forgotten our date with King Edwin's altogether larger "palace." At some time in the future, when we have mastered three-dimensional timber construction, and have the necessary resources, we will rebuild one of the halls from Yeavering. It will probably be that associated by the excavator with the reign of King Edwin (AD 617–33). Some 25m long by 14m wide (ca. 80 ft. × 46 ft.), this would be the largest timber building reconstruction of any period in Britain.

Reflections

We have so far enjoyed mixed reactions to our farmland creation and its buildings. People generally seem to sense that it is different; taken with the images of that part of the new museum building already constructed, the reality of the seventh-century church, and the grass and trees around both, many speak of enjoying a sense of peace and renewal in an unexpectedly green corner of an otherwise fairly desolate postindustrial landscape on South Tyneside. Our achievement on the farm itself excites admiration, especially from local people who can easily remember its former appearance; and for many it is simply a farm, attractive mainly for its animals. Our semi-wild, fierce-looking pigs, academically representing the importance of the pig in Anglo-Saxon society, are especially popular; people love feeding them, the sheep, and our geese and hens. This would be so whether or not they are labeled "early medieval" and no harm in that; we all have to begin somewhere, and present-day suburban ignorance of the elements of farming is often as great as is that of Bede and early Christianity.

We have to attract people into our Anglo-Saxon landscape, for it is their entrance fees that enable us to continue; and we are happy to engage their interest at any level. Best of all is when a visitor becomes interested enough to volunteer as a helper. We run a successful school program throughout most of the year, and it is the fifteen thousand children each year who most use the landscape we have created. There, now, they can study aspects of the environment along the stream and in the pond, both of which look already as if they had been put there by nature thousands of years ago instead of by us five years ago. There is an important lesson in that alone. But the main educational use is archaeological and historical, both within as strong an agricultural as a religious framework. The animals in particular are a marvelous educational resource, making a "day on the Anglo-Saxon farm" as popular with children and their teachers as "a day in Bede's monastery."

Among the many lessons learned so far is the rediscovery of just how labor-intensive farming is—or, at least, is when you cannot use machinery. With only two cattle as our seventh-century power source, the dependence on manual labor is both sobering and a serious management problem. We can never run this farm by employing labor, so we simply need and have to rely on lots of volunteers. Building up such a source of help is critical to our survival. We have also relearned what a wide range of resources a premodern farm demands and what a drain on resources it is, and certainly would have been, to go and acquire food and all sorts of materials, often from some distance. We can begin to appreciate, the hard way, what is actually meant by a monastic estate, and our respect for early medieval long-term silvicultural management is considerable.

Yet, for all our aspirations, we also know now for certain that it is quite impossible to re-create a "true" past, for none such existed or exists; that is particularly so of a past as specific as our core idea. Furthermore, quite apart from philosophical and theoretical objections, the demands of our own time, populist and statutory, make it very difficult even to remain close to our principles. How, for example, do you accommodate in an early medieval landscape, with any pretensions to former realism, rain shelters for the visitors, seats for the tired and breathless, railings beside the pond, and other safety precautions as defined by law and insurance companies? There are legally required health and sanitary facilities for the animals (whose standard of living is rather higher than many peoples' today), equal access over the whole site for everyone regardless of their personal challenges, and a road and turning circle strong enough to bear an ambulance and fire-engine. These are all very desirable, some even essential, no doubt, but hardly the elements defining the view that a famous monk looked out on here thirteen hundred years ago. At the physical level alone, our creation can never be more than a severely compromised approximation to what a seventh-century landscape with buildings may have looked like, in its form and very being almost certainly saying more about us and the late twentieth century than about Bede and his time.

Postscript

In the intervening time since writing the first draft of this essay (1998), the Jarrow Hall has been completely refurbished and the large museum building completed. The Hartlepool "monastic cell" has also been built (figure 6.12), but a construction of a large hall based on archaeological evidence from Yeavering was not realized when a feasibility study indicated that it would cost some £300,000 (about $435,000) and, for health and safety reasons, involve the use of some very inauthentic modern construction techniques. The farm itself has come to be much better managed; some of the intended tree cover is established. No further systematic experimental work on other buildings or agricultural processes has, however, been conducted. The authors' official roles at Bede's World have ended, so this chapter does not now necessarily reflect current management policy or practice.

References

Colgrave, B., and R. A. B. Mynors
    1969   Bede's *Ecclesiastical History of the English People*. Clarendon Press, Oxford.

Daniels, R.
    1988   The Anglo-Saxon monastery at Church Close, Hartlepool, Cleveland. *Archaeological Journal* 145: 158–210.

Fowler, P. J.
    1997   Farming in Early Medieval England: Some Fields for Thought, and discussion thereof, in Hines (ed.), pp. 245–268.

Gates, T.
    1982   Farming on the Frontier: Romano-British Fields in Northumberland. In *Rural Settlement in the Roman North*, edited by P. Clack and S. Haselgrove. Council for British Archaeology Group 3, Durham, pp. 21–42.

1983   Unenclosed Settlements in Northumberland. In *Settlement in North Britain 1000 BC–AD 1000,* edited by J. C. Chapman and H. C. Mytum. British Archaeological Reports, British Series 118, pp.103–148.

Gates, T., and C. O'Brien
1988   Crop Marks at Milfield and New Bewick and the Recognition of Grubenhauser in Northumberland. *Archaeologia Aeliana 5th series,* 16: 1–9.

Hill, P.
1997   *Whithom and St. Ninian. The Excavation of a Monastic Town 1984–91.* The Whithorn Trust/Sutton Publishing, Stroud, Glos., U.K.

Hines, J., ed.
1997   *The Anglo-Saxons from the Migration Period to the Eighth Century. An Ethnographic Perspective.* Boydell Press, Woodbridge, Suffolk, U.K.

Hooke, D.
1985   *The Anglo-Saxon Landscape. The Kingdom of the Hwicce.* Manchester University Press, Manchester.
1997   The Anglo-Saxons in England in the Seventh and Eighth Centuries: Aspects of Location in Space, and discussion thereof, in Hines (ed.), 65–99.

Hooke D., ed.
1988   *Anglo-Saxon Settlements.* Blackwell, Oxford.

Hope-Taylor, B.
1977   *Yeavering: An Anglo-British Centre of Early Northumbria.* HMSO, London.

Lerche, G.
1994   *Ploughing Implements and Tillage Practices in Denmark from the Viking Period to about 1800 Experimentally Substantiated.* Kristensen, Horning.

O'Brien, C., and R. Miket
1991   The Early Medieval Settlement of Thirlings, Northumberland. *Durham Archaeol. J.* 7: 57–91.

Powlesland, D.
1997   Early Anglo-Saxon Settlements, Structures, Form and Layout, and discussion thereof, in Hines (ed.), 101–124.

Rackham, J., ed.
1994   *Environment and Economy in Anglo-Saxon England; A Review of Recent Work on the Environmental Archaeology of Rural and Urban Anglo-Saxon Settlement in England.* Council for British Archaeology, York.

Rahtz, P.
1976   Buildings and Rural Settlement. In *The Archaeology of Anglo-Saxon England.* D. M. Wilson, ed., pp. 49–58, Methuen, London.

Reynolds, P. J.
1979   *Iron Age Farm: The Butser Experiment.* British Museum, London.

van der Veen, M.

1992   *Crop Husbandry Regimes. An Archaeobotanical Study of Farming in Northern England 1000 BC–AD 500.* J. R. Collis Publications, University of Sheffield.

Suggested Further Reading:

The following three volumes, all central to considerations of the matter in this chapter, have been published since it was written (see above):

Dark, P.

2000   *The Environment of Britain in the First Millennium AD.* Duckworth, London.

Fowler, P. J.

2002   *Farming in the First Millennium AD: British Agriculture between Julius Caesar and William the Conqueror.* Cambridge University Press, Cambridge.

Hawkes, J., and S. Mills, eds.

1999   *Northumbria's Golden Age.* Sutton, Stroud.

ANN E. KILLEBREW ■

Chapter Seven

Reflections on a Reconstruction of the Ancient Qasrin Synagogue and Village

One of the most professionally challenging and rewarding, but at the same time trou-bling, projects I have been involved in as a field archaeologist working in Israel for the past twenty-six years was the excavation and reconstruction of a Byzantine vil-lage house at Qasrin. This was a moment of truth because I was forced to face how little I, as a twentieth-century archaeologist, really understood the material culture of daily life during the fourth to eighth centuries AD. The rewarding aspects of this endeavor were the enjoyment and enthusiasm of visitors to the site following the reconstruction and the realization that it is not necessarily the ancient remains them-selves, but rather how they are presented and how the story is told. With the recon-struction of the Qasrin Byzantine house, the most ordinary aspects of everyday life, rather than the monumental synagogue, became the focal points of the visitors' experience. However, in retrospect, I am troubled by several of the results of the reconstruction: the inevitable damage to the original remains; the manufacture of a world that creates the appearance of "authenticity" and "truth" or "fact" to the public, but in reality never existed; the emphasis on reconstructing particular aspects of Qasrin's history, resulting in a distortion of the archaeological record; and, like many other heritage sites in Israel and throughout the world, the apparently inevita-ble connection between modern politics and site presentations (see e.g., Silberman 1997; Killebrew 1999).

History of the Site and Excavations

The ancient village of Qasrin[1] is located in the central Golan Heights, approximately eight miles northeast of the Sea of Galilee. In 1884, Gottlieb Schumacher (1888: 194) first identified the site during his survey work in the Golan and later revisited

---

1. "Qasrin," a hebraized form of the Syrian village name "Kisrin," will be used in this article to designate the ancient site while "Katzrin" will be employed to indicate the modern Jewish town.

the site when he described "Kisrin" as a "small Bedouin winter village with a group of beautiful oak trees and old ruins." Subsequent to Schumacher's groundbreaking exploration of the Golan, the region remained largely "terra incognita." During Syrian rule, the region was a military zone closed to archaeological research, until the Arab-Israeli Six-Day War in 1967 when the region was conquered by Israel and reopened to exploration.

Modern archaeological survey in the Golan recommenced following the 1967 Israeli occupation of the region. Shmaryahu Gutman and Claire Epstein (1972) were two of the first archaeologists to lead systematic surveys in the region. Within the abandoned modern Syrian village of Kisrin, Gutman discerned a monumental entrance and lintel that he correctly identified as belonging to an ancient synagogue (Gutman and Epstein 1972: 270). The Qasrin synagogue is not unique. It is one of dozens of ancient synagogues and churches known in the Golan dating to the Byzantine period (fourth to seventh centuries AD), an era when this normally marginal region was heavily settled by Jewish, Christian, and pagan populations (Ma'oz 1981; 1985; Dauphin 1982; Dauphin and Schonfield 1983). Additional surveys in the Golan by Dan Urman (1985) from 1969 to 1971 uncovered numerous architectural elements originally belonging to the Qasrin synagogue and also identified several ancient Hebrew and Aramaic inscriptions. Due to the site's modern significance as a monument of ancient Jewish settlement in the Golan, a series of excavations were conducted inside the synagogue from 1971 to 1972 (D. Urman), 1975 to 1976 (M. Ben-Ari), and 1978 (Z. Ma'oz; see Ma'oz and Killebrew 1993: 1219 for a summary). The establishment in 1977 of the modern Jewish city of Katzrin, capital of the Golan Heights, next to the ancient synagogue site, best illustrates the symbolic and political significance of ancient Qasrin.

In 1981, the Israeli Knesset passed the Golan Heights Law, another political milestone that formally annexed the region to the state of Israel. Though not internationally recognized, this law has had significant implications for the administration of the Golan's antiquities and resulted in the transference of jurisdiction from the military government to the Israel Department of Antiquities, now known as the Israel Antiquities Authority.

My involvement with Qasrin began during a visit to the site in 1981, together with Rachel Hachlili, professor of archaeology at the University of Haifa. Zvi Ma'oz, then the military government's staff officer of Archaeological Affairs of the Golan, invited us to codirect salvage excavations at the site. Rachel Hachlili, one of the leading experts in ancient synagogues, and I gladly accepted. My original interest in excavating Qasrin was solely academic. I was intrigued by the opportunities offered by a generous budget to investigate daily life during the Byzantine period through the excavation of the village associated with the synagogue, generally not the focus of most archaeological excavations of synagogues in the past.

Our excavations, sponsored by the Katzrin Local Council, the Golan Research Institute, the Israel Government Corporation for Tourism, and the Israel Department of Antiquities, began in 1982. From 1982 to 1984, Rachel Hachlili, Zvi Ma'oz, and

I conducted a new series of excavations in the synagogue. From 1983 through 1990, I directed excavations in the adjacent village. We uncovered approximately 1,500 square meters, or nearly 10 percent of the site. During the course of the excavations, we identified nine occupation periods. Ceramic remains from the Middle Bronze II, Iron II, Hellenistic, and Late Roman periods indicated that the site had been occupied during these periods. The most substantial architectural remains dated to the Late Roman/Byzantine/Early Islamic periods (third or fourth to mid-eighth centuries AD), when the site was a Jewish village with a synagogue; the Mamluk period (thirteenth to fourteenth centuries AD), when the site was a Moslem village with a mosque constructed inside the ruined synagogue, and the modern period (late nineteenth century to 1967 AD), when the village was inhabited by Bedouin and a settled population under Syrian administration (Ma'oz and Killebrew 1988, 1993; Killebrew and Fine 1991; Killebrew 1997).

From Research to Presentation

From the beginning of the excavations, the main focus of the project's sponsors was the Byzantine synagogue and contemporary Jewish village in order to develop tourism in the region and to promote a clear political message—because Jews inhabited the Golan in antiquity, modern-day claims to Israeli sovereignty over the Golan have visible historical justification. In fact, one of our first activities was to restore the synagogue to its original state during the Byzantine period by dismantling the poorly preserved remains of the later Mamluk mosque, constructed after the synagogue had gone out of use. Since removal of later structures is an action that occurs daily at countless archaeological sites, this destruction action can be supported or argued from an archaeological perspective. I reasoned that as an academic and a professional archaeologist, I could ignore the political implications of the dismantling of later additions to the synagogue structure. I knew that we had excavated all periods of occupation with equal care and documentation. I believed that my research was one thing and the goals of the Katzrin Local Council were an entirely separate matter. From their perspective, the purpose of the excavations was to uncover as much as possible of the Jewish village, to present the site with its implicit modern message to the public, and to promote economic development for the region.

Not only did I naively believe I could remain aloof from the modern politics of the site's development and presentation, I also felt I could remain unengaged with the tourists and many visitors to the site. Initially I saw the excavations solely in light of my own research goals; visitors were seen, at best, as bothersome intrusions who had to be tolerated and hopefully ignored. However, during the years I directed excavations at the site my perspective began to change. The Qasrin excavations were made possible through public funds and, certainly, I realized that I owed something in return to the public that knowingly or unknowingly supported our work. Also, as the excavations progressed, I became increasingly convinced that the material remains of daily life we were excavating in the village houses were potentially far more fascinating to the visitor than the more monumental synagogue.

Thus, with much enthusiasm and little experience, we decided that the best way to present the site was through complete reconstruction of one domestic house unit—an approach that was still possible in the mid-1980s in Israel, and especially in the remote Golan, when all archaeological sites were under the jurisdiction of the Israel Department of Antiquities. This type of unilateral decision would be quite impossible today following the reorganization of the department into the Israel Antiquities Authority (IAA) with the passing in the Knesset of the Antiquities Authority Law 5749-1989 in 1989. This law increased the power of the IAA and outlined twelve functions under the authority's jurisdiction, including the preservation and restoration of antiquities. Today the Israel Antiquities Authority must approve all conservation, restoration, and on-site presentation activities (Rabinovich 1994).

Reconstructing the Village House

During the course of excavations at the site, we uncovered the synagogue and sections of three large domestic structures to the east (figure 7.1). Each house, or multi-generational family compound, consisted of several interconnected nuclear family units that together could number as many as fifteen rooms. Two main types of family units were common—one a "courtyard" house, or an open courtyard surrounded by a series of roofed rooms; and the second, more typical unit, which consisted of a large multipurpose room (referred to in the contemporary Rabbinic literature as a *traqlin*), divided from a small storage area by a wall with openings, or windows, that allowed contact between the two spaces. Above the smaller storage area, an upper floor, or sleeping loft, was typically constructed. Each of these units had an associated courtyard, sometimes shared with another nuclear family unit within the same complex, or *insula*. We selected one particularly well-preserved unit, that we termed "House B," to reconstruct one nuclear family unit belonging to the more common second house type (figures 7.2, 7.3).

Our first source of information was from the excavation itself and from excavations at contemporary Roman and Byzantine sites or ancient depictions. The beginning point of our reconstruction was the basic plan of House B, the stratigraphic analysis of its architectural development, collapsed architectural elements such as stone beams and corbels, excavated information regarding open and roofed areas, locations of various installations, and, of course, the artifacts themselves.

Luckily, in addition to the evidence from the excavation of House B, we had several other sources of information that proved to be very helpful in the reconstruction of the house, including a number of Byzantine period structures still standing

Figure 7.1. General aerial view of village and synagogue excavations (photographer, Zeev Radovan).

Figure 7.2. Aerial view of House B, before restoration (photographer, Zeev Radovan).

Figure 7.3. Aerial view of House B, after restoration (photographer, Zeev Radovan).

at several villages and towns in the Golan and southern Syria. One of these presently uninhabited villages is Farj, located several miles to the east of Qasrin (Dauphin 1984). In this village, periodically inhabited until 1967, dozens of houses dating back to the Byzantine period still stand, sometimes to the second story (figure 7.4). Several of these houses are nearly identical to the domestic units excavated at Qasrin (figure 7.5). These still-standing structures provided invaluable information regarding the size and location of windows, construction of roofs, evidence for the second-story sleeping loft over the storage room with a window wall, and many other architectural details that were not preserved at Qasrin. Working closely with architect Lawrence Belkin, we meticulously researched and discussed each detail of the Qasrin architectural reconstruction based on our excavation results and these additional primary sources of information.

Archaeological evidence for other contemporary sites was also utilized in our attempts to replicate many other items of daily life. These include ovens, mats, baskets, rope, and metal and wooden objects that were not often preserved in the damp Golan climate, but were preserved at other sites in the arid Judean Desert. Using local materials, our reconstructions were based on Roman-Byzantine period artifacts, such as baskets, mats, rope, wooden implements, and furniture that were preserved at caves and other sites in the Judean Desert (see e.g., Yadin 1963: esp. 123–156). Occasionally we were able to base our reconstruction on Byzantine period objects copied in stone, such as stone doors found associated with the tombs

Figure 7.4.   View of Byzantine house with window wall in Farj, Golan Heights. Note two storied original Byzantine house still standing with a pre-1967 modern Syrian addition on the third floor (photographer, Ann E. Killebrew).

at Beth She'arim (Mazar 1973: 221–222; Avigad 1976: 21, 48–51, 90–93, 116–118) that imitate their wooden counterparts.

A second important source of information was ethnographic work I conducted in Buqata, a northern Golan Druze village whose inhabitants, until 1967, lived in houses very similar to those we excavated in the ancient Qasrin village. During the 1980s, I surveyed several of these traditional houses that were still in use and inter-

Figure 7.5. Photo of restored window wall in the Qasrin house (photographer, Zeev Radovan).

viewed their residents. Not only were architectural plans nearly identical, several of the interior features of the Byzantine houses, such as internal window walls, remained in use through most of the twentieth century. Although care must be taken when comparing and drawing analogies between cultures separated by almost fifteen hundred years, one cannot ignore the continuity in architectural tradition and material culture from the Byzantine period nor the remarkable similarities in details specific to the Golan and its characteristic basalt stone construction. In one of the Buqata village houses, the window wall was used as a shelved storage space or closet, which probably was one of its ancient functions as well (figure 7.6). It was also possible to document functional use of space and other elements of traditional life that were not preserved in the archaeological record such as the mud plastering of the floors and walls and construction of ceilings. Several objects and installations of daily use placed in the reconstructed house were based on my ethnographic work in Buqata in addition to previous ethnographic studies of abandoned Syrian villages carried out during surveys following the 1967 war (Roth 1984) and published research into the traditional Palestinian house (Hirschfeld 1995).

A third source of information was experimental archaeology that I utilized in an attempt to replicate elements of Byzantine period material culture. Early on, we decided that the house and its interior should be self-explanatory, without signs, and should aim to re-create to the best of our abilities the atmosphere of a home. Every-

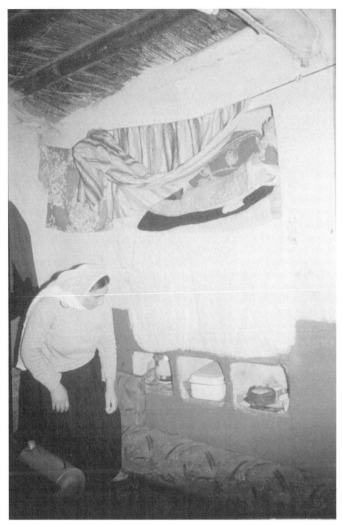

Figure 7.6.   Example of a window wall used as a closet in a village house, Buqata, Golan Heights (photographer, Ann E. Killebrew).

thing should be touchable and accessible to the visitor. Thus, we ruled out the use of any authentic ancient artifacts and decided to create replicas of many of the objects of daily use.

One of our major endeavors was the production of replicas of the seventh- and eighth-century AD pottery assemblage. I worked closely with potter and artist Gideon Kari for six months, who successfully created copies of the original ceramic repertoire using the techniques of the ancient potters (figures 7.7, 7.8). In fact, the

Figure 7.7. Potter Gideon Kari, with replicas of Byzantine period storage jars. The authentic storage jar appears in the center (photographer, Ann E. Killebrew).

replicas were so successful that most archaeologists cannot identify them as copies without close inspection. Though expensive to replicate, after over ten years of being on open display in the reconstructed house without guards or display cases, very few of the vessels have been stolen or intentionally broken. This is especially remarkable because, before the opening of the restored "Talmudic Village" house, vandalism of the archaeological site and especially of the remains inside the village houses was a serious problem. Perhaps this change in the public's attitude can be attributed to a certain new respect for the remains created by a sense that the reconstructed and restored House B was now a "home."

The Druze workmen in our project, especially the older men who lived in traditional villages before 1967, were closely involved in the archaeological experiments and reconstruction. Several of them were stonemasons and builders of houses similar to those we excavated in Qasrin. Their knowledge was of invaluable help throughout the reconstruction of the house itself and the various household installations such as ovens, chimneys, and dovecotes. Oven production was an especially complex task, requiring the use of two very specific clays from the region. Using a traditional local clay recipe for the ovens, we mixed together one bucket of red hamra clay, two and a half buckets of yellow calcite-rich clay, two and a half buckets of clean sifted earth, water, and large amounts of straw temper to fashion the heating installations. Both types of ovens commonly used in the Byzantine period, a sunken

Figure 7.8. View of storage jar replicas in the restored Qasrin Byzantine house (photographer, Danny Syon).

cylindrical oven used to produce flat bread and a domed freestanding oven used to bake, were manufactured at a separate location using a coil technique, and then fired at a low temperature for at least twelve hours (figures 7.9, 7.10). After cooling, the ovens were moved to their final location. The final product was an oven that was suitable for regular heating for cooking and subsequent cooling, and remarkably resembled those we excavated.

Mud plaster covered the interior walls (and possibly the exterior walls) of the Qasrin houses. Again, I discovered there was a definite "art" to wall plastering. After a series of rather unsuccessful experiments using modern, weather-resistant materials, I came to the conclusion that the traditional method, using clean, sifted earth mixed with water and large quantities of straw, was the most effective type of wall plaster. A thick layer of mud plaster was first applied to the stone walls, paying close attention to fill up the cracks between the basalt building stones. Then a second thick layer was spread evenly over the wall, completely covering the stones. Lastly, after the plaster had partially dried and cracks had formed, a thin watered-down layer of mud plaster was applied to the wall, covering up as much as possible the unsightly cracks. It was a labor-intensive and time consuming project and requires yearly re-plastering of the walls.

A final source of information was contemporary Rabbinic and other written texts from the period, especially the *Mishnah* and *Talmud*. Though the purpose of

Figure 7.9.   Production of a replica of Byzantine-period ovens at Qasrin (photographer, Ann E. Killebrew).

the Rabbinic texts was largely legal religious rulings and commentaries, indirectly they do shed valuable light on numerous aspects of daily life during the Byzantine period. I worked closely with Steven Fine, currently the director of the Jewish Studies Program at the University of Cincinnati and an expert on Rabbinic sources. These texts filled in many of the gaps in our knowledge of daily life, especially relating to perishable objects made from organic materials and, even more importantly their uses in daily life. One example of the value of the written sources is illustrated in a passage from the *Tosephta* (Baba Kamma 2: 9) that mentions a legal ruling regarding a broken bench. From this source, we were able to conclude that benches were a very common type of seating in domestic settings during the Byzantine period and thus reconstructed two benches in the multipurpose room (figure 7.11). The Rabbinic sources at times also provided unexpected insights into the material culture of the period. To my great surprise, beds are mentioned on numerous occasions and clearly indicated that everyone, even the poorest members of society, slept on beds (see e.g., *Tosefta* [Ketubot 6: 8] mentioning the obligation of the community to provide an orphan with a bed; figure 7.12; see Killebrew and Fine 1991).

The Rabbinic sources were especially useful in restoring the final functional area of the house—the open courtyard. This is the most private and least accessible

Figure 7.10.   Firing replica of Byzantine-period oven at Qasrin (photographer, Ann E. Kille-brew).

part of these village houses where most household tasks took place. Much of this reconstruction is based on ethnographic research considered in light of the Rabbinic sources and contemporary ethnographic studies and surveys (figure 7.13).

The reconstruction was completed and opened to the public in May 1989. Previous to the opening of the reconstructed house, Park Qasrin drew approximately thirty thousand visitors annually. Within several years, numbers reached one hundred fifty thousand to two hundred thousand visitors a year, mainly due to the attraction of the reconstructed house. This level of visitation equals that of several of the most popular archaeological parks located on major tourist routes in the country. Another change following the opening of the reconstructed house was a shift in patterns of visitation within the archaeological park. In total, the average time that a typical tourist or group spends at the site is approximately a half an hour. Before the opening of the "Talmudic House," approximately five to ten minutes were spent in the village, with the majority of the time spent in the synagogue. Based on my personal observations of visitor behavior and conversations with numerous tour guides, the focus of the visit to the archaeological site shifted from the synagogue to the village after the opening of the reconstructed house. Now approximately twenty to twenty-five minutes are spent in the village and the remaining time in the synagogue.

Figure 7.11. Interior view of multipurpose room (*traqlin*) inside the reconstructed Qasrin house (photographer, Danny Syon).

Reflections on the Reconstruction

More than ten years have gone by since the reconstructed house was opened to the public. On a personal level, I have very mixed feelings about this project and the impact on the site itself, on the visitors, and on site presentation and interpretation in general. I am extremely pleased that such a low-budget project, implemented following years of meticulous research on every element of the reconstruction, has met with such public approval. To this day, the reconstruction is adequately maintained and the reconstruction retains its popularity. What is most rewarding is the positive reaction of the largest visitor population to the park—the children—to the reconstruction. They are free to touch, climb, sit, and explore all elements of the house. The Qasrin Park management has developed very successful educational programs built around the reconstructed house based on activities from traditional daily life as one of its themes. This encourages a positive attitude toward archaeology among younger audiences—something that is essential for the continuity of our profession.

However, upon reflection, there are several aspects of the reconstruction that I feel less comfortable about. First and foremost is the presentation of only one of the three main periods of occupation, the Byzantine period during which the village was Jewish. During the other two main periods of occupation—the Mamluk and modern periods—the site was Islamic in its identity. The visitor to the site today is

Figure 7.12.   Interior view of restored second story sleeping loft at Qasrin (photographer, Danny Syon).

largely unaware of these other no less important periods of occupation, thus creating an incomplete view of the history of the site. The result is an intentional, though perhaps not entirely accurate, political message about the past and, by implication, about the political future of the region. This is best illustrated by the recent addition to the archaeological park of a multi-media presentation supporting Israeli retention of the Golan, which is part of a highly visible political campaign against returning the Golan to Syria (see, e.g., Rabinowitz 2000).

Though the Jewish heritage of Qasrin is certainly one of many legitimate interpretations of the site and its significance, a different selection of the main occupational period to be reconstructed could convey an entirely different political message. Just imagine the very contemporary and perhaps more accurate implications if *both* the Byzantine synagogue and the Mamluk mosque had been presented to the public! I would recommend that archaeologists recognize that all heritage is politicized and contested (see, e.g., comments in the 2000 Getty Conservation Institute research report, Avrami, Mason and de la Torre 2000: 6–7) and take as active a role as possible from the beginning of the project and remain involved through the completion of the public presentation. However, it should also be recognized that the influence of the archaeologist is often limited and he or she seldom determines the message of a site. Rather, it is the individual administrator or agency that funds

Figure 7.13.   Outdoor courtyard of the reconstructed Qasrin house (photographer, Danny Syon).

the project, as in the case of Qasrin, that usually decides upon the message and means of presentation.

In addition, I have serious concerns regarding the damage that inevitably is imposed on the original remains below a partial or complete physical reconstruction. No matter how much care is taken, the original remains are affected. In the case of Qasrin, it was necessary to dismantle and rebuild the ancient walls of the house in order to support the reconstruction and ensure the safety of hundreds of thousands of visitors. These houses were never constructed for wear and tear produced by such intense visitation and it would have been irresponsible on our part not to reinforce the structure with metal rods and cement, both materials that cause serious damage to the original materials.

On a conceptual and philosophical level, one of the difficulties with the Qasrin reconstruction is the mixing of architectural elements from different periods or stages of the building's use, as is the case with most attempts to re-create an earlier structure. Unfortunately, this is almost unavoidable, even when great care is taken, and in effect creates an idealized, homogenized "fantasy" building that never existed except in its modern reincarnation.

Another important issue is the possible confusion in the visitors' minds about what is original and what is reconstructed. Though we made great efforts at Qasrin to mark where the original structure ends and the reconstruction begins, it is not always clearly distinguishable by most visitors. Inevitably, both the original and reconstructed elements become merged in their understanding of the archaeological past. Thus the reconstruction, which is at best a well-researched interpretation and at worse a modern ideological expression of the site's perceived significance, can become part of the "authentic" past in the eyes of the public. This is best illustrated at the site of Knossos on Crete where the spectacular reconstruction of the Minoan palace is now part of the protected history of the site even though it is common knowledge that the restoration is inaccurate.

All of these concerns have been raised on countless occasions and incorporated into several international charters (see especially the 1964 Venice Charter: International Charter for the Conservation and Restoration of Monuments and Sites, the 1990 Charter for the Protection and Management of Archaeological Heritage, and the 1994 Nara Document on Authenticity). Interestingly, in spite of all the very legitimate concerns expressed in these internationally accepted cultural heritage policy documents, reconstruction remains the most popular and appealing method of site presentation to the general public at many sites throughout the world. During a recent heritage workshop in the Moselle region, Germany, I was surprised to see the continued popularity of total reconstructions such as those at the recently restored Roman villa at Borg and Roman temple at Tawern (Kuhnen 1999: 146–147). At the latter site, the restoration was done at the request of the local Tawern villagers who provided the funding necessary for the work.

In recent years, serious attempts have been made to develop "virtual" and "nonintrusive" on-site digital reconstructions, such as the prototype in situ "Timescope" operating at the site of Ename in Belgium (Callebaut and Sunderland 1998; Pletinckx, Callebaut, Killebrew and Silberman 2000). However, this approach is very expensive, requiring great expertise and high maintenance costs. The reason that in situ physical reconstructions still remain highly popular with the public is probably because they enable the visitor to "understand" the ancient remains in a direct and technologically uncomplicated visual way.

What became of my cherished goal of serious archaeological research? With the completion of the excavations and reconstructed house, the Katzrin Local Council had no further need of the archaeologists' services, and funding for research was terminated. Thus, to this day, the final excavation report and publication have yet to appear due to lack of funding required to process and write up the findings. This perhaps is my greatest disappointment and should be a tale of caution to all archaeologists involved in publicly funded archaeological heritage projects. Adequate budget for the scientific publication of the excavation must be negotiated during the initial stages of the project.

Many times, I have asked myself, if I had the opportunity, would I do the Qasrin house restoration again? In light of all the problematic aspects of this project, I console myself with the knowledge that there are thousands of similar, still-unexcavated Byzantine period houses in the Golan and our work at Qasrin can be seen as an opening research statement regarding the interpretation of these houses. So after some soul-searching and hesitation, my answer would still be yes, I would undertake the restoration. Not only did I professionally benefit from the experience (or at least was forced to face how much I did not understand about the past), I also believe that hundreds of thousands of people have enjoyed the site in a way that never would have been possible without the reconstruction. My most serious reservations are about the dominant public "message" of the site. If there is anything that we, as archaeologists, have learned, it is that history, especially in the ancient Near East, is multilayered. Rather than stressing specific ownership over human heritage, archaeologists' most important task in public presentation should be to illustrate the multivocal and multicultural nature of our shared past.

References

Avigad, Nahman
  1976   *Beth She'arim Report on the Excavations during 1953–1958. Volume III: Catacombs 12–23*. Rutgers University Press, New Brunswick, N.J.

Avrami, Erica, Randall Mason, and Marta de la Torre
  2000   *Values and Heritage Conservation Research Report*. The Getty Conservation Institute, Los Angeles.

Callebaut, Dirk, and John Sunderland
  1998   Ename: New Technologies Perpetuate the Past, *Museum International* 198: 50–54.

Dauphin, Claudine
  1982   Jewish and Christian Communities in Roman and Byzantine Gaulanitis: A Study of Evidence from Archaeological Surveys. *Palestine Exploration Quarterly* 114: 129–142.
  1984   Farj en Gaulanitide: Refuge Judéo-Chrétien? *Proche Orient Chrétien* 34: 233–235.

Dauphin, Claudine, and Jeremy Schonfield
  1983   Settlements of the Roman and Byzantine Periods on the Golan Heights. Preliminary Reports on Three Seasons of Survey (1979–1981). *Israel Exploration Journal* 33: 189–206.

Gregg, Robert C. and Dan Urman
  1996   *Jews, Pagans, and Christians in the Golan Heights: Greek and Other Inscriptions of the Roman and Byzantine Eras*. South Florida Studies in the History of Judaism 140. Scholars Press, Atlanta, Ga.

Gutman, Shmaryahu, and Claire Epstein
  1972   The Golan. In *Judaea, Samaria and the Golan, Archaeological Survey 1967–1968*, pp. 244–292, edited by Moshe Kochavi. Carta, Jerusalem, Israel.

Hirschfeld, Yizhar
1995   *The Palestinian Dwelling in the Roman-Byzantine Period.* Franciscan Printing Press, Jerusalem.

Killebrew, Ann E.
1997   Qasrin. *In The Oxford Encyclopedia of Archaeology in the Near East.* Vol. 4, pp. 381–383, edited by Eric M. Meyers. Oxford University Press, New York.
1999   From Canaanites to Crusaders: The Presentation of Archaeological Sites in Israel. *Conservation and Management of Archaeological Sites* 3: 17–32.

Killebrew, Ann E., and Steven Fine
1991   Qatzrin—Reconstructing Village Life in Talmudic Times. *Biblical Archaeology Review* XVII (3): 44–57.

Kuhnen, Hans-Peter
1995   *Archäologie zwischen Hunsrück und Eifel Führer zu den Ausgrabungsstätten des Rheinischen Landesmuseums Trier.* Schriftenreihe des Rheinischen Landesmuseums Trier Nr. 15. Rheinisches Landesmuseum, Trier.

Ma'oz, Zvi U.
1981   The Art and Architecture of the Synagogues in the Golan. In *Ancient Synagogues Revealed,* pp. 98–115, edited by Lee I. Levine. Israel Exploration Society, Jerusalem.
1985   Comments on Jewish and Christian Communities in Byzantine Palestine. *Palestine Exploration Quarterly* 117: 59–68.

Ma'oz, Zvi U., and Ann E. Killebrew
1988.   Ancient Qasrin Synagogue and Village. *Biblical Archaeologist* 51(1): 5–19.
1993.   Qasrin. In *The New Encyclopedia of Archaeological Excavations in the Holy Land.* Vol. 4, pp. 1219–1224, edited by Ephraim Stern. Israel Exploration Society, Jerusalem, Israel.

Mazar, Benjamin
1973   *Beth She'arim Report on the Excavations during 1936–1940. Volume I: Catacombs 1–4.* Rutgers University Press, New Brunswick, N. J.

Pletinckx, Daniel, Dirk Callebaut, Ann E. Killebrew, and Neil A. Silberman
2000   Virtual-Reality Heritage Presentation at Ename, *IEEE MultiMedia* April–June 2000: 45–48.

Rabinovich, Avraham
1994.   Inside the Israel Antiquities Authority, *Biblical Archaeology Review* 20 (2): 40–45.

Rabinowitz, Allan
2000   Katzrin: Talmudic Village. *Jerusalem Post,* 1 June 2000.

Roth, Yehuda
1984   *Survey of the Southern Golan.* Museum Ha'aretz, Tel Aviv, Israel (in Hebrew).

Schumacher, Gottlieb
1888   *The Jaulân.* Bentley and Son, London.

Silberman, Neil A.
   1997   Structuring the Past: Israelis, Palestinians and the Symbolic Authority of Archaeological Monuments. In *Archaeology of Israel: Constructing the Past, Interpreting the Past.* Journal for the Study of the Old Testament Supplement Series 237, pp. 62–81, edited by Neil A. Silberman and David Small. Sheffield Academic Press, Sheffield.

Urman, Dan
   1985   *The Golan: A Profile of a Region during the Roman and Byzantine Periods,* BAR International Series 269. BAR, Oxford.

Yadin, Yigael
   1963   *The Finds from the Bar Kokhba Period in the Cave of the Letters.* Israel Exploration Society, Jerusalem, Israel.

RONALD F. WILLIAMSON ■

Chapter Eight

Replication or Interpretation of
the Iroquoian Longhouse

It has been said that the past is an artifact of the present and that its strangeness is domesticated by our own preservation of its vestiges (Lowenthal 1995: xvii). In our attempt to become at ease with the past, however, we can easily lose sight of the fact that the past was as complex as the present. This is no more apparent than in the attempt to reconstruct the multidimensional lifeways of prehistoric peoples on the basis of one-dimensional data recovered from the archaeological record. While this is a lesson that many historic site management and interpretive agencies learned decades ago, some prehistorians remain convinced that precise replication of the Iroquoian longhouse is both an achievable and a significant objective.

It is argued here that such an objective is not achievable in the context of the thousands of multifunctional longhouses that were erected over the course of half a millennium by various northern Iroquoian populations across a vast landscape. Both the archaeological and ethnohistoric records suggest that there would have been many structural designs through time and space. While it should be noted that the prehistorians involved in the replication debate were simply considering structural design issues and were all aware of the broader issues associated with the investigation and presentation of the North American aboriginal past, it is also argued that the significance of achieving a particular roof line on a longhouse pales in relation to the preparation of a sound cultural interpretive program in which to present the structure to the general public. In this way, replication scholarship can be seen to have taken a back seat to the recognition and presentation of the inherent cultural values of such places, whether they are reconstructions or re-creations.

Indeed, there has been a meaningful debate in recent years on the methods used by agencies to interpret the past of others. In Canada, for example, the national historic site program has been transformed in the past few decades from one focused on military and political history consumed with the passion to replicate, to one reinventing heritage interpretation in the context of historical and natural landscapes and the economic, social, and cultural histories of the many peoples who contributed to, and were affected by, the building of the nation. Indeed, many of these sites can trace their development from early- to mid-nineteenth-century work programs where replication, in the absence of much data, was the goal, through the 1960s when new expertise and innovative technologies promised more accurate replication and authenticity to the realization in the last few decades that conservation was possible, but not replication. It was also realized that conservation did not necessarily imply extensive renovation with one particular period in mind, but recognition of the contribution of all eras in the past. Indeed, the 1980s saw a holistic and analytical attempt to understand the fundamental values of historic places and to recognize the multiple layers of meaning reflected in their inherent values. In this way, the central organizing principle of "ecological integrity" of the previous decade was replaced with the notion of "commemorative integrity" where value-based management acknowledges that there is no single correct way to interpret a site (Cameron 1997).

This evolution of interpretive programming has been examined by Laura Peers (1996) for a number of Canadian historic sites. She argues that, originally, most sites emphasized the role of Europeans in establishing colonial culture in the wilderness by employing costumed interpreters of traders and priests with few, if any, aboriginals in sight. Most of these sites were funded by the provincial and/or federal governments, which clearly favored sites that interpreted themes of national and regional importance while discouraging the commemoration of minorities, labor, and other divisive themes (Peers 1996: 34).

The initial national interpretive agenda was about politically and socially important white men, colonialism, settling of the land and extending the fur trade into the interior, and bringing the ethnics or aboriginals under control. It was the Canadian version of "winning the west" where the Indian, interpreted as the exotic other, was to be subjugated (Peers 1996: 49). This past was created to legitimize the social and political structures of the day. The historic sites, in their very structure of palisade, logbuilding, and aboriginal house structure on the exterior of the palisade, enacted a story that has been known and reinforced since the time of the historical events themselves, a kind of "theatre of convention and power" where the powerful nation-state overwhelms the weak tribal entities (Peers 1996: 45–47). It is a story where there was always an "inevitable progression from the simplicity of the Native American to the complexity and sophistication of the Anglo-American" (Norkunas 1993: 23). As Peers argued, this is a past as a source and vehicle for myth in the sense that what was interpreted at these sites had little to do with the past.

All of this changed with the realization of the historical impact of administrative culture on the nature and structure of "authentic reconstructions" (Gable and Handler 1993: 26). Indeed, with the new social history of the 1960s and the 1970s, administrative culture was challenged by both white and minority scholars in their presentation of this highly selective, culturally and racially homogeneous view of the past. By the early 1980s, Peers argues that minority lives began to appear in site interpretations and in the planning and review documents officially sanctioned by the bureaucracies. Lower Fort Gary, for example, had gone from being "a little

Scottish village on the Red" to a multicultural community of the past, portraying race, class, and gender relations in the fur trade (Peers 1996: 69).

Longhouse Reconstructions

The reconstruction and presentation of Iroquoian villages has occurred largely in the context of the former rather than the latter interpretive framework described above, at least in the sense that few of the existing sites are managed by aboriginals or have involved aboriginals meaningfully in their interpretation. Moreover, these issues are largely ignored, in the literature at least, in favor of a polemic regarding the one and only authentic way to build an Iroquoian longhouse. Not only does focusing on such a debate neglect the important social and political issues associated with the heritage values attached to such places, but it risks presenting prehistoric aboriginal life as simple or one-dimensional in the expectation that Iroquoians, through time and space, ascribed to a single house-building convention.

The term "Iroquois" is usually applied to the five Iroquoian-speaking groups that made up the League of Iroquois of upstate New York. These groups were the Mohawk, the Oneida, the Onondaga, the Cayuga, and the Seneca. There were, however, other Iroquoian speaking groups including the Susquehannock, situated south of the League; the Erie, located on the south shore of Lake Erie; and those groups living in Ontario. The latter included the Huron and Petun, historically located around the southern end of Georgian Bay, and the Neutral located around the western end of Lake Ontario (figure 8.1).

Several years ago, in an attempt to explain the detached way in which North American archaeologists have treated aboriginal peoples, Bruce Trigger (1980) examined the relationship between that treatment and the development of American archaeology, focusing on the underlying stereotypic images of native people, which initially precluded the realization of continuous prehistoric cultural progress. He challenged archaeologists to convince native people that archaeology has an important contribution to make to the study of aboriginal history, for the sake of that history, and that archaeology can enrich knowledge of aboriginal life and cultural development prior to European contact. This results in freeing aboriginal history from an exclusive reliance on written sources, which are largely a product of, and reflect Euro-American culture. He also challenged archaeologists to work with native people in reconstructing that history.

The current longhouse construction debate is occasioned by the desire of archaeologists and site managers, involved in efforts to interpret Iroquoian history, to replicate as authentically as possible, the prehistoric Iroquoian house structure within the context of a model segment of a larger community. The initial reconstruction of Iroquoian villages and house structures dates back to the same period as the construction of many of the national historic sites, although the impetus to build

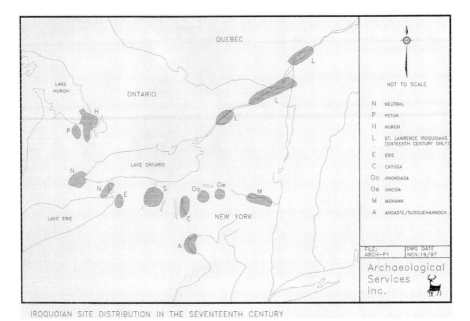

IROQUOIAN SITE DISTRIBUTION IN THE SEVENTEENTH CENTURY

Figure 8.1.   Locations of Iroquoian tribes in the seventeenth century. (All figures in chapter 8, courtesy of Ronald Williamson.)

them had little to do with government initiatives and funding and national agendas and more to do with archaeological experimentation, private enterprise, and the educational programming aspirations of local conservation authorities and museums. Unfortunately, few of these early enterprises were associated with aboriginal groups. At least nine Iroquoian villages and several single longhouses have been reconstructed in eastern Canada, a number of which appear on original archaeological sites. A portion of the Middle Iroquoian Nodwell site, located in Port Elgin, Ontario, on Lake Huron, was one of the first to be reconstructed in the early seventies by J. V. Wright. He devoted part of a chapter of his book on the site to the documentation of his efforts at reconstructing the site. The longhouses are no longer standing. Another reconstruction has been underway for some time at the prehistoric Lawson site, in London, Ontario, adjacent to the London Museum of Archaeology. A third reconstruction, and that of a Huron village, is located in Midland, Ontario, not far from Ste. Marie among the Hurons, itself a reconstructed seventeenth-century Jesuit mission, complete with its own longhouse, symbolic of a significant native presence at the mission. Another reconstruction, and one of the earliest to have been constructed, is located near Delaware, Ontario, on the property of Longwoods Road Conservation Area and is representative of a twelfth-century Early Iroquoian site. The remaining reconstructions include one located west of Toronto at Crawford Lake Conservation Area and another, now abandoned, on private land in

Fort Erie, Ontario. The Pinetree Native Friendship Centre in Brantford, Ontario, built the most recently reconstructed village with the help of the City and Six Nations Reserve. Two other longhouses have been built by aboriginal bands on their reserves. The currently operating village reconstructions each attract between thirty and eighty thousand visitors annually, the majority of which are students enrolled in either native studies or archaeology programs.

In terms of house forms, there have been as many construction designs as there have been longhouses previously constructed—the staff of each claiming vigorously that their house style best represents the traditional Iroquoian structure. The problem of design is, nevertheless, significant since contemporary aboriginals are no longer familiar with prehistoric house designs and construction methods, and the Jesuits or other seventeenth-century witnesses rarely provided explicit descriptions of structural detail other than to report that houses were bark covered, that they were as high as they were wide, that they contained four foot high bunklines, and that the roof structures were arbor-shaped. Later descriptions by Lafitau and others are largely secondhand and many, such as those recorded at eighteenth-century forts, are too late to be entirely reliable in that houses may have already undergone considerable design change due to European influence. Moreover, archaeological plans of longhouses provide little structural information beyond ground level.

The outlines of longhouses can be traced by removing topsoil on settlements to expose small dark stains in the subsoil. Some of these stains are presumed to be the decayed remains of posts once placed deeply into the ground as part of the construction of dwellings. The patterns produced by these posts, in addition to their diameter and depth, constitute the entire archaeological record relating to house construction, as historical descriptions or illustrations of longhouses, also do not offer any conclusive comment on this wall-roof relationship.

Differences of opinion, therefore, exist concerning their three-dimensional form, as discussed most recently by Mima Kapches (1993), J. V. Wright (1995), and Dean Snow (1997). These differences pertain especially to the nature of the roof superstructure and its relationship to the exterior house walls. Indeed, Wright's arguments were made in response to an article by Mima Kapches (1993) concerning a possible Huron unit of measurement and its implications for longhouse architecture. Kapches stated that the exterior walls of Wright's Nodwell site longhouse reconstructions were weight bearing. Wright alternatively argued that the mainly 3-inch diameter wall posts were incapable of providing the structural strength for such large and tall houses and that large interior posts must have provided the main structural strength through a series of pi-frames onto which the rafters, the walls, the main joist verticals, and the lateral joists were attached (Wright 1974: 295). Wright's diameters and locations of the vertical pole elements of his houses were determined by fitting them into the actual archaeological post molds of the house floors. Specifically, he hypothesized that a pi-frame was composed of two large vertical posts set approximately 10 feet (3 m) apart, which supported a horizontal beam whose ends extended 5 feet (1.5 m) beyond the vertical posts on each side. A series of these pi-frames, running the length of the house, constituted the structural framework of the dwelling.

Figure 8.2 illustrates a similar design used in the construction of houses at the Tawiscaron site in Fort Erie, Ontario. Again, large interior posts provide the main structural support through a series of symmetrical frames onto which horizontal, longitudinal poles, cross-frame joists, the ridgepole structure, and the walls are attached. While not pi-frames, as described by Wright (1995), these extend the length of the house and are joined by longitudinal poles, which constitute the structural framework of the dwelling. The exterior wall posts of the house, using this design, were attached to the longitudinal poles attached to the upper ends of these frames. Two additional small diameter poles were then tied to these upper ends and to the ridgepole, thereby forming the roof structure.

The exterior wall posts of longhouses, using these designs, were attached to longitudinal poles resting on the ends of the frames, and function largely to both create the wall and to form a frame to which the wall bark was attached. On the other hand, Kapches believes that the Iroquoian roof was constructed by bending the wall posts over an interior frame with their ends lashed together at the center of the roof (figure 8.3). In this way, the exterior wall posts formed both the walls and the rafters of the structure. Kapches argues that "the natural tension of these wall posts to spring outward would significantly strengthen the roof of the house" (Kapches 1993: 147), a belief for which there is no structural or architectural evidence.

Figure 8.2.   Longhouse frame from Tawiscaron, Fort Erie, Ontario (now destroyed).

Figure 8.3. Longhouse frame from Ska nah Doht, Longwoods Road Conservation Area, Delaware, Ontario.

Wright noted, however, that the relatively small diameters of the exterior house wall post molds preclude the exterior house walls acting as the main support for the roof superstructure. The larger interior posts would have functioned as the major structural strength of the building (i.e., the pi-frames). Also, the outer vertical elements of the pi-frames (on either side of the central corridor) would have acted as attachment points for the 5-foot wide benches that ran along both sides of the longhouse. Based on historical descriptions, which consistently state that long-houses were as tall as they were wide, for a 20-foot wide longhouse, Wright uses a ratio of 4:1 to interpret a structure with 16-foot high exterior walls and a 4-foot high roof erected around the pi-frame. Poles with only a 3-inch butt diameter to fit into the exterior wall post molds of the archaeological floor plan could not have extended much higher than 16 feet (4.8 m), where they and the transverse roofing poles were then connected to the two longitudinal eave poles along either side of the structure.

Wright further argued that Kapches's longhouse construction design, if it used cedar poles, as some of the archaeological evidence suggests, would have required post molds three or more times larger in diameter than those recorded in the archaeo-logical floor plans, such that in a 20-foot (6 m) wide house, wall posts would have to have been a minimum of 30 feet (9 m) long to allow for a 2-foot placement in the soil and a one foot overlap with their adjoining mate from the opposite side of the longhouse. According to Wright's materials survey, cedars with a butt diameter of only 3 inches range from 9.5 to 17.5 feet (2.9 to 5.3 m) long, falling short of the length needed to match the bent wall-roof post design with the exterior house wall post mold diameters. Moreover, the rafter portion of the bent wall posts would have to have borne the snow load, yet would have been the area of smallest diameter and thus the weakest portion of the post.

Dean Snow (1997) in his examination of aspects of the interior family spaces of Iroquoian longhouses, as well as their overall structural design, generally supports Wright's model of longhouse construction over that of Kapches, although he disagrees with Wright's 4:1 ratio for wall-to-roof height, concluding instead that the arched roof accounted for about half the overall height of the longhouse. Snow suggests that those houses built according to Kapches's design result in "houses that are either too squat or too tall to fit the documentary evidence, with berths that are too shallow and aisles that are too wide because of the need to set interior posts far apart, and will usually fail structurally if built at full scale" (1997: 76). While the observation that this design style fails to fit the seventeenth- and eighteenth-century documentary evidence is correct, his contention that they fail structurally when built at a full scale is not. The houses at Longwoods Road Conservation Area, built in that style (figure 8.3), survived more than a decade without substantial reconstruction.

On the other hand, Snow notes that houses built according to Wright's cross-section plan, have outside walls that are much too high in proportion relative to overall house height given descriptions of the roof shape in the archival record, although this is not the case for the Fort Erie houses (see figure 8.2). He suggests that perhaps flatter roofs, such as that shown in the Fort Frontenac drawing (Snow 1997: 75; figure 8.6), occurred in parts of Northern Iroquoia where snow loading was less. Snow notes regional differences in design, in that Mohawk longhouses had end storage compartments that were rounded at the corners, giving a generally round floor plan, but walls that were carried straight up to the eaves. On the other hand, archaeological examples indicate that Ontario longhouses had sloping wigwam-style outer end compartment walls. End storage compartments were generally rather lightly framed, as opposed to the substantially built living compartments. In the event of house expansion, the temporary ends would have been rebuilt into more substantial compartments.

In terms of materials, Wright and Snow prefer eastern white cedar for the wall posts, although Wright argues that the longitudinal and transverse beams as well as the rafters of the roof superstructure probably consisted of other strong but relatively flexible species such as white elm, maple, and especially white ash. He suggests that the barks used to cover the structures would have been mainly white elm and white cedar with the elm bark being used as the roof sheathing and the cedar for the exterior wall sheathing. Elm bark, being heavier and thicker than cedar, could have better accommodated snow loads on the roof, while its smooth interior face forming the ceiling would have better withstood potential sparks from the central hearths. Cedar bark, being thinner, lighter and more pliable would have been better suited for wall sheathing. He also concluded that the cordage necessary for lashing the various poles together and fastening the bark sheathing would have been manufactured from the cambium layer of the basswood tree, which has been documented in numerous historical and ethnographic documents.

In summary, Wright and Snow believe that archaeological settlement pattern as well as materials survey data in conjunction with historical, and, in Wright's case, linguistic evidence, all indicate that Kapches's design is simply not possible if one accepts the consistent observation of contemporary Europeans that Iroquoian longhouses were as high as they were wide, observations supported by the only known scale drawings of Iroquoian longhouses. Wright believes that the adherence to the other construction method, of bending poles from either side of the house and lashing them together at the apex of the roof, may be traced to a single reference, Lamothe Cadillac's description of a late-seventeenth-century Huron longhouse at Mackinac, where wall posts were inserted in the ground and bent over to form the roof (Kinietz 1940: 41). The Huron may have borrowed this style from local Algonquian house building (see also Murphy 1991).

In a passing comment, however, Wright does note that according to the Jesuit *Relations*, the Huron, when away from their permanent villages, had other construction options for building their houses, including the bending of saplings together to form roof structures. This suggests that the Huron had a repertoire of house building techniques and constitutes an interesting and unexplored element to this debate. While Snow acknowledges that "Northern Iroquoian longhouses varied considerably and that there were undoubtedly regional differences" (1997: 81), particularly that the heavy pi-frame construction proposed by Wright was perhaps necessitated by the greater average width of Ontario Iroquoian longhouses over New York Iroquoian houses and the need for withstanding heavier snow loads, it is unlikely that there was only one Iroquoian design for constructing longhouses, even within a single community.

Archaeological Examples of Construction Variability

There is simply no doubt that longhouses varied considerably, both temporally and spatially, among contemporaneous Iroquoian-speaking groups on account of locally available construction materials, regional environmental demands, and sociocultural variables, such as the function or the specific sociopolitical context of the house.

For example, figure 8.4 illustrates the plan of an early-thirteenth-century Early Iroquoian longhouse that was surrounded by a palisade (Williamson 1990). The structure is 20 feet (6 m) wide, narrow by later Iroquoian standards, and was probably constructed by bending 16- to 20-foot (4.8 to 6 m) wall posts over to form the roof structure, in the style described by Kapches and as shown in figure 8.3. Contrary to Wright's assertion that this style of longhouse originated with Kinietz's

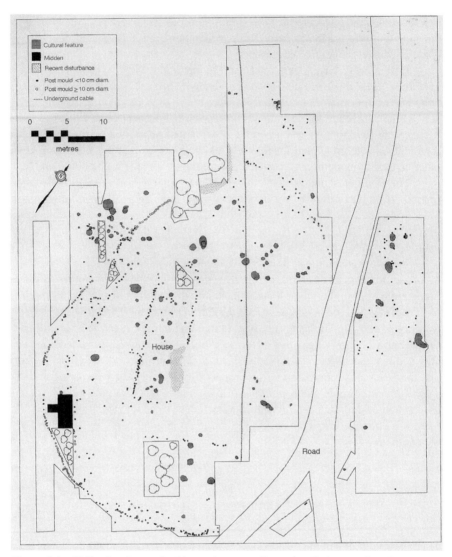

Figure 8.4.   Kelly site plan, early-thirteenth-century Iroquoian, Delaware, Ontario.

1940 description of a late-seventeenth-century Huron longhouse at Mackinac, the Longwoods Road Conservation Area structures, constructed in 1970–1971, were fashioned on the evidence of even narrower Early Iroquoian structures at the DeWaele Site, excavated by William Fox (1976). The site architects, using cedar poles, constructed the Longwoods houses in keeping with the principle of least effort and the seventeenth-century descriptions of a bark covered structure with an arbor-shaped roof. Not only have these houses withstood the test of time, managing the southern Ontario snow loads, but they have functioned to introduce over half a million visitors to prehistoric Iroquoian lifeways. There is simply no evidence whatsoever that this was not the house design employed by Early Iroquoians, until such time that their houses expanded, in both length and width (Dodd 1984), to accommodate larger extended families within the amalgamated communities of the early fourteenth century (Williamson and Robertson 1994). Indeed, Iroquoian houses change substantially through time from the late tenth or early eleventh century small and elliptical houses (see Kapches 1987; Fox 1986) to the larger, longer, and wider structures of the Middle to Late Iroquoian period.

Despite the gradual standardization and refinement of the Iroquoian structure during the Middle to Late Iroquoian period, great variation in house plans has also been recorded within a number of sites (Finlayson 1985; Williamson and Robertson 1995; Robertson et al. 1995). Houses 6 and 7 at the fourteenth century Wiacek site (figure 8.5) situated near Barrie, Ontario, for example, would appear to stand in marked contrast to Houses 1, 2, and 3, both in terms of their overall size and form and with respect to their relatively peripheral location at the eastern edge of the site (see also, Lennox et al. 1986). Similar buildings have been documented on many other contemporaneous sites in Ontario (e.g., Channen and Clarke 1965: 7–10; Dodd 1984: 281; Robertson and Ramsden 1996; MacDonald and Williamson 2001).

Given its relatively open construction, it is most probable that House 6 served as a sheltered activity area, or a temporary warm weather dwelling, while House 7 was probably capable of sheltering a small group of people during cold weather, or on a year-round basis. The potential identity of such occupants is an intriguing question, particularly if one assumes that by the Middle Iroquoian period the residence patterns of the growing kinship units were becoming more cohesive and formalized, with individual longhouses representing individual corporate groups related by ties of kinship. House 7 may, therefore, indicate a fissioning of one of the groups occupying the adjacent longhouses, the arrival of a small group of new members to the community, or simply a continuation of the flexible economic and residence patterns characteristic of the preceding Middle Woodland and Early Iroquoian periods, in which people were free to pursue seasonal subsistence activities in either extended or nuclear family units (Robertson et al. 1995: 50).

On the other hand, it is possible that House 7 may indicate an Algonquian presence at the site. Interaction between the Iroquoians of south-central Ontario and their Algonquian neighbors appears to have been well developed from the earliest phases of Iroquoian settlement in the region (Wright 1966: 41; Trigger 1976: 170–171; Warrick 1990: 350–352). By the historic period at least, groups of Algonquians frequently passed the winter months in Huron villages (Tooker 1991: 25; Trigger 1976: 166–168). Unfortunately, the archaeological evidence for such a practice is far from conclusive, in part hindered by a general lack of settlement pattern data for Algonquian sites. In a consideration of a small sample of "cabins" from Ontario

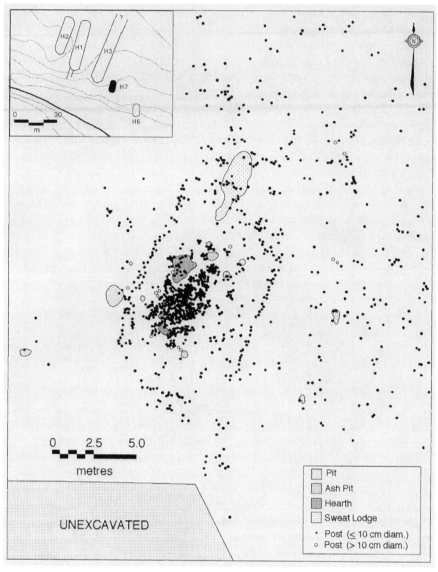

Figure 8.5.   Wiacek Site—House 7, fourteenth-century Iroquoian, Barrie, Ontario.

Iroquoian sites, Mima Kapches (1984: 64) wisely cautioned against simplistic interpretations of such anomalous structures as indicators of an Algonquian presence,
pointing out that the ethnographic records also make reference to the Huron building
temporary shelters in the Algonquian manner. Any of these structures could easily
have been constructed in the manner described by Kapches (1993).

A final case study should serve to dissuade researchers from assuming a
homogeneous house design for the occupants of any particular Iroquoian community. House 4, at the fifteenth-century Parsons site, situated in north Toronto, was
located immediately to the east of House 5 (figures 8.6 and 8.7). It stands in marked
contrast to the other documented houses by virtue of its narrowness, for this structure measured only 16.7 feet (5 m) in width, whereas the remaining houses all measured between 24 and 25.3 feet (7.2 and 7.6 m) in width. The narrowness of the
structure may indicate that House 4 is somewhat later in date than either of its immediate neighbors (Houses 3 and 5). Moreover, only 13.3 feet (4 m) separated House
4 from House 5 to the west, and little more than 6.7 feet (2 m) separated House 4
from House 3 to the east, whereas Houses 5, 3, 7, and 8 were all separated by dis-
tances of approximately 28.3 to 40 feet (8.5 to 12 m). House 4 may, therefore, have
been proportioned to fit within the limited space available between the larger and
earlier Houses 3 and 5.

Regardless of the temporal relationship that may have existed between House

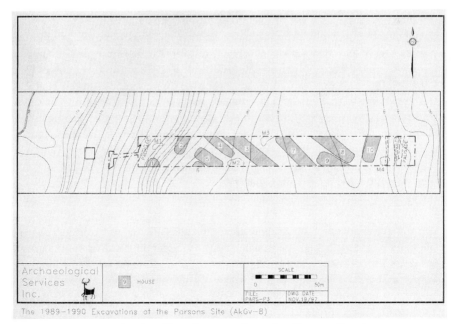

Figure 8.6.   Parsons site plan, fifteenth-century Iroquoian, Toronto, Ontario.

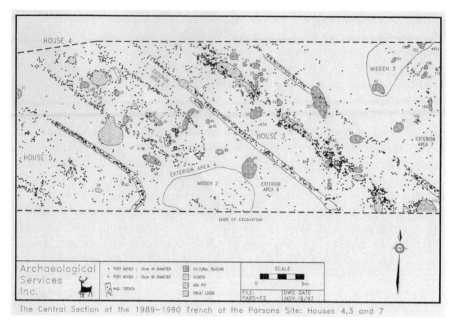

Figure 8.7. Parsons site, Houses 3, 4, and 5.

4 and its immediate neighbors, the occupation of this structure appears to have been complex. In the first place, it would appear that the construction of the house occurred over at least two phases, involving a transition from two separate structures to a single one that incorporated architectural elements of the earlier structures. The existence of a small structure, in the area of the extreme southern end of House 4, is suggested by the fact that both side walls appear to consist of two rows of single line posts, and by a marked discontinuity in the alignment of the east side wall related to the later phase of occupation. It is this latter discontinuity that suggests that House 4 evolved from two smaller structures to a single larger house. While the northern end wall of the original small southern structure is poorly defined, it would appear that the building measured between 26 and 33 feet (8 and 10 m) in length, possibly being somewhat open-ended and incorporating a sheltered activity area or vestibule.

The original end of the more northerly house is attested to by the presence of a short section of wall trench adjacent, but at an angle, to the final east side wall joining the two structures, and by a group of ten posts forming two short lines at a right angle to the final west side wall. There was, therefore, originally an open area between the two structures that extended from Feature 25 on the north to Feature 33 on the south.

The wall posts related to all phases of the occupation of the house had a mean diameter of 6.4 cm, a range of 4 to 18 cm and a standard deviation of 1.74. This mean diameter is significantly smaller than that of the other houses, suggesting that smaller diameter posts were sufficient for the house and that it may have been proportionally lower in height. Such architectural variability, although running counter to the normative stereotype of the Iroquoian longhouse, should not be surprising. It should, however, serve as a cautionary note concerning formulaic or normative analyses of construction techniques (Robertson et al. 1995: 34–36).

Summary and Conclusion

In summary, it should be assumed that Iroquoians had a sufficiently detailed knowledge of their environment to construct their houses to withstand the elements particular to their region. Also, the houses were likely constructed with respect to the principle of least effort, in that those construction materials found within the region were the most cost effective relative to overall value, design considerations, and energy expended.

These factors would have played the leading role in the prehistoric housing industry. For example, in that wood was methodically harvested for village construction and likely chosen for its uniformity in diameter and height, it is likely that the available quantities of certain lengths of trees partially determined the height of the wall, provided a minimum height was attained to allow for the proper convection of smoke out of the house. Another example would be the frequent use of cedar to bark houses (as clearly indicated in the Brébeuf *Relation* of 1635—JR 14: 43–45). This is especially true when cedar saplings were used for the construction of palisades and house structures (see, for example, Lennox 1984: 130–131). Cedar saplings were probably often used on account of their former availability in low-lying areas, their manageability, and their resistance to deterioration. It would have been unreasonable when cutting literally tens of thousands of large-diameter cedar trees for palisade and support posts, to cut additional trees for bark alone, although large sheets of elm bark are admittedly easier to apply. For local reconstructions then, house designs should probably conform to regional environmental demands, the dimensions of nearby excavated Iroquoian houses of the target period under interpretation, and the safety standards set by the local Public Works Department and building inspectors.

Despite having just argued for a variety of longhouse design styles through space and time, I am not at all sure why a discussion concerning the structural design of longhouse roof structures is that consequential. Is the primary aim of reconstructing these three-dimensional houses to: (1) present an accurate reflection of what we cannot possibly know, in other words, what went on at the 16-foot level above the ground and beyond the gaze of most tourists; or (2) introduce to people the lifeways of the aboriginal occupants of this region in an exciting and dynamic way? Should this debate not be about how to interpret, on the basis of archaeological and ethno-historical data as well as oral histories, the use of longhouses so as to best represent Iroquoian life, a debate about how to best reveal the meanings and relationships of this cultural heritage to the public through firsthand involvement with the site? While it is true that there is a desire on the part of tourists for authenticity, their indulgence in the values that they associate with the past goes far beyond that desire; they also want to experience the exotic, where living history is the delivery of another culture's cosmology (Peers 1996: 35).

Until very recently, while other Iroquoian village reconstructions were offering a glimpse into the prehistoric cultural heritage of Ontario, only the Fort Erie site had involved native people exclusively in the construction of the village and in the interpretive programs offered to the general public and school groups. It was, in fact, partly owned by the Ontario Native Women's Association whose regional members actively participated in the direction of the entire complex. The goal was to provide an accurate as possible representation of a prehistoric Iroquoian village segment and an educational program that allowed students or members of the public to actively learn about past Iroquoian lifeways.

Aboriginal staff members are now involved, however, at a number of these prehistoric site reconstructions as well as at Ste. Marie among the Hurons and at a number of other Parks Canada historic sites such as Lower Fort Gary, Old Fort William, the Northwest Company Fur Post, and Colonial Michilimackinac, among others. Peers has argued that the aboriginals staffing the National Historic sites have come to represent opposition to the power and perspectives of the economically and politically dominant class of North American society, thereby challenging, through the opportunity to present Native voices, the hegemonic function of public history, national history, and tourism (Peers 1996: 5). Moreover, for all of those sites, as well as the prehistoric reconstructions, the knowledge of past ways of life and traditional beliefs informs contemporary struggles to reclaim lands and lives in aboriginal communities. The native interpreters are playing themselves or more accurately are representing themselves in the present as well as their ancestors in the past. Peers calls this acting as "being as well as doing" in that it constitutes reflections of intimate connections to the history that they depict. It is a living history where the lives of the present are the lives of the past (Peers 1996: 10).

An important result of the inclusion of aboriginal peoples in the interpretive staff at both the prehistoric site reconstructions and the national historic sites is that they are finally being visited by aboriginals. Typically, the way that a tourist reads meaning into his or her experience at a living history site is related to the social and political relationships between the tourist's culture and that upon which he or she gazes. Until recently, the aboriginal tourist would have been uncomfortable with that experience, but now they are provided with reconstructions of aboriginals in charge of their own lives.

Peers has argued, that "if society, hegemony and history, and therefore these sites, are in process, there is room for contestation, revision and negotiation by many voices in that process, just as there was in the past" (Peers 1996: 69). This suggests that the message of these sites can be more complex than the simple reinforcement of the social order and that public history is becoming less organized, less homogeneous, and less threatening than that of only a short time ago. This is good news for those of us who believe that, as anthropologists, we should continue to play a role in the contextualization and interpretation of the historical lives of contemporary peoples (Hill 1992). It is with these developments in mind that I would suggest we move the debate about Iroquoian village reconstructions from the roofs to the floors.

References

Cameron, C.
 1997 Heritage Conservation Today. Paper presented at the Heritage: Next Generations Conference, 14 February 1997, Ontario Heritage Foundation, Toronto.

Channen, E. R., and N. D. Clarke
 1965 The Copeland Site: A Precontact Huron Site in Simcoe County, Ontario. *Anthropology Paper 8*. Ottawa: National Museum of Canada.

Dodd, C. F.
 1984 Ontario Iroquois Tradition Longhouses. *Archaeological Survey of Canada, Mercury Series* 124. Ottawa: National Museum of Man.

Finlayson, W. D.
 1985 The 1975 and 1978 Rescue Excavations at the Draper Site: Introduction and Settlement Pattern. *Archaeological Survey of Canada, Mercury Series* 130. Ottawa: National Museum of Man.

Fox, W. A.
 1976 The DeWaele Site: A Late Glen Meyer Village. In *The Late Prehistory of the Lake Erie Drainage Basin*, edited by D. Brose, pp. 173–192. The Cleveland Museum of Natural History, Cleveland, Ohio.
 1986 The Elliott Villages (AfHc-2)—An Introduction. *Kewa* (1): 11–17.

Gable, Eric, and Richard Handler
 1993 Colonialist Anthropology at Colonial Williamsburg. *Museum Anthropology* 17(3).

Hill, Jonathan D.
 1992 Overview in Contemporary Issues Forum: Contested Pasts and the Practice of Anthropology. *American Anthropologist* 94 (4): 809–815.

Kapches, Mima
 1984 Cabins on Ontario Iroquoian Sites. *North American Archaeologist* 5(1): 63–71.
 1987 The Auda Site: An Early Pickering Iroquois Component in Southeastern Ontario. *Archaeology of Eastern North America* 15: 155–175.
 1993 The Identification of an Iroquoian Unit of Measurement: Architectural and

Socio-Cultural Implications for the Longhouse. *Archaeology of Eastern North America* 21: 137–162.

Kinietz, W. Vernon
1940   The Indians of the Western Great Lakes, 1615–1760. *Museum of Anthropology, Occasional Contributions* 10, University of Michigan, Ann Arbor.

Lennox, P. A.
1984   The Hood Site: A Historic Neutral Town of AD 1640 National Museum of Man, *Archaeological Survey of Canada, Mercury Series Paper* No. 121: 1–183.

Lennox, P. A., C. F. Dodd, and C. R. Murphy
1986   The Wiacek Site: A Late Middleport Component, Simcoe County, Ontario. Ministry of Transportation and Communications, Toronto.

Lowenthal, David
1995   *The Past Is a Foreign Country.* Cambridge University Press, Cambridge.

MacDonald, Robert I., and Ronald F. Williamson
2001   Sweatlodges and Solidarity: The Archaeology of the Hubbert Site. *Ontario Archaeology.* Vol. 71.

Murphy, Carl
1991   A Western Basin Winter Cabin from Kent County, Ontario. *Kewa* 91 (1): 3–17.

Norkunas, Martha K.
1993   *The Politics of Public Memory.* SUNY Press, Albany.

Peers, Laura
1996   Playing Ourselves: Native Histories, Native Interpreters, and Living History Sites. Ph.D. Dissertation, McMaster University, Hamilton, Ontario.

Robertson, D. A., and C. N. Ramsden
1996   Settlement Patterns. Archaeological Services Inc.: Draft Report on the Salvage Excavation of the Dunsmore Site (BcGw-10), Vespra Township, Simcoe County, Ontario, edited by D. A. Robertson and R. F. Williamson. Manuscript on file, Archaeological Services Inc., Toronto.

Robertson, David, Stephen Monckton, and Ronald F. Williamson
1995   The Wiacek Site Revisited: The Results of the 1990 Excavations. *Ontario Archaeology* 60: 40–91.

Snow, Dean
1997   The Architecture of Iroquois Longhouses. *Northeast Anthropology* 53: 61–84.

Thwaites, R. G.
1896–1901   The Jesuit *Relations* and Allied Documents, 73 Volumes. Burrows, Cleveland, Ohio.

Tooker, E.
1991   *An Ethnography of the Huron Indians, 1615–1649.* Reprinted. Syracuse: Syracuse University Press. Originally published 1964, *Bureau of American Ethnology Bulletin* 190, Washington D.C.: Smithsonian Institution.

Trigger, B. G.
  1976   *The Children of Aataentsic: A History of the Huron People to 1660.* McGill-Queen's University Press, Montreal.
  1980   Archaeology and the Image of the American Indian. *American Antiquity* 45: 662–676.

Warrick, Gary
  1990   A Population History of the Huron-Petun, AD 900–1650. Ph.D. Dissertation, Department of Anthropology, McGill University, Montreal, Quebec.

Williamson, Ronald F.
  1990   The Early Iroquoian Period of Southern Ontario. In *The Archaeology of Southern Ontario to AD 1650*, edited by C. J. Ellis and N. Ferris, pp. 291–320. Occasional Publication of the London Chapter, Ontario Archaeological Society, 5. London, Ontario.

Williamson, Ronald F., and David A. Robertson
  1994   Peer Polities Beyond the Periphery: Early and Middle Iroquoian Regional Interaction. *Ontario Archaeology* 58: 27–48.

Williamson, R. F., and D. A. Robertson, eds.
  1998   The Archaeology of the Parsons Site: A Fifty Year Perspective. *Ontario Archaeology* 65/66.

Wright, J. V.
  1966   The Ontario Iroquois Tradition. *National Museum of Canada Bulletin* 210, National Museum of Canada, Ottawa.
  1995   Three Dimensional Reconstructions of Iroquoian Longhouses: A Comment. *Archaeology of Eastern North America* 23: 9–21.

JOE P. DISTRETTI AND CARL KUTTRUFF ■

Chapter Nine

Reconstruction, Interpretation, and Education at Fort Loudon

Fort Loudoun is the site of a mid-eighteenth century British fortification in east Tennessee. Administered by the Tennessee Department of Environment and Conservation, it is one of several archaeological and historic sites acquired by the state for preservation and interpretation of the state's prehistoric and historic past. Fort Loudoun State Historic Area consists of a preserve of 1,200 acres (486 hectares) bounded by Tellico Lake. The central features of the facility are a reconstructed fort and an interpretive and administrative center. Also within the park are the site of a Federal Period blockhouse, parking areas, picnic facilities, boat launches, maintenance buildings, and staff housing. With the need for public education in history and archaeology, reconstructed archaeological sites, if properly interpreted, can provide excellent opportunities. Fort Loudoun is one such model of historical reconstruction and interpretation. It is perhaps unique, however, in that virtually none of the original site is preserved.

History

To place the decision that was made to reconstruct Fort Loudoun in proper context, we briefly examine the history of the fort. It is important to consider that its history includes not only its brief four-year occupation in the mid-eighteenth century but also that of the near two-and-one-half centuries since its abandonment by the British. Especially germane to the decision to reconstruct is the last seventy years of its history beginning in the mid-1930s.

Fort Loudoun was the westernmost fort in a series of British forts that extended westward from Charleston, South Carolina. Located among the Overhill

Cherokee villages, construction of Fort Loudoun began on 5 October 1756 and was completed by 30 July 1757. Part of the fort was located on a narrow ridge adjacent to the Little Tennessee River. The remainder was on level ground south of the ridge. Two companies of South Carolina provincial militia built the fort, while one company of British regulars held garrison duty during construction and for the remainder of its eighteenth-century occupation (Kelley 1961a). Two early plans of the fort show that it was constructed with an outer ditch on three sides and an earthen parapet on all four. The interior was enclosed with a log-palisade with four diamond-shaped bastions. The contemporary documentation, and now the archaeology, both verify numerous buildings and other constructions that were within the fort.

British relations with the Cherokee remained friendly and mutually beneficial through the fall of 1759. But, soon after that, the situation began to deteriorate. Cherokee pressure against the garrison at Fort Loudoun gradually increased and by the spring and summer of 1760, the siege of Fort Loudoun was intensified to the point where the garrison was facing starvation. On the morning of 9 August 1760, the commander surrendered to the Cherokee and the garrison abandoned the fort and attempted to return to South Carolina (Kelley 1961a; Kuttruff 1988).

The Cherokee occupied the fort for a short period immediately after the surrender, and the abandoned supplies were removed to nearby Cherokee towns. Two years later Henry Timberlake traveled through the valley and mapped the location of the fort in relation to the nearby Cherokee towns. His account and later ones by visitors to the Federal-period Tellico Blockhouse in the 1790s described the fort as in ruins and overgrown (Williams 1948). Despite its decay, Fort Loudoun was always a known landmark of the region. Its location appears never to have been forgotten or lost by the local citizenry. Nineteenth- and early-twentieth-century accounts of the fort and its location attest to its perceived historical importance for the local area. In the 1930s, the site was acquired by the state of Tennessee.

Archaeological Investigations

The first archaeology carried out at Fort Loudoun was a Works Progress Administration's (WPA) clearing and excavation in 1936 (Cooper n. d. [ca. 1936]; Kelley 1961b; Kuttruff 1988). Those investigations determined the locations of the palisade line and several of the interior structures. The palisade line was marked with a low stone wall, and the barracks and powder magazine with stone constructions. At the close of those excavations, the site, held in trust and administered by the Fort Loudoun Association, opened to the public with a minimum of interpretation. During the 1940s and early 1950s, interest in, and activities at, the fort waned. However, in the mid-1950s and the early 1960s, the association renewed their interest in the site and conducted limited excavations to provide information on specific features for reconstruction and interpretation.

Reconstruction of the palisade line began in the 1960s and was completed by the end of that decade. The public interpretation program consisted of a display of artifacts in a small visitor center museum, a brochure providing a limited history of the site, and a key to a self-guided walking tour of the fort. The Fort Loudoun Association conducted a great deal of documentary research during this period and published an excellent, concise history of Fort Loudoun (Kelley 1961a).

This placid period in the history of the fort changed radically in the early and mid-1970s. The proposed completion of the Tellico Dam and flooding of the lower portion of the Little Tennessee Valley by the Tennessee Valley Authority (TVA) would virtually inundate all but a small portion of the fort site. Attempts from several fronts were unsuccessful in halting construction of the dam. Fort Loudoun, a National Historic Landmark since 1965, clearly was in danger of being completely lost.

Instrumental in insuring that the site was adequately mitigated were locally prominent individuals, the Fort Loudoun Association, the Department of Conservation, individuals within TVA, and certain state and local political figures. Each of the constituencies that were involved had its own reasons and priorities for promoting the eventual excavations and reconstruction. These reasons varied from compliance with federal Cultural Resource Management (CRM) regulations, economic benefits, personal and political gain, sustenance of the Fort Loudoun Association, an historic preservation motive, and public education goals.

Put in perspective, the decision to reconstruct Fort Loudoun and to develop the area into the interpretive and educational institution that it is today derived from the multivariate interests just noted as well as engineering requirements. The first mitigation solution proposed was the construction of a levee around the site, leaving the site as it was, surrounded by a lake. Geologists and engineers determined that the area within the levee would fill with water along with the area outside the levee. Without the option of preserving the site, the TVA decided to conduct a virtually total excavation and data retrieval program.

Between the excavations and the subsequent flooding of the area, there would be nothing remaining to show for the former eighteenth-century site. To offset this, the construction program included a 250,000 cubic yard (191,139 cubic meter) landfill to be placed over the original site on which a reconstruction would be built. The new surface, contoured to replicate the original surface, was to be eight meters above the old one, so as to be above the projected high lake pool level. Upon that landfill, TVA was responsible for constructing the palisade line and surrounding ditch, and replicating the stonework on the fort interior that had been previously reconstructed. Control of the area reverted from the Fort Loudoun Association to the state Department of Conservation. TVA and the Department of Conservation would jointly fund a new interpretive and administrative center. The Department of Conservation would design and implement the interpretive exhibits, and, as funding allowed, continue reconstructions on the interior of the fort. The final excavations began in May 1975 and continued through August 1976. Funded by TVA and under the direction of Kuttruff, those excavations were to recover as much information and material as possible from the interior of the fort and the surrounding areas during the eighteen months before flooding was supposed to have occurred (Kuttruff 1988). Flooding finally happened in 1979.

The archaeology included the hand excavation of about eight thousand square meters, or approximately 93 percent, of the interior of the fort. Hand and machine excavated trenches across the ditch and parapet determined their extent and configuration. The remaining portions of the moat on the east, south, and west sides were then similarly cleared. Machine and hand excavations cleared the remainder of the moat on the east, south, and west sides of the fort. During pan-scraping operations for landfill, a large area to the south of the fort was examined for archaeological remains. Cultural features were present over some eight thousand square meters of a much larger area exposed. One hundred sixty-two pit features, twelve structures, and hundreds of postmolds were defined, mapped, and excavated. The occupations represented by these features and structures spanned the prehistoric continuum from the Archaic period onward. Of particular importance was the location and excavation of three house structures, nineteen pit features, one burial, and numerous artifacts from the Cherokee Indian village of Tuskegee. Settlement had begun at this site around 1757, in direct response to the establishment of Fort Loudoun, and lasted until the village was destroyed in 1776 by a military expedition (Kuttruff 1988).

Interpretive Program

As discussed above, the decision to build a fort reconstruction was mostly a political and economic one to satisfy a number of varied and vested interests. Up to this point, the focus of the project had been on compliance and construction. After the excavations and initial constructions were nearly complete, attention shifted toward interpretation of the site and its educational potential.

Although no detailed development plan was formulated prior to the excavations, the planned partial reconstruction of the fort and interpretive center *implied* that there would be exhibits and an interpretive program. The archaeological and historical research was therefore oriented in anticipation of future site development. In fact, the archaeological team did much additional research to benefit the future reconstructions and interpretations.

Once the archaeology was complete and the historical documentation had been accumulated, we were, on the one hand, at a significant advantage over many other reconstruction sites in that all of the known historical records relating to the history of the fort had been assembled. There was the additional advantage of having a total inventory of the archaeological features that had been present within and surrounding the fort. Being able to combine these two nearly complete sets of data provided a unique or, at least, rare opportunity for authenticity in replication of the fort. This was particularly true in terms of the structures located within the fort, their placement, size, and some details about their original construction. We therefore could choose from a complete inventory of types and numbers of buildings for the reconstruction.

While the potentials just noted were certainly positive, they were offset by some negative factors. The original site of the fort, now under landfill, in effect, no longer existed. Once the lake was created, the surroundings were completely altered. Instead of being situated on a small river, the new fort surface was virtually an island within a large expanse of lake (figure 9.1). These two factors, among others, were central considerations in determining the focus of many of the interpretations. An *Interpretive Development Guide* that set forth the overall objectives and themes was subsequently developed by the project archaeologist and staff of the Exhibits Section of the Department of Conservation (Kuttruff 1981a, 1981b). The *Guide* listed the structures to eventually be reconstructed (under the direction of Distretti). The major themes selected for presentation and interpretation included the natural environment of the valley, the history and occupation of Fort Loudoun, the archaeology, and the fort reconstructions.

Figure 9.1. Aerial view of the island-like appearance of the site of Fort Loudoun after completion of the landfill, reconstruction of the palisade line, and flooding of Tellico Lake. (Photograph courtesy of Tennessee Valley Authority.)

Interpretive Themes, Reconstructions, and Interpretations

A full discussion of the way in which the various interpretive themes were presented has been detailed in other papers (Kuttruff 1990; Kuttruff and Distretti 1991). Since the focus of this chapter is on reconstruction, the remainder concentrates on the reconstructions and their ultimate use in the interpretation scheme.

In interpreting the fort reconstruction, consideration of the artificiality of the site and the alteration of its surroundings was critical. Because of fiscal and manpower limitations, only a few structures and other features could be built. Seven structures, in addition to the palisade and powder magazine that had been completed by TVA, were selected to be built. Structures were chosen to illustrate the range of functionally different buildings that were within the original fort. The structures that have been built include, to date, the blacksmith shop, a temporary troop quarters building (adapted for modern storage and restrooms in the fort), a barracks building, the storehouse, a temporary officer's quarters, and the guardhouse (figure 9.2). Gun platforms have also been constructed in all four bastions. A model of the fort,

Figure 9.2. View of several reconstructed buildings within the fort. The size, shape, and placement were determined by the archaeological investigations. (Courtesy, Fort Loudoun State Historic Area.)

located in the interpretive center, complements the fort construction, showing what a "complete reconstruction" would look like. The model shows all the buildings known to have existed, and underscores the complexity of the original installation. The reconstructions also present the several different methods of building construction available at the time of construction of the original fort. Illustrations and text in the interpretive center provide visitors with insights into how the historical, archaeological, and historic architectural information were combined to develop the reconstructions. The range of construction techniques was utilized in the new buildings. The actual construction of these buildings has provided ongoing activity within the fort, and permitted visitors to see the various construction techniques in process.

The selection of building materials was compromised by the prohibitive cost of replicating or fabricating authentic materials, such as hand-hewn timbers and split clapboards. For practical reasons, the structures have to last for a relatively long time; therefore, materials such as preservative-treated logs for the palisade were considered absolutely necessary. Nonetheless, efforts were made to insure that the constructions were sympathetic to the originals. Attempts were also made to obscure features that were not in keeping with the intent of the constructions. Given the compromises in building materials and public amenities, these efforts have provided an appearance of authenticity consistent with the historical documentation and archaeology. Visitors are made aware of these constraints and are informed that the reconstructions are not necessarily exact replicas, but show the range of available construction techniques that may have originally been used at Fort Loudoun.

Since a reconstructed fort is a focus of the site, a discussion of eighteenth-century fortifications is presented in the interpretive center. In addition to the fort model, there is a diagram of Fort Loudoun with the parts of the fort, such as bastions, curtains, and palisades, appropriately labeled. Accompanying text provides definitions and explains the purpose of the several parts of the fort. Other eighteenth-century fort plans and archaeological site plans illustrate the range of size, shape, and complexity of frontier forts. Because of budgetary restraints and security reasons, the reconstructed buildings do not have a full complement of typical furnishings and accoutrements to create a lived-in look. Portions of the exhibits in the interpretive center help alleviate the otherwise static reconstructions.

Difficult if not impossible to replicate for interpretive purposes is the density of a great number of living things and the noise within a relatively small fort, which at Fort Loudoun included officers, soldiers, Indians, cattle, horses, pigs, chickens, and dogs. Replicating some of these ambiances on a short-term and small-scale basis with historical re-creations or living history exhibits is an important part of the interpretive program at Fort Loudoun. Throughout the year, a number of "living history" garrison weekends are held. During those times, a company of historians, including park personnel and volunteers occupy the fort and its reconstructed buildings. The buildings come to life with activities that were typical of the fort period. The fort and the buildings have a used and lived-in look, where the visitors can see the range of furnishings and accoutrements. Some of the demonstrations, such as

parades, musket and cannon drill, and other activities maintain the historical interpretation (figure 9.3). The goal of the reenactors is, however, education of the public
about Fort Loudoun and the eighteenth century. To this end, the historical interpretation (historic present) is compromised to the benefit of explanations, and answers to
questions by the interested visitors. Through its reconstructions and costumed garrison days, the site becomes more than just a static display of buildings and grounds.
The living history programs engage the senses, bringing to life the fort environment
and the daily garrison life.

Parenthetically, since the reconstructed Fort Loudoun is a "new" site, there
are no constraints on activities, such as fires and excavations that have to be imposed
on the garrison. There is not the necessity of having to protect the archaeological site
from present-day activities that would otherwise be detrimental to a more pristine or
in situ site. Visitation has been high—beyond original expectations, approaching
two hundred and fifty thousand in recent years. History-oriented visitation, including numerous school groups and college history classes, begins in mid-March and
continues into early June. This is supplanted by summer, water-related recreational
visitation from June through mid-September. By early October, visitation shifts
again to history-oriented groups and continues through mid- to late November,
depending on the weather and how long the fall colors last.

Figure 9.3.   Musket drill during a Garrison Weekend at Fort Loudoun. (Courtesy, Fort Loudoun State Historic Area.)

Conclusion

Public interpretation of historic and prehistoric archaeological sites, such as Fort Loudoun, is a viable means of presenting the results of archaeological and historical research directly to the public. That the project archaeologists and historians designed the implemented interpretive program is significant. Regional and site-specific interpretations, such as those presented at Fort Loudoun, are important in the interpretation of archaeological and historical materials and information. The opportunity to have a reconstructed fort and have it placed essentially on-site allows the visitor to relate to the historical information more readily than if the information is procured off-site in a more abstract manner. Sites like Fort Loudoun, with their reconstructions, provide an educational resource for local school groups and for those studying local or regional history. They also serve historic preservation goals of official commemoration of significant aspects of cultural history and enhance public awareness of the historical past.

References

Cooper, Hobart S.
  n.d.   Archaeological Excavations Fort Loudoun, Monroe County, Tennessee. Report on file, Hobart S. Cooper Papers, McClung historical Collection, Knox County Public Library, Knoxville, Tennessee (ca. 1936).

Hamer, Philip M.
  1925   *Fort Loudoun on the Little Tennessee.* Edwards and Broughton Printing Company, Raleigh, North Carolina.

Kelley, Paul
  1961a   *Historic Fort Loudoun.* Fort Loudoun Association, Vonore, Tennessee.
  1961b   Fort Loudoun: The After Years, 1760–1960. *Tennessee Historical Quarterly* 20 (December): 303–322.

Kuttruff, Carl
  1981a   Interpretive Proposal for Fort Loudoun Historic Area, Monroe County, Tennessee. Report on file, Tennessee Department of Conservation, Division of Archaeology, Nashville.
  1981b   Interpretive Development Guide for Fort Loudoun Historic Area, Monroe County, Tennessee. Report on file, Tennessee Department of Conservation, Division of Archaeology, Nashville.
  1988   Fort Loudoun: Historic Occupations. Report on file, Tennessee Department of Conservation, Division of Archaeology, Nashville, Tennessee.
  1990   Fort Loudoun, Tennessee, a Mid-Eighteenth Century British Fortification: A Case Study in Research Archaeology, Reconstruction, and Interpretive Exhib-

its. In *The Politics of the Past,* edited by Peter Gathercole and David Lowenthal, pp. 265–283. Unwin Hyman, London.

Kuttruff, Carl, and Joe P. Distretti
1991 Fort Loudoun, Tennessee: Archaeology, Reconstruction and Public Interpretation. Paper prepared for a National Interpreter's Workshop, Charleston, South Carolina, November 1991.

Williams, Samuel Cole
1948 *The Memoirs of Lieutenant Henry Timberlake 1756–1765.* Continental Book, Marietta, Ga.

MARION BLOCKLEY ■

Chapter Ten

The Ironbridge Gorge
Preservation, Reconstruction, and Presentation
of Industrial Heritage

The Ironbridge Gorge provides a fascinating case study in the development of conservation and presentation philosophy over the past thirty years. The international significance of Great Britain's role as the first industrialized nation was symbolized by the inscription of the Ironbridge Gorge onto the World Heritage list in 1986. The pioneering work of the amateur industrial archaeologists of the 1950s (Rix 1955) and the demolition of Euston Arch and other iconic industrial structures in the early 1960s generated a wave of concern for the protection of the industrial heritage (Raistrick 1972) which culminated in the impassioned plea by Michael Rix to establish national parks of industrial archaeology in which he stated "Ironbridge Gorge is a prime candidate for such a designation" (Rix 1964).

However, this sense of urgency to conserve the physical evidence of early industry led to an overemphasis on the concept of the industrial monument. One of the main criticisms that has been levelled at the practice of industrial archaeology by historians and archaeologists alike is that it has been substantially descriptive rather than analytical, without a broader research agenda regarding the origins and social and economic effects of industrialization (Gould 1995; Palmer and Neaverson 1995, 1998; Riden 1973; Trinder 1982). Henry Hodges in *Artefacts*, his classic text on the history of technology makes the following disclaimer, "the study of technology must always be, to the archaeologist at least, of secondary importance, for a history of technology, no matter how complete, cannot pretend to describe more than a single aspect of mankind" (Hodges 1971: 13).

Despite an apparent lack of protection until recent years, there is an embarrassment of riches of resources surviving from the last two hundred and fifty years in comparison, say, with the material culture of the entire prehistoric or early medieval periods. Uniquely, the industrial heritage resource also includes documentary footage, company archives, and the testimony of the surviving workforce to illuminate and inform our understanding of industrial processes and working practices. This is particularly well exemplified in the case study of Broseley Pipeworks below. Consequently, the lack of a clear research agenda has, until recently, hampered a strategic approach to the selection of buildings, landscapes, townscapes, machinery, and other artifacts for conservation and public presentation. Indeed, should our limited resources be more effectively targeted on the preservation of company archives, oral testimony of the workforce, documentary film footage, and aerial photographic survey rather than the presentation of building shells and entire landscapes of extraction?

For the purposes of this chapter, industrial archaeology and industrial heritage will refer to the material culture of the last two hundred and fifty years. However, there is an argument that without a clearly defined research agenda regarding the social relations and symbolic meanings of the structures and processes of "industrialization" the descriptive catalogue of industrial monuments should include the massive civil engineering projects (Boethius, A. and Ward-Perkins 1970); ironworks (Cleere and Crossley 1985); extractive industries (Burnham 1997); or potteries and brickworks of the Roman Empire. Further, the worldwide development and distribution of techniques of manufacture, such as bronze casting in the prehistoric period, is surely of equal if not arguably far greater significance than the developments of the eighteenth century in Europe (Singer et al. 1954, 1956, 1957).

Similarly, the remarkable developments in science and technology within early medieval China, some six or seven centuries before the industrial revolution of the eighteenth century (Needham 1965), also emphasize the somewhat narrow chronological focus of industrial archaeology and heritage studies in Europe and North America.

From the 1960s onward, the lobby for the preservation of industrial monuments, without any established criteria for the selection process, led to the preservation of a random sample of industrial buildings, containing water wheels and steam engines or associated with key people or events. The relatively recent establishment of survey programs by English Heritage to create national inventories has belatedly made the selection process more representative of the whole range of industries (Cherry 1995; Stocker 1995). However, there is still an emphasis on the preservation of monuments rather than the scientific study of industrial buildings and structures to learn about their technological and social context. Unlike mainstream archaeology with its various research agendas, industrial structures are largely still viewed as "objects," icons of early industry. The recent designation of the Ironbridge Gorge Museums among the non-national museums housing collections of national significance was dependent on its claim that the structures and monuments of industrialization were a significant element of its collection (Ironbridge Gorge Museum Trust 1997; Museums and Galleries Commission 1994).

The meaningful analysis of industrial complexes requires the use of archaeological concepts such as function, context, and typology. The assumption that form follows function is used in the development of typologies of industrial structures;

however, they are particularly susceptible to adaptation according to the availability of capital for investment, market forces, or the introduction of new technologies. The current development of listing criteria for industrial buildings attempts to take into account these specific problems in order to correct the formerly random selection of structures on aesthetic or other grounds (Cherry 1995).

The flexibility to apply both scheduling and listing legislation to industrial structures, buildings, and landscapes can be very beneficial in protecting machinery in situ. The recent scrutiny of the existing Schedule of Ancient Monuments indicates that industrial monuments have been underrepresented in the schedules and a comprehensive national research program has been implemented industry by industry as part of the Monuments Protection Programme (Stocker 1995). The Nuffield Survey of Ironbridge Gorge carried out by the Ironbridge Institute was a pioneering attempt at a detailed survey of an industrial landscape (Clark and Alfrey 1986, 1987, 1988). The thematic surveys of listed buildings by the Royal Commission on the Historical Monuments of England have led to the establishment of new criteria for listing industrial buildings. These now recognize their informational and associative value as well as their aesthetic appeal. The criteria also include the completeness of a site to enable the context of buildings to be considered as well as evidence for the evolutionary change of buildings.

Conservation area designation provides a useful measure protecting those industrial buildings and complexes which individually do not merit listing but collectively are worthy of preservation. Thus outbuildings and boundary walls within the Ironbridge Gorge World Heritage Site are protected within the boundaries of the conservation area, by conservation area legislation, rather than its status as a World Heritage Site, which currently provides no additional legislative protection. The local planning authority has recently introduced an Article 4 direction for the World Heritage site to provide it with additional powers of protection.

Legislation alone does not provide adequate protection, unless it is effectively administered by central and local government, with the informed, active interest of the local community. The lime kilns along the wharfage in Ironbridge are a salutary reminder of this point. Despite being designated as a Scheduled Ancient Monument within a World Heritage Site, planning permission was granted by the local planning authority for a bungalow to be built on top of the kilns. It is therefore a major priority for the interagency group of organizations and local authorities, which has developed the management plan for the Ironbridge Gorge World Heritage Site, to ensure an effective system of development control, informed by a comprehensive database linked to a geographic information system (Interagency Group 1997) (DOE/DNH 1994).

The machinery housed within industrial buildings is fundamental to the understanding of industrial processes. Unfortunately, listing does not provide an effective means of protecting machinery in situ, and, often at the point of decommissioning, plant and machinery are shipped out and sold off for their scrap value. The building shells of the former lead mining complex at Snailbeach in the South Shropshire hills were imaginatively protected using conservation area legislation (Hampson 1997). The empty fragmented buildings scattered among the slopes of a bluebell wood form a romantic if largely unintelligible set of ruins for ramblers and hill walkers. Access to the site has been kept low key so as not to conflict with the needs of the local residents in this remote rural community. Yet ambiguous trail leaflets, inadequate signage, and way marking confuse visitors who trespass inadvertently on private property. Undoubtedly ruins generate their own sublime romance, but surveys carried out with visitors indicate confusion or lack of awareness of the true nature of industrial monuments with their architectural references to medieval gothic. The Darby furnace itself in Coalbrookdale is viewed by many as a shrine for "the cradle of the industrial revolution." Yet stripped of its waterwheel and bellows and shrouded by a massive cover building separating it from its landscape context, its significance remains obscured (figure 10.1).

Undoubtedly the cover building provides a good weatherproof cover for the ruined structure; elsewhere in the Gorge excavated incomplete structures are vulnerable to water penetration and root/frost damage. Repointing and waterproof caps for the ruined walls allow these structures to be maintained as monuments but add little to their visual appeal or context as a wildlife habitat. The solution adopted in Finland and the United States is to create a cover building in the style of the original profile of the complete kiln from surviving depictions, incorporating an element of recon-

Figure 10.1.   Cover building over the Darby Furnace in Coalbrookdale. (Courtesy of Marion Blockley.)

struction/interpretation as well as conservation. Scheduling of a site provides additional protection for machinery and will help prevent asset-stripping and loss of information. Traditionally, large machines such as steam engines were displayed as sculptural objects in splendid isolation in the science and technology galleries of museums, with no reference to the structures that originally housed them (Horne 1984: 110–115). While understanding of industrial processes is best provided by working exhibits—the conservation implications of this are considerable. Unique machinery shouldn't run the risk of damage, whereas heavily restored and repaired machinery can be used. However, some machines and structures, such as kilns or cooling towers, if not used regularly, will suffer permanent damage as a result.

Within a museum gallery it isn't generally feasible to provide an authentic power source such as steam or water, and working exhibits are usually powered by a quiet, odor-free electrical motor which itself creates a completely false impression. Individual working machines cannot convey the noise and smell of an entire factory floor. Modern health and safety regulations ensure that the working looms at sites like Styal Mill, Helmshore textile mill, and Calderdale industrial museum in the north of England are only run for short periods and that demonstrators wear ear protection. Industrial collections within museums are also particularly difficult to manage because of their sheer bulk. Only relatively recently has the need for a more strategic approach to the development of collecting policies for industrial museums been fully appreciated (Ball and Winsor 1997).

Relocation or Preservation In Situ?

Within the Ironbridge Gorge it is interesting to look back with hindsight at the decisions that were taken over the siting of the open-air museum of relocated buildings. When it was accepted that the then fashionable (1960s) Scandinavian model for museums would be an appropriate choice for the Gorge, the question was where to site it? Two options were put forward. First, an area of derelict industrial land of low amenity and historical value at Blists Hill at the west end of the Gorge was considered. The second was located around "the cradle of the industrial revolution" at Coalbrookdale itself, where many of the most significant eighteenth-century monuments, workers' housing, and ironmasters' houses survived in situ. A Colonial Williamsburg scenario was considered where the historic landscape would be "socially engineered" to present Coalbrookdale in its eighteenth-century prime. Late-twentieth-century buildings, including council houses, which detracted from the "purity" of the presentation would be removed and "appropriate" eighteenth-century properties would be imported to fill the "gaps" in the landscape (Madin and Partners 1965). With hindsight, this is an intriguing prospect and would clearly have led to the destruction of the vibrant community based around the still functioning Glynwed Foundry, successors to Allied Ironfounders who claim their proud pedigree from the eighteenth-century ironmasters of Coalbrookdale. How different the landscape of Coalbrookdale would have been with tight controls over traffic, signage, access, and private ownership of property.

One of the fundamental conservation versus presentation debates that has been addressed over the years at Ironbridge is the choice to relocate monuments and buildings to an open-air museum or to preserve them in situ. In the early years of the museum, there was a clearly stated assertion that it was perfectly acceptable to "cherry-pick" the most significant monuments depicting developments in industrialization throughout Shropshire and relocate them to the Blists Hill Open-Air Museum (Morton 1968: 41–43). Thus, the value of these surviving structures could be fully realized only when placed within a museum framework to explain the curator's perception of the development of industrialization. The world's first iron aqueduct, designed by Thomas Telford in 1896 and still situated on the derelict Shropshire Union Canal at Longden-on-Tern, was an item for relocation to Blists Hill. The bridge at Cound, near Cressage on the A458 Bridgnorth to Shrewsbury road, was designed by Thomas Telford. In the late 1960s it was argued that the bridge could no longer support road traffic and should, therefore, be relocated to Blists Hill. Again, fortunately with hindsight, it remains in its original landscape setting and measures are planned to control traffic use. Similarly, the charcoal furnace at Charlcote would have been removed from its remarkable South Shropshire, complete industrial landscape context to illustrate the development of ironworking.

The beam engines "Samson and David," built by Murdoch Aitken of Glasgow for the Lilleshall Company's Priorslee ironworks in 1851, and still active until 1952, were relocated to the original entrance to the Blists Hill Open-Air Museum in 1971. They were intended to form the centerpiece of a concourse building at the entrance to the museum, but they have remained for the last twenty-seven years beneath the "temporary" steel frame protective canopy. The removal of Samson and David was very expensive and would have been much more so had it not been decided to remove the condensers. Without the condensers it will be impossible ever to steam the engines again, although it should be possible to turn them over by an electric motor. The intention of the curator at that time was to reerect them in the engine house of the Blists Hill blast furnaces. Unfortunately they were too large to be accommodated in the existing engine house and to display them in a truly authentic setting would have involved the building of a new engine house and the relocation of blast furnaces to be blown by the engines. The Museum Trust therefore decided that since the engines could not reasonably be displayed in an authentic setting they should be separated from the rest of the museum exhibits, where it was hoped to achieve "a high degree of authenticity" (Trinder 1985). In the cover building, visitors could explore "Samson" and "David" at close quarters to admire their Doric ornamentation and to see the mathematical beauty of James Watt's parallel motion, but no attempt was made to suggest that they were working exhibits.

The Wrought Ironworks at Blists Hill Open-Air Museum is an interesting example of the dilemma of working exhibits. As an open-air museum of relocated buildings, the potential existed to illustrate authentic working processes, authentically powered. The rolling mill came from the Atlas Works in Bolton, the last surviving wrought iron rolling mill in existence. The building housing it is in fact only part of a structure from Woolwich Royal Naval dockyard (itself now an open-air museum). The process of the wrought iron rolling is spectacular and dramatic when working, particularly at night. Further, although there is a market for wrought iron in the restoration of historic buildings and structures, such as Clevedon pier, it was not possible to combine the production of wrought iron with the needs of the market. As a result, surplus accumulated at certain times and the process itself, archaic and perhaps inherently flawed, proved difficult and unreliable to operate on a regular basis despite optimistic projections (Smith 1979). The costs of regularly operating the machinery as a working exhibit for the general visitor proved prohibitive. Now the exhibit remains static and unintelligible, although the layers of corrosion and dust clothe it with a false air of authenticity next to the in situ, authentic and tidily restored but confusingly gothic ruined blast furnace, the early-twentieth-century fairground, and a relocated Victorian school.

As a result, the open-air museum at Blists Hill, in common with other open air industrial museums, displays working processes with the use of exhibit demonstrators, but on a small-scale, craft level. This, of course, leads to the criticism of nostalgia and sanitization. The attractive quaint aspects of craft production are presented at the expense of the reality of the 12-hour working day in the steelworks, coal-mine, or textile mill (Stratton 1996; Trinder 1984 and 1986; West 1988). One good solution to this problem is the approach at the Jackfield decorative tile works where a commercial business is housed. It demonstrates the process of producing encaustic tiles within the former pattern store of Mintons, Maw and Company, adjacent to the Jackfield Tile Museum (Herbert 1979 and Stratton 1996).

The Decorative Tile Works at Jackfield Tile Museum is a commercial venture which has the huge benefit of allowing visitors to experience some of the atmosphere, sounds, smells, and mess of a real factory rather than merely a museum exhibit. As with all working factory tours there have to be compromises to accommodate visitor flow and health and safety requirements. The processes of manufacturing with production streamlined for efficiency helps the museum to interpret the "division of labor" ethic that dictated the original layout of the Craven Dunnill "model" factory, which occupied this site before conversion to the Jackfield Tile Museum (figure 10.2). As with the original Victorian factory, production is laid out following a logical progression. Clay preparation and biscuit production, including both pressing and slip-casting are concentrated in Craven Dunnill's original press shop. Biscuit firing is carried out next door, where tiles originally were dried prior to them being loaded into the coal-fired biscuit kilns. Next to this is the decoration area where screen-printing and tube-lining takes place, followed by the final glaze firing. Production is linear, a small-scale version of what originally happened in the factory, progressing from the raw material at one end of the site to the finished product at the other. However, as a commercial operation, certain activities have to be

Figure 10.2.   Decorative tile works at Jackfield. (Courtesy of Marion Blockley.)

batched for the sake of efficiency so it is not always possible, for example, for people to see tube-lining. This commercial enterprise enhances people's insight and understanding of the principles of division of labor fundamental to any large Victorian enterprise, and guides draw visitors' attention to the way in which the current commercial operation reflects the original Victorian concept.

Effective Presentation of Industrial Heritage: Why Do Open-Air Museums Work?

Despite the critiques of cultural historians regarding authenticity, industrial open-air museums like Blists Hill remain popular with visitors. Partly, this is because they aim to re-create an entire "way of life" using relocated buildings and collections as stage sets for their costumed interpreters. Visitor research carried out by McIntosh at Rhondda Heritage Park indicates that the main motivation for visiting was "a significant desire to experience past ways of life and work and to retrace industrial heritage, especially that of nostalgic and emotional significance" (McIntosh 1997: 16). It is easy to criticize nostalgia, but it does allow visitors to relate to past and present lifestyles. This recognition that intellect is engaged through emotional responses to sensory perceptions is fundamental to interpretative theory (Ham 1983;

Tilden 1957). Drawing on cognitive theory, Sam Ham identified three principles for effective communication with "non-captive audiences," people who do not suffer the additional incentive of academic assessment: 1) The information presented must be entertaining to retain interest, 2) it must be ordered into meaningful "chunks" so that it is easy to process and 3) it must be relevant to them and their own experience (Ham 1983: 12).

He agrees with Freeman Tilden (1957), the father of heritage interpretation, that people relate things that are relevant to them and retain memory of these rather than others. Ham also identified that verbal participation was a significant element in visitor enjoyment. Further participation by observing and doing was even better. These activities are known as "active" rather than "passive" learning and underpin the popularity of the open-air museums using costumed demonstrators. A dialogue with a coherent interpreter involving questions and answers is active learning, whereas reading a text panel, guidebook, or listening to an audio tour is passive. The former is more likely to be successful and is termed by Hein as "discovery learning" (1995: 220).

McIntosh's research, partly carried out at Blists Hill, indicated that 72.2 percent of visitors to industrial heritage sites visit for "learning-related reasons," although only 14.6 percent came specifically for "child-related reasons" (McIntosh 1997: 76). She also found that just over half the visitors surveyed at industrial heritage sites came for "generalist reasons," "somewhere for a nice day out," or "sightseeing," rather than a specific interest in industrial heritage (McIntosh 1997: 11). This has serious implications for the presentation of industrial heritage. These findings are borne out by research into heritage site visitors carried out for the National Trust (BDRC, 1995).

The use of costumed interpreters at open-air museums like Blists Hill can stimulate the visitor's interest and imagination. It is also *a responsive mode of communication* and, done well, can communicate on a series of different levels. It is less effective with large groups and the museum may lose control over some of the interpretations presented (Risk, P. 1994).

The Social Context of Industrial Heritage Presentation

Industrial heritage museums have been criticized for their focus on nostalgia and failure to engage with contemporary economic realities (West 1988). The author has great difficulty acknowledging the tangible benefits of detailed research into industrial archaeology in regions struggling with the reality of mass unemployment. Others have criticized the elitist/capitalist interpretation of eighteenth- and nineteenth-century British heritage broadly defined. Industrial archaeologists have tended to focus on developments in technology and the processes of industrialization, emphasising progress rather than negative impacts. At Ironbridge, the curator of Coalport

China Museum has gone some way toward addressing these issues with the installation of a social history gallery in a museum of china, displayed in the decorative arts tradition. Certainly, there has been a refocusing of the interpretative themes at various industrial heritage sites and museums over the last few years in conjunction with efforts to look at social reform and the social and economic impacts of industrialization.

Some argue that the revitalization of former industrial districts such as the Lace Market in Nottingham (Daniels and Rycroft 1993) has effectively disenfranchised the indigenous workforce. Former industrial areas are regularly re-created to present "establishment" perspectives and memorialize elite individuals (Tunbridge and Ashworth 1996). In the London Docklands, Short (1989) describes the tension between "yuppies" (young urban professionals) and "yuffies" (young urban failures).

In the past, retention of industrial structures was often a result of local enthusiasm rather than a clear strategic approach. One of the main challenges for the selection of industrial sites for conservation and preservation is the assessment of their long-term maintenance. A purely academic case can be made for the historical significance of many industrial sites and landscapes, but the scale and complexity of industrial sites, landscapes, and even whole townscapes makes their long-term maintenance particularly costly. Over the last fifteen years, the lobby for conservation and public presentation of the industrial heritage for its intrinsic historical significance has adopted a high profile, citing Ironbridge as a successful model for emulation (Ball and Stobart, 1996; Butler and Duckworth 1993; Goodall 1993; Liddle 1989). However, market forces dictate and there are clear indications of an oversupply of Industrial Heritage attractions in the domestic tourist market (Mullins 1998). How many Ironbridge Gorge museums can we realistically expect the tourist market to support? The origins, development, and financial model for the Ironbridge Gorge Museum Trust are quite specific and do not necessarily transfer easily to other less scenic locations.

It is a commonplace among conservation professionals that objects and structures don't retain their original cultural meaning. The uninteresting damp pile of stones and brick under a large glass and steel pyramid viewed from my office window in Coalbrookdale is, for some, literally a shrine to one of the great men of the industrial era. Yet to Abraham Darby and his workforce, the furnace was a tool, and no doubt an uncomfortable workplace. Industrial structures are viewed by many as icons of an innovative industrial past rather than functional structures in a manufacturing environment, shrouded by dirt, waste, and noise, and marked by considerable effort. William Lipe in his seminal and often recycled paper (Darvill, 1993; Lipe, 1984) defined the various values and historical frames of reference used by academics and conservation professionals. They included cultural, intellectual, psychological, and historical frames of reference. Importantly, he referred to the associative or symbolic value of monuments which underpin the criteria for listing. Industrial structures have been selected for preservation by virtue of their association with the pioneering engineers Abraham Darby (I, II or III) or Thomas Telford or other great heroes such as Richard Trevithick. It is not entirely frivolous to note the apparent absence of great heroines of the industrial age. Where is the public presentation of the significant role of the Darby women in Coalbrookdale or Philippa Walton at the Royal Gunpowder Mills, Waltham Abbey, Essex (RCHME 1994 31–32)?

Industrial structures selected for their associative or symbolic value often tend to be innovative or spectacular at the expense of the typical or representative, less spectacular sites. These can still have informational value as an excellent education resource (see below, Broseley Pipeworks). This normally can only be fully realized when the site itself has been augmented by the addition of appropriate interpretative media, whether fixed or portable, to make the full information accessible (Goodey 1993).

Finally, industrial heritage assets can have an economic value to justify their continued existence in contemporary society as heritage attractions for tourism or with a viable adaptive reuse (Binney et al. 1990; Prentice et al. 1993; Streeten 1995). The selection of structures for their economic benefit is ultimately subject to aesthetic values. Further, the success of heritage attractions is ultimately bound up with public perception and the acceptance of certain elements of past culture in the contemporary landscape (McIntosh 1997). Sites selected for conservation and preservation in situ on the grounds of historical significance often run into financial difficulties due to a dependence on visitor income. Competition for leisure time is intense, and, unless industrial heritage sites are imaginatively presented and their significance revealed in a way which engages with a wide range of varied audiences, their long-term survival is threatened and the considerable costs of conservation and maintenance cannot be justified. There is a strong case to be made for "preservation by record" for many large industrial complexes in order to retain their informational value. Further, the importance of company archives, including documentary film, oral testimony of the workforce, and comprehensive aerial photographic records of large industrial complexes prior to decommissioning, could be considered a more informative and economically sustainable resource for the retention of information regarding former industrial processes. It is worth noting that the obsession with the survival of original, "authentic" fabric is a preoccupation of European and North American conservation professionals. In the Asia-Pacific region it is the continuity of tradition or set of skills embodied in an individual that is important, rather than retention of original fabric in situ. Thus individual craftsmen can be designated as national heritage assets for the skills that they retain, while total rebuilding of historic timber structures in situ is entirely acceptable.

Sites need to be chosen for their continued relevance to the local community. Local enthusiast-driven initiatives have led to the creation of a number of preserved steam railways and stationary steam engines all over the country. However, they struggle to find the recurrent costs of maintenance unless integrated into local authority economic development strategies (Alfrey and Putnam 1992). It is interesting to note that the original proposal for the creation of an open-air museum at Ironbridge was made to the Dawley (later Telford) Development Corporation on the grounds that it would improve the corporation's strained relations with the local community by paying homage to their industrial antecedents (Madin and Partners 1965). Local authorities frequently select industrial heritage sites as a catalyst for economic regeneration, for exploitation as a tourism product, or to enhance local pride (Barker and Harrop et al. 1994). The danger in this approach is that local economic development and competition between local authorities drive these choices for development rather than the intrinsic merit of the site and appropriateness of the proposed development. The intense competition between local authorities has led to duplication of tourism products and stagnation in the market (Ball and Stobart 1996; English Tourist Board 1993; Green 1994).

Broseley Pipeworks

The old Smitheman's Crown Pipeworks is situated in Broseley, a small industrial town just south of the Gorge, currently subject to a recommendation by the Ironbridge Institute for inclusion within the World Heritage Site. The site consists of a row of 1880s cottages converted into workshops, with a small coal-fired bottle kiln to the rear (see figure 10.3). The original works was taken over by Southorns Tobacco Pipe Manufacturers and remained in use until the end of the 1950s. After that, the site was left virtually untouched. The bottle kiln was stacked with saggars and the row of former cottages left with most of the original tools, equipment, and pipe molds in situ as well as orders, receipts, and letters dating back to the 1880s still impaled on their office spikes. In 1991, Bridgenorth District Council and Ironbridge Gorge Museum Trust developed a proposal to preserve the site and plan a museum. The contents were purchased, photographically recorded in situ and then carefully removed so that, in 1993, extensive restoration of the buildings could take place. This same approach was adopted by the Ironbridge Institute when recording the in situ contents of the Smith and Pepper Jewelery Factory, now the popular Jewellery Quarter Discovery Centre, part of the City of Birmingham Museum (Mason 1992).

The pipeworks buildings were in a poor state, renovation of the structure absorbed most of the budget, and there was little left over to develop the interpretation and public presentation of the collection and the social history of the site. A Heritage Lottery Grant enabled work on the museum phase to go ahead. Whereas in the 1970s the complex might have been recorded brick for brick, dismantled, and removed to the Blists Hill site for public presentation and access, its retention in situ capitalizes on the important historical associations of its site and enhances the social context for displaying the collections, oral history, and film footage. Immediately to the rear of the pipeworks on Duke Street is the site of the Quaker burial ground where Abraham Darby I is buried. Unfortunately, the precise location cannot be ascertained as individual graves were not marked, following Quaker convention.

Figure 10.3. Clay pipe kiln at Broseley Pipeworks abandoned with its contents in the 1950s. (Courtesy of Ironbridge Gorge Museum Trust.)

One disadvantage of the in situ location is the lack of space for visitor services, particularly parking. The site of the former congregational chapel immediately adjacent to the Quaker burial ground is now the car park for the museum. Hardly a peaceful or appropriate setting for the last resting place of the hero of the industrial age in Coalbrookdale. The schoolroom to the former chapel acts as ticket office and shop for the museum. Overlooking the graveyard is a two-story cottage that provides accommodation for the resident craft demonstrator.

The public presentation of the site has tried as far as possible to retain the atmosphere of the original pipeworks. On the ground floor, original equipment and benches have been left in situ, and enablers demonstrate techniques of clay tobacco pipe production. The top floor houses museum gallery-style didactic interpretation with a combination of panels and showcases. However, visitors gain little impression of the impact of smoking on health and are not provoked to think about its impact on people's lives and the local economy. Overall they come away with a nostalgic impression of a quaint local industry. This impression is reinforced by a fascinating video of film footage shot in 1938 within the pipeworks, showing the making of churchwardens (long-stemmed pipes). The first floor has been "conserved as found" from the 1950s with floor and wall surfaces left in their original "distressed" state with evidence of wear and the accretion of waste from the manufacturing process in situ. The museum interpretation and display has benefited hugely from the reminiscences of the women who worked in the pipeworks until its closure. The oral history archive tells us who worked at which bench and even what music they danced to from the constantly playing radio. Undoubtedly this site has huge benefits from its preservation in situ, and gains tremendous atmosphere and sense of authenticity. A useful comparison can be drawn with the urine-stained carpets and tasteful 1960s nylon curtains expensively conserved and retained by English Heritage at Brodsworth, a country house near Doncaster in the north of England.

However the pipeworks has proved extremely difficult to manage as a viable site. The constraints of the original building with equipment in situ and poor floor loading make visitor circulation difficult. These small factories were never designed for visitor circulation or to meet modern health and safety or disability access legislation (English Heritage 1995a, 1995b; DDA Act). Second, the location in Broseley is difficult to find, away from the tourist honeypot site of Ironbridge. Adequate parking and a visitor traffic circulation route have to be found within the densely settled core of a residential conservation area without compromising the integrity of the town.

With the benefit of hindsight, concern is now being expressed about the economic benefits generated by many industrial heritage developments. Inflated claims have been made in support of European Regional Funding applications regarding the creation of employment in former industrial regions. A good example would be the repackaging and selective presentation of the South Wales deep mining industry (Prentice et al. 1993). These claims need to be tested against the diversion of capital investment from other activities, and allowance made for jobs displaced from other sectors.

Beneficial Adaptive Reuse: John Rose Building, Coalport

A good example of the beneficial adaptive reuse of a large complex of industrial workshops is the John Rose building at Coalport, part of the china museum complex (figure 10.4). For many years, the site remained a derelict eyesore following an arson attack. The buildings were owned by Telford Development Corporation and were purchased by the Ironbridge Gorge Museum Trust to prevent unsympathetic reuse. A complex package of funding was put together using the European Regional Development Fund, Heritage Lottery Fund and Architectural Heritage Fund, The Museum Trust, and eighteen local companies. Shropshire County Council was involved as a partner in developing sheltered workshops for people with specific learning difficulties, and a shop to sell their crafts at the east end of the complex. The Youth Hostels Association was installed as tenant for the majority of the building, which provides additional accommodation, seminar rooms, and a restaurant for the large numbers of school groups who visit the Gorge for field study. The museum gained the additional benefit of a restaurant/cafe, which can be used by visitors.

Designation of a site as a Scheduled Ancient Monument or Listed Building does not mean that it is necessarily appropriate for development as a museum or tourist attraction for public presentation. The site may be so incomplete as to remain unintelligible unless some form of reconstruction or simulation is attempted, whether in situ, via computer-generated graphics, or a conventional site interpretation panel.

Figure 10.4. Coalport Chinaworks. The partially restored Shropshire canal running through the site, reconstructed kiln in the foreground, and the site of John Rose's china factory, now a youth hostel, to the left of the canal. (Courtesy of Ironbridge Gorge Museum Trust.)

The Coalport Replica Kiln: In Situ Reconstruction

At Coalport the museum site is dominated by the distinctive and graceful shape of the bottle oven, so characteristic of the urban landscape of the potteries (see figure 10.4). These structures are commonly described as bottle kilns or ovens, but they are in fact only the outer protective casing of the kiln or oven within. Known as "hovels" these structures served only to take away the smoke during firing as well as creating a draught and protecting the kiln or oven within from the elements. The large hovel at Coalport has no kiln structure within it and it serves as a dramatic gallery space for the display of Coalport china. It was felt that the process of kiln firing was not easily explained on the site so a full-size replica of a kiln within the second hovel at Coalport was attempted. No two kilns were ever alike and they were frequently rebuilt, repaired, and adapted because of their extreme working conditions; however, the Coalport reconstruction is typical of many.

Preservation by record may be a more realistic response or a portfolio of alternative uses may be appropriate. Too many industrial heritage sites have been turned into industrial museums emulating the example of Ironbridge, Beamish, or the Black Country Museum. All current surveys indicate that visitor levels cannot be maintained and there is an oversupply (Mullins 1998; de Haan 1997). Further, the influx of National Lottery money for the creation of new capital projects will lead to still further oversupply and market congestion. For the long term, there needs to be a model for the management of industrial heritage sites with a clear strategy for their imaginative public interpretation and the effective management of visitors. At Ironbridge this approach is being adopted by the Strategy Group of partner organizations for the World Heritage Site as part of the process of developing, implementing, and revising the management plan for the World Heritage Site.

References

Alfrey, J., and T. Putnam
  1992 *The Industrial Heritage—Managing Resources and Uses.* Routledge, London.

Alfrey, J. and C. Clark
  1993 *The Landscape of Industry: Patterns of Change in the Ironbridge Gorge.* Routledge, London.

Ball, R. and J. Stobart
  1996 Promoting the Industrial Heritage Dimension in Midlands Tourism: A Critical Analysis of Local Policy Attitudes and Approaches. In *Tourism and Culture: Towards the 21st Century*, edited by M. Robinson, N. Evans, and P. Callaghan. Conference Proceedings, University of Northumbria, Newcastle, September 1996. Centre for Travel and Tourism, Sunderland. Vol. 2, 21–38.

Ball, S., and P. Winsor, eds.
1997   *Larger and Working Objects: A Guide to Their Preservation and Care.* MGC, London.

Barbour, J.
1994   The Sellafield Visitor Programme, Inception to Refurbishment. *Environmental Interpretation, Interpreting Working Industry* 9(3): 5–6.

Barker, M., and K. Harrop
1994   Selling the Industrial Town: Identity, Image and Illusion. In *Place Promotion: The Use of Publicity and Marketing to Sell Towns and Regions,* edited by Gold and Ward. John Wiley and Sons, Chichester.

B.D.R.C. Consultants Ltd.
1995   *Visiting Houses and Gardens Review for the National Trust.*

Binney, M., F. Machin, and K. Powell
1990   *Bright Future: The Re-use of Industrial Buildings.* SAVE Britain's Heritage, London.

Boethius, A. and J. B. Ward-Perkins
1970   *Etruscan and Roman Architecture.* Harmondsworth, London.

Burnham, B.
1997   Roman mining at Dolaucothi. *Britannia* (28): 325–336.

Butler, D. and S. Duckworth
1993   Development of an Industrial Heritage Attraction: The Dunaskin Experience, in *Built Environment,* 19(2): 116–136.

CEI
1994   Environmental Interpretation. *Interpreting Working Industry,* July 1994. CEI, Manchester.

Cherry, M.
1995   Protecting Industrial Buildings: The Role of Listing. In *Managing the Industrial Heritage,* edited by Palmer and Neaverson, 119–124.

Clark, Catherine
1993   *English Heritage Book of Ironbridge Gorge.* Batsford, London.

Clark, C., and J. Alfrey
1986   *Coalbrookdale.* Unpublished Nuffield Survey Report No. 1. Ironbridge Institute, Ironbridge.
1987a   *Coalport and Blists Hill.* Unpublished Nuffield Survey Report No. 2. Ironbridge Institute, Ironbridge.
1987b   *Benthall and Broseley Wood.* Unpublished Nuffield Survey Report No. 3. Ironbridge Institute, Ironbridge.
1988   *Jackfield and Broseley.* Unpublished Nuffield Survey Report No. 4. Ironbridge Institute, Ironbridge.

Cleere, H., and D. Crossley
1985   *The Iron Industry of the Weald.* Leicester University Press, Leicester.

Cossons, N.
  1973   The Ironbridge Project. *Museums Journal* 72 (4): 135–139.
  1979   Ironbridge—The First Ten Years. *Industrial Archaeology Review* III (2): 179–186.

Crossley, D.
  1994   Early Industrial Landscapes. In *Building on the Past, Papers Celebrating 150 Years of the Royal Archaeological Institute*, edited by B. Vyner, pp. 244–263. Royal Archaeological Institute, London.

Daniels, S., and S. Rycroft
  1993   Mapping the Modern City: Alan Sillitoe's Nottingham Novels. *Transactions of the Institute of British Geographers,* NS, 18(4): 460–480.

Darvill, T.
  1993   Valuing Britain's Archaeological Resource. Professor of Archaeology and Property Management, Inaugural Lecture, Bournemouth University 26 February 1992. Bournemouth University, Poole.

de Haan, D.
  1997   Recipe for Success. *Museums Journal,* 97(7): 26–27.

DOE and DNH
  1994   Planning Policy Guidance Note 15 (PPG15): Planning and the Historic Environment DOE/DNH, London.

English Heritage.
  1995a   *Developing Guidelines for the Management of Listed Buildings.* English Heritage, London.
  1995b   *Industrial Archaeology, a policy statement by English Heritage.* English Heritage, London.

English Tourist Board
  1993   Experience the Making of Britain. *Industrial Heritage Year Campaign Evaluation Survey.* ETB, London.

Gold, J. R., and S. V. Ward, eds.
  1994   *Place Promotion: The Use of Publicity and Marketing to Sell Towns and Regions.* John Wiley and Sons, Chichester.

Goodall, B.
  1993   Industrial Heritage and Tourism. *Built Environment,* 19(2): 93–104.

Goodey, B.
  1993   Planning for the Interpretation of the Industrial Heritage. *Interpretation Journal,* Winter 1993, 54: 5–9.

Gould, S.
  1995   Industrial Archaeology and the Neglect of Humanity. In M. Palmer, M. and Neaverson, eds., 1995: 49–54.

Green, S.
  1994   Industrial Tourism: An Overview. Environmental Interpretation, *Interpreting Working Industry,* 9(3): 16–17.

Ham, S.
    1983   Cognitive Psychology and Interpretation: Synthesis and Application. *Journal of Interpretation*, 8(1).

Hampson, L.
    1997   Snailbeach Lead Mine: How an Unique Industrial Enclave Was Formed, Survived, Then Disappeared into Obscurity and Was Then Reclaimed. Dissertation submitted for M.Soc.Sc. in Industrial Heritage, University of Birmingham (Ironbridge Institute).

Hein, G.
    1995   The Constructivist Museum. *Journal of Education in Museums* 16: 21–23.

Herbert, A. T.
    1979   Jackfield Decorative Tiles in Use. *Industrial Archaeology Review* 3(2): 146–152.

Hewison, R.
    1987   *The Heritage Industry: Britain in a Climate of Decline.* Methuen, London.

Hodges, H.
    1971   *Artefacts.* John Baker, London.

Horne, D.
    1984   *The Great Museum.* Pluto Press, London.

Horne, M.
    1997   I.G.M.T. Annual Visitor Survey 1997.

Hunter, M., ed.
    1996   *Preserving the Past, the Rise of Heritage in Modern Britain.* Sutton, Stroud. Interagency Group 1997 Draft Management Plan for Ironbridge Gorge World Heritage Site.

Ironbridge Gorge Museum Trust
    1997   Application for Designation, January 1997.

Liddle, B.
    1989   The Case for Modern Industrial Tourism. *Area* 21(14): 405–406.

Lipe, W.D.
    1984   Value and Meaning in Cultural Resources. In *Approaches to the Archaeological Heritage*, edited by H. Cleere. CUP: 1–11, Cambridge.

Madin, J. and Partners
    1965   A Case for an Open Air Museum. Presented to Dawley Development Corporation June 1965 (not published).

Mason, S.
    1992   Past into Present: The Jewellery Quarter Discovery Centre. *Museum Development* March 1992, 26–32.

McIntosh, A.
    1997   *The Experience and Benefits Gained by Tourists Visiting Socio-Industrial Heritage Attractions*, OU Doctural Thesis, Milton Keynes, not published.

McWhirr, A.
    1982   *Roman Crafts and Industries*. Aylesbury, Shire.

Morton, G. R.
    1968   The Ironbridge Gorge Museum Trust—Blists Hill Open Air Museum. *West Midlands Studies* (2): 39–44.

Museums and Galleries Commission
    1994   Standards in the Museum Care of Larger and Working Objects: Social and Industrial History Collections. MGC, London.

Muter, W. G.
    1979   *The Buildings of an Industrial Community: Coalbrookdale and Ironbridge*. Phillimore, London.

Needham, J.
    1965   Science and Civilisation in China. In *Mechanical Engineering*. Cambridge University Press, Cambridge.

Palmer, M. and P. Neaverson, eds.
    1995   *Managing the Industrial Heritage: Its Identification, Recording and Management*. Proceedings of a seminar held at Leicester University in July 1994, Leicester Archaeology Monographs No.2., School of Archaeological Studies, University of Leicester, Leicester.

Palmer, M. and P. Neaverson
    1998   *Industrial Archaeology, Principles and Practice*. Routledge, London.

Prentice, R. C., S. F. Witt, and C. Hamer
    1993   The Experience of Industrial Heritage: The Case of Black Gold. *Built Environment*, 19(2): 137–146.

Raistrick, A.
    1972   *Industrial Archaeology: An Historical Survey*. Hodder and Stoughton, London.

RCHME
    1994   The Royal Gunpowder Factory, Waltham Abbey, Essex: An RCHME Survey, 1993. RCHME, London.

Riden, P.
    1973   Post-Post-Medieval Archaeology. *Antiquity* 57: 210–216.

Risk, P.
    1994   People-based Interpretation. In *Manual of Heritage Management*, edited by R. Harrison, pp. 320–330. Butterworth-Heinemann, Oxford.

Rix, M.
    1955   Industrial Archaeology. *The Amateur Historian*, (2) 8: 225–229.
    1964   A Proposal to Establish National Parks of Industrial Archaeology. *Journal of Industrial Archaeology* I (3): 184–192.

Short, J.
    1989   Yuppies, Yuffies, and the New Urban Order. *Transactions of the Institute of British Geographers* NS, 14(2): 173–188.

Singer, C., E. J. Holmyard, and A. R. Hall, eds.
1954–1957   *A History of Technology*, Vol. 1 (1954), Vol. 2 (1956), Vol. 3 (1957), Clarendon Press, Oxford.

Smith, S.
1979   The Construction of the Blists Hill Ironworks. *Industrial Archaeology Review* III (2): 170–178.

Stocker, D.
1995   Industrial Archaeology and the Monuments Protection Programme in England. In M. Palmer and P. Neaverson, eds., pp. 105–113.

Stratton, M.
1996   Open-Air and Industrial Museums: Windows onto a Lost World or Graveyards for Unloved Buildings? In *Preserving the Past: The Rise of Heritage in Modern Britain*, edited by M. Hunter, pp. 156–176. Alan Sutton, Stroud.

Streeten, A.
1995   Management and Funding for England's Industrial Heritage. In M. Palmer and P. Neaverson, eds., 1995: 125–131.

Tilden, F.
1957   *Interpreting Our Heritage*. University of North Carolina Press, Chapel Hill.

Trinder, B.
1982   *The Making of the Industrial Landscape*. Dent, London.
1984   A Philosophy for the Industrial Open Air Museum. In *Proceedings of the Association of European Open Air Museums,* 11th Conference.
1986   The Open Air Museum as a Reflection of the Industrial Landscape. In *Proceedings of the Association of European Open Air Museums,* 12th Conference.

Tunbridge, J. E., and G. J. Ashworth
1996   *Dissonant Heritage: The Management of the Past As a Resource in Conflict.* John Wiley, Chichester.

West, B.
1988   The Making of the English Working Past: A Critical View of the Ironbridge Gorge Museum. In *The Museum Time Machine, Putting Cultures on Display*, edited by R. Lumley, pp. 36–62. Comedia/Routledge, London.

BRUCE W. FRY ■

Chapter Eleven

Designing the Past at Fortress Louisbourg

In 1961, the government of Canada embarked upon an ambitious program of reconstructing key elements of Louisbourg, a fortified seaport on the Atlantic coast built by the French in the eighteenth century. The endeavor took far longer and consumed far more resources than originally envisaged, but the government commitment remained remarkably constant over more than two decades. During that time, research teams carried out extensive archaeological and documentary investigations to provide as much authentic detail as possible to the design and reconstruction process. This chapter outlines some of the difficulties that arose in the course of the work and evaluates the degree to which the archaeological contributions were reflected in the end product.

A Past That Never Was

In 1995, the Fortress of Louisbourg National Historic Park commemorated the 250th anniversary of the first siege of Louisbourg—when the French stronghold fell to an enthusiastic and essentially amateur expedition from New England (Rawlyk 1967; Baker 1978). The anniversary was celebrated in the tradition of historic reenactments: a Grand Encampment of dedicated colonial and Revolutionary War aficionados, costumed and equipped in painstakingly authentic eighteenth-century style, bivouacked under the walls of the fortress; and there was much exuberant firing of black-powder arms, banging of drums, skirling of bagpipes, and marching up and down. As an added touch, a flotilla of Tall Ships sailed through the narrow channel and anchored in the harbor. All in all, it was a great success: Tourist traffic was backed up for miles on the only highway access; the modern town and the historic site were packed with visitors, and the reenactors were thoroughly satisfied with their experiences, everyone reveling in a past that, of course, never was.

The year 1997 marked another anniversary, less spectacular and largely unnoticed: the thirtieth anniversary of the target date originally intended for completion of the reconstruction. After all, 1967 was a significant year for Canada, which was celebrating its one hundredth year as a country with extravaganzas, the largest of which was Expo '67, the world's fair held in Montreal. It seemed only fitting that the largest and most prestigious National Historic Site in the Parks Canada system should also be ready as a showcase. In fact, although visitors could view the work in progress, there was little that was completed, and any form of official opening had to be delayed another two years. By 1969, only the King's Bastion, with its impressive barracks building, chapel, and governor's quarters, was actually in shape to be open to the public, but an official opening had for so long been part of the planning that it was unstoppable. Jean Chretien, now prime minister but then the minister responsible for Parks Canada, gamely plodded, clad in oilskins, through mud and puddles to proclaim to a bedraggled group of staff and local dignitaries that Louisbourg was well and truly open.

Coincidentally, 1997 also saw the inauguration of a postgraduate certificate program in Historic Sites Conservation, a joint venture of the University College of Cape Breton and the Fortress of Louisbourg. Prominent on the program, not surprisingly, was an appraisal of Louisbourg as a "heritage experience" and an outdoor museum. From a perspective of thirty years, it also allowed some of us who had been associated with the site in the early years to focus on the history of the reconstruction and to attempt an evaluation of its successes and failures.

The 1967 goal epitomized the development of the reconstruction: From the beginning, Louisbourg was an unabashedly political venture, attracting the attention of the highest levels of government as well as the media. A succession of ministers and senior bureaucrats closely monitored progress and made periodic inspections. Governors-general and a prime minister also came on ceremonial visits.

Political and Economic Motivations

The interest in Louisbourg was predominantly socioeconomic: In a region of chronic unemployment, an alternative to the faltering coal and steel industries became a political holy grail. A Royal Commission recommended the partial rebuilding of Louisbourg as a boost to tourism (MacLean 1995: 20–22); politicians and bureaucrats were quick to realize the kudos to be won from providing immediate jobs in construction and related trades, and the reconstruction, undertaken by the National Parks Branch (now Parks Canada) as an engineering project, began in 1961.

Despite the economic agenda, the Royal Commission report emphasized the historical significance of Louisbourg in the context of national identity, and the government of the day, taking a remarkably long-term view, committed itself to the project on behalf of future generations. A cabinet memorandum grandly, if scarcely originally, proclaimed as its goal: "that the future may learn from the past." Unfor-

tunately, those charged with the task did not learn from the recent past of comparable undertakings.

Indeed, the first few years of the Louisbourg project are almost exact parallels
to the work at Jamestown in the 1930s (cf. Harrington 1994: 4–5). Although there
was a resident project manager, he had to clear all major decisions with his superior,
the chief of the park's engineering division, who was in the nation's capital, Ottawa,
over a thousand miles away. There were draftsmen on site, but the professional
architects were in Ottawa, and none were experienced in restoration work. The architect responsible for designing the barracks building (comprising governor's wing,
chapel, and officers' quarters, as well as soldiers' barracks) in the King's Bastion
was a partner in private practice in Montreal. The research effort was similarly fragmented; a small group of historians, specifically hired for the project, worked in
isolation in Ottawa. The main source of information enabling the engineers to begin
design and construction came not from researchers on staff but from a general consultant on loan from the government of Ontario on a part-time basis. The consultant's qualifications were that he had worked on the restoration of Fort Henry, a
nineteenth-century British fort, and on the creation of Upper Canada Village. Upper
Canada Village is a pioneer settlement made up of rural nineteenth-century buildings moved from previous locations in the St. Lawrence valley when the seaway was
constructed in the 1950s.

Archaeology at Louisbourg: The Battle of the 1960s

The archaeological investigation of the site had an equally inauspicious start. As a
preliminary to the Royal Commission, an art historian from the Royal Ontario
Museum succeeded, with a series of small test pits, in locating the corners of several
buildings throughout the town. He also found the strategic elements of the fortifications, thereby confirming the rich potential of the site (Harper 1962). The Historic
Sites Division of the National Parks, overruled in favor of an engineering management regime, carried out some archaeological work at the Royal Battery located on
the harbor shore across from the town site proper. However, appalled at the engineers' disregard for anything but their own priorities and consequent lack of concern
for the archaeological remains, the Historic Sites Division quickly disassociated
itself from the Louisbourg project; for the next two decades, it had little input into
planning and development.

To his credit, the general consultant had envisaged and strongly recommended, "A comprehensive research program in both history and archaeology is the
only basis for an authentic restoration of Louisbourg" (Way 1962: 1). But, with no
archaeological background or experience, he was ill equipped to locate a qualified
archaeologist, much less to synthesize historical and archaeological data. Faced with
little support from the Historic Sites Division in Ottawa, the Louisbourg managers

initially hired on contract an anthropologist with no knowledge of, and indeed, little apparent interest in, eighteenth-century sites; his report of the 1962 season was very generalized (Howard 1962 a, b).

The situation improved considerably with the appointment in the spring of 1963 of Edward Larrabee as senior archaeologist: Now Louisbourg had someone with experience in historical archaeology and military sites. Larrabee, having worked on contract for the U.S. National Park Service, was in contact with all the major practitioners of what was then a very young discipline. He was, moreover, a meticulous organizer and planner. Working with the senior historian, Larrabee quickly came to realize the sheer size of the task and the impossibility of the reconstruction schedule already in place.

Thus was created a bitter dichotomy. While moving rapidly to assemble an archaeological team and to allocate discrete elements of the King's Bastion complex to its members, Larrabee sought to formalize a process whereby research information would first be synthesized and then presented to the engineers as reconstruction recommendations. The engineers, unable to comprehend the depth and intricacy of the research needed, were not sympathetic to anything that threatened to delay schedules. With the perversity that characterizes large public institutions, the bureaucracy, having acknowledged Louisbourg's historical significance and endorsed the principle of carrying out a thorough, credible job, became anxious for progress and for visible results. And, of course, political pressure began to mount as the long-term vision became mired in short-term concerns and impatience. Questions were asked in Parliament, and the *Toronto Globe and Mail* depicted:

> The new battle of Louisbourg. . . . The archaeologists and historians, barricaded behind maps, diaries, rusty cannons and piles of building stone, are defending their position bravely. Their argument is this: Don't spoil the job to meet a deadline. Without thorough historical research, it won't be a true reconstruction; it will be a pretentious fake. (Mortimore 1964: 16)

More diplomatically, Larrabee, in distinguishing between "applied" and "salvage" archaeology, alluded to the pressures of year-round excavation in the face of reconstruction deadlines while arguing for "An ordered dialogue between the [research] disciplines that would allow for accurate reconstruction and would document the steps by which it was reached" (Larrabee 1971: 13–14). But the "ordered dialogue" would mean that research would play a major role in setting the schedule of the reconstruction, a heretical notion, and one that managers in Louisbourg and Ottawa perceived to represent intransigence on the researchers' part. Senior bureaucrats felt that a change in approach was necessary.

The ensuing change was quite radical. At the beginning of 1966, the engineer in charge of the project was discreetly moved to one side and the park superintendent appointee, not originally due to assume the position until after 1967, was given full responsibility for the reconstruction. Attrition in the research ranks was close to 100 percent. Larrabee's contract was not renewed, and the team of American archaeologists he had brought in drifted off in different directions; all but one of the historians in Ottawa, given an ultimatum to relocate to Louisbourg, resigned. The survivors faced a formidable challenge: to re-create a research team and to provide a steady flow of reliable data to meet a modified but still tight schedule.

Blending Research into the Planning and Design Process

The new manager, John Lunn, represented a breakthrough in that he was neither an engineer nor a career bureaucrat but a museologist. Although not an archaeologist, he had been museum curator of an important Romano-British site in England at the time of its much-publicized excavation, so he was at least able to understand the complexities of archaeological research and the need to correlate it with historical research. Moreover, he sought to end the research-reconstruction dichotomy by bringing the researchers into the planning and design process rather than relegating them to the role of information providers at the bottom of the line. Now all the various disciplines were located at Louisbourg and research was clearly established as part of the management structure: A succession of senior archaeologists and historians, responsible for their respective teams of researchers and for ensuring that the findings were made intelligible to the design and construction specialists, reported to a research director.

Ironically, the "ordered dialogue of the disciplines," advocated by Larrabee, came to fruition in the form of a design committee, although perhaps not quite as he had envisaged it. Rather than a series of traditional research reports interpreted and distilled by senior researchers from the respective disciplines, the design committee provided an ongoing exchange of ideas through the evaluation of original documentary sources and archaeological records. The debates were frequently noisy and heated, never boring, and all design decisions had to successfully overcome challenges as to credibility, just as research findings were subject to intense scrutiny. In the process, Louisbourg pioneered the interdisciplinary team approach to all aspects of historic sites management that has now become accepted practice across the Parks Canada system (MacLean 1995: chapters 2–3).

Nevertheless, the political pressure for some kind of showing by the centennial year of 1967 remained, and the pace was relentless. Archaeologically, once the bulk of the work on the King's Bastion was finished, attention turned to the fortification front ending at the Dauphin demi-bastion, site of the main entrance to the town as well as a heavily armed semi-circular battery that defended the harbor. At the same time, excavations began along the quay and in Block One, the government block in the town comprised of the king's storehouse, the chief engineer's residence, the artillery shed, and the town bakery. It was Lunn's plan that, once the information on these areas was available, sufficient "lead time" would exist to allow the research to assume a more manageable pace.

Excavation directly related to the reconstruction in fact continued until 1975, when a representative array of defensive works, government facilities, private residences, and commercial properties had been uncovered. The quantities of artifacts were astonishing, enhanced in many instances by the state of preservation. Louisbourg is a low-lying site on a poorly drained peninsula, much of it barely above sea level, which has risen nearly three feet since the eighteenth century. As a result, many foundations and cellars, wells and privies are inundated—ideal conditions for the preservation of otherwise perishable organic materials such as wood, leather, and even cloth. This was the archaeological record that provided, together with extensive documentation, the basis for the reconstruction of an area that covers approximately one-third of the original site.

Infusion of Archaeological Authenticity

How well did that reconstruction succeed, and to what extent were the archaeological findings respected in the final product? Several factors have to be taken into account in arriving at an overall assessment: the original stated goals of the project; the quality of the research; the rigor of the design process; and finally, the impact of the site on visitor—the quality of the site as a tourist attraction and outdoor museum or "heritage learning experience."

Given the political pressures and high profile that accompanied Louisbourg's development, it is surprising that no detailed, formal management plan existed prior to the early 1970s. Initial recommendations and recorded government decisions had been couched in general terms such as "a symbolic reconstruction . . . sufficient to furnish a comprehensive representation of the material and cultural forms set up on a strange land" or again, "The Fortress of Louisbourg is to be restored partially so that future generations can thereby see and understand the role of the Fortress as a hinge of history. The restoration is to be carried out so that the lessons of history can be animated" (government documents quoted in MacLean 1995: 21–23). Determination of the specific area appears to have been based on informal agreement with the general consultant and recognition that it would be too costly and time-consuming to attempt anything like a total reconstruction of the entire site. In a period of government expansion and nationalistic fervor, Lunn adroitly exploited this degree of imprecision for several years, arguing the reconstruction would only be representative and convincing if a sufficiently wide streetscape giving depth to the quay front was created. Once he had approval in principle for this approach, he then made the case for more time and more funding, delaying any official opening for two years and the actual completion of reconstruction by a further six years. By the time he completed a formal plan, work on most of the properties in question was in progress: The goal was neatly tailored to fit the outcome.

The tensions of the early years masked an underlying commitment to what was perceived to be authenticity; there was never any express intention to dispense with research evidence. Rather, the tensions arose through attempts to meet short-term, arbitrary deadlines while maintaining "authenticity" even as researchers were collating information. The dilemma produced elements of comic relief: the engineers, in an effort to placate an impatient minister, built rampart walls on the King's Bastion to a height they considered "safe." But shortly thereafter, archaeological excavations on a related feature (the glacis slope in front of the rampart) demonstrated convincingly that the safe height was too high by approximately two feet; construction crews began jack-hammering the top of the wall to its more accurate elevation. The top of the rampart was separated from the parapet above by a cordon or belt course; the general consultant recommended a "typical" thickness for this course in the absence of specific evidence. Several hundred feet of sandstone were cut and placed before archaeologists found cordon stones of a different thickness in the rubble in the ditch. Stonemasons thereupon set about the laborious task of trimming their work by one and one-half inches.

There was indeed an obsession with detail, right down to the thickness of floor planks and slate shingles, also reflected in the training of craftsmen who worked in stone, wood, and iron to make accurate reproductions of archaeologically recovered artifacts. Compromises were made, of course: The French had built with weak, poorly setting lime mortar, and were constantly plagued with maintenance problems; the reconstruction made no attempt to repeat the method, but used modern Portland cement. Today, after thirty years of weathering and gathering moss, the walls have mellowed and no longer have a harshly modern look. In overall structural appearance, perhaps the most visible shortcoming is in the brickwork—no amount of aging will soften the look of mass-produced brick fired to high temperatures, so that it can emulate the crumbly, irregular, and warm characteristics of the original, but a supply of authentic looking "heritage" brick did not exist in the 1960s.

Throughout the construction phase, the design committee relied upon a hierarchy of evidence to support its decisions. At the highest level was archaeological "as found" evidence, followed by documentary sources of varying degrees of reliability, the highest being the French engineers' reports, specifications, and plans. Only when there was no likelihood of direct evidence for a particular structural element was a "typical" source considered, again within a hierarchy of reliability. Louisbourg itself provided evidence that could be extrapolated from one area to another in many cases, both for structural elements such as doorways, fireplaces and gun embrasures and for artifacts such as building hardware or domestic tablewares. Otherwise, researchers drew upon comparative material in France and in other French colonies as well as contemporary documentary sources, published and archival. On occasion, the evidence was contradictory, confronting the design committee with the necessity of having to make what amounted to arbitrary decisions; when all else failed, different options were reviewed and voted upon!

The craftsmen working on structural materials were soon joined by dress designers and costume makers, who, working with eighteenth-century specimens from museums and from documents, strove for the utmost accuracy in military uniforms and period dress. A design team assured quality control over outside suppliers making reproduction ceramics, pewter, and glass and clay pipes, by providing original examples and examining everything for accuracy in dimension, color, and texture. Louisbourg, in its structures, furnishings, and costumed animators thus reflected the archaeological evidence, or, more properly, the sum of the research evidence derived from archaeological, documentary, and analogous sources. In this sense, it may be regarded as an "authentic" reconstruction. The vast amounts of material recovered, however, meant that researchers were not able to complete comprehensive studies but had to concentrate on selected contexts: The collection now houses more than five million artifacts. Site-wide studies of different categories are still in progress today, and as the reconstructed buildings themselves are now showing signs of age and an urgent need for repair—indeed, in the case of some all-timber buildings, a total rebuilding—researchers continue to provide any new information that might modify the earlier designs.

The archaeological contribution was extensive and intensive. Despite the turmoil of the first seasons, a small team of permanent staff formed again, and, supplemented by seasonal contractors, systematically excavated the designated reconstruction areas, feeding information through the design committee. The search for grand patterns in the archaeological record and for generalizing laws about human behavior that was the hallmark of archaeological thinking during the 1960s found little expression at Louisbourg. This was *applied* archaeology, seeking specific evidence on a particular site, its structures, inhabitants, and history. Nor was there any preoccupation with demonstrating the capability of the archaeological record alone to interpret and explain the past; throughout the reconstruction phase, researchers took for granted the interdependence of archaeological and documentary sources. No excavations on town site properties took place without being preceded by a structural history, and the historian who had prepared the report was frequently in the field to consult with the archaeologist.

In contrast, the growing concern in the United States with the loss of archaeological sites due to natural and human activity that began to manifest itself in the late 1960s, and which had coalesced into the concept of cultural resource management (CRM) by 1974 (Fowler 1982), was of practical relevance to Louisbourg. Archaeological excavation being by its nature essentially destructive, archaeologists have always had to confront the issue of what to do with the structural remains they have uncovered: stabilize them, use them as a basis for restoring the original intact structure (i.e., reconstruction) or simply rebury them (Fry 1969). From the beginning, the Louisbourg project struggled with this issue.

To an engineer untrained in restoration or preservation work, and ignorant of any notion of heritage value inherent in ruins, the matter was straightforward: Old fabric—unstable, incapable of bearing loads to modern specifications, and not firmly anchored on bedrock—should be replaced. Within the King's Bastion, only some of the casemates (massive, vaulted chambers set deep in the ramparts) had withstood the ravages of siege, demolition, and time sufficiently to be stabilized and incorporated into the reconstruction. Subsequent to Lunn's assumption of control, the atmosphere favoring the preservation of original fabric improved somewhat, but the record is spotty at best. Dressed sandstone surrounds to features such as windows, doorways, fireplaces, and gun embrasures, as well as quoins at the angles of buildings and fortification walls, have been incorporated into the construction if their condition was sound enough. Otherwise, they survive as oversized archaeological artifacts and as museum objects. Here and there, original cobblestone or brick floors and drains survive, encased in a modern structure, but the fragile nature of most features, especially in the private dwellings within the town, meant that losses were high. Preservation of original fabric has never been an overriding priority for the construction forces at Louisbourg, especially when measured against requirements for structural soundness and service access in reconstructed buildings.

The archaeologists thus found themselves in the front line of an ongoing campaign to preserve as much as possible and to minimize damage caused by the installation of such services as pipelines and access roads. Their concern, moreover, was not just for features in the reconstruction zone. Two-thirds of the town site, after all, remained outside of the developed area, some of it in dire need of attention. Defenses located right on the shoreline were particularly susceptible to erosion: The Princess half-bastion was found to be losing parts of its walls as early as 1963 (Fry 1971). The construction managers initially failed to appreciate the irony of spending large amounts at a National Historic Site to demolish and then rebuild one part of the site while, in another part, original features were disappearing into the sea. Parks Canada management, however, was gradually becoming more conscious of its network-wide CRM responsibilities. In 1980, the Atlantic regional office authorized funds for the erection of a barrier in front of the Princess half-bastion, followed a short while afterward by a protective covering of the deteriorating ruins of the hospital—a large building occupying an entire town block outside the reconstruction area. Still, later, in 1993, the ruins of the Royal Battery, outside the town, were likewise protected from further erosion, having first been a focus of attention in 1961–1962 and thereafter neglected.

Beyond the walls of the town and its harbor defenses, the historic park encompasses some twenty-five square miles of undeveloped land, mostly low, forest-covered hills interspersed with peat bogs, and also some coastal areas north and south of the fortress. Extensive remains of French fieldworks, thrown up in an attempt to guard against British landings, and of British encampments and siege works, survive in good condition throughout the area.

Outside the main gate was a thriving suburb of fishermen's dwellings and taverns, which extended around the harbor. They were destroyed during the sieges, and nineteenth- and twentieth-century settlers who founded modern Louisbourg later chose their sites. Some traces of the settlements outside the walls still remain, usually exposed through coastal erosion after severe storms. Although the management plan of 1973 did not take these features into account, the archaeological staff began

Figure 11.1.   Excavation of the Dauphin demi-bastion and gate, wooden drawbridge in fore-ground. (Courtesy of Parks Canada.)

systematic surveys in 1986, incorporating all the outlying sites into an overall CRM strategy for the park.

The ultimate shortcoming of archaeology at Louisbourg is neither theoretical nor methodological; rather, it is in professional delivery. Moving from applied archaeology, in which results were fed directly into the design and reconstruction process, to a CRM posture, little was published after the mid-1970s, with the exception of a report on the fortifications (Fry 1984). Portions of the artifact collection are scrupulously indexed and catalogued, stored in controlled conditions to the highest conservation standards, and readily accessible whether by type or by archaeological context. The contexts themselves are listed property by property in "events" follow-ing the recording concept developed by the archaeologists excavating medieval Win-chester in England. Preparation of the listings, in the form of a five-volume finding

Figure 11.2. View of the reconstructed section of the town and fortifications, Dauphin Gate in foreground. (Photo: Parks Canada.)

aid, was a monumental task taking more than four years (Harris 1982). It includes historical summaries of each town site property that has been excavated, a summary of the excavations with site plans, provenience lists, and an analysis of the sequence of events represented in the archaeological deposits. It is currently available, however, only to staff or to visiting researchers, although there is a long-term plan to distribute the information more widely, possibly electronically. Everyday visitors to Louisbourg see little of the collections, although exhibits within the King's Bastion barracks and in several houses in the town provide useful background to the years of research and design that went into the end product.

Conflicts in Public Interpretation

Visitors have to grapple with several layers of somewhat contradictory interpretive concepts as they wend their way through the streets and in and out of buildings.

Figure 11.3.   Excavations within the town, showing typical fieldstone masonry cellar and cobbled floor. (Photo: Parks Canada.)

Leaving a shuttle bus outside the walls, they approach the main gate, where guards halt them and challenge them to identify themselves; France is on the verge of war, and the garrison is on the alert for English spies. Once inside the town, visitors encounter costumed animators who reinforce the message that they are reliving a "moment in time" in the summer of 1744. Early in the reconstruction, a consensus emerged that the place should appear as it was at the height of its growth and prosperity, when the fortification walls had recently been completed and were not too

Figure 11.4.   Reconstructed entranceway to King's Bastion and Barracks, protected by defensive works and troops on guard duty; visitors encounter interpretive guides in period uniforms and civilian dress here and throughout the reconstructed area. (Photo: Parks Canada.)

dilapidated. This would have been in 1744, shortly before the first siege and New England occupation.

But modern reality inevitably intrudes. A site capable of absorbing thousands of visitors has to make provision for amenities and must comply with contemporary health and safety regulations; the eighteenth-century illusion is jarred by washrooms, heating and sprinkler systems, and by museum-style exhibits located randomly throughout the site. Some buildings, indeed, exist only as facades, and are not furnished or open to the public, but contain services and equipment needed for daily operations. The illusion is further diluted by supposedly French inhabitants and soldiery speaking English with a resolutely Cape Breton lilt, and by stalwart lasses in soldiers' uniforms. The form is there, but not the substance: Interiors are clean and dry, streets and ditches are free of filth and refuse, the air is no longer redolent with the odor of drying cod. The difficulty, if not the impossibility, of re-creating the past through reconstruction and animation is a lesson that Louisbourg has had to learn and is still attempting to transcend (cf. Lowenthal 1985).

The fixation with 1744, while it simplified construction decisions, restricted the scope of the interpretive message, ironically precluding any explanation of the site's role in the eventual fall of New France, historical themes that staff are now addressing (MacLean 1995: 73–4; chap. 4). Regrettably, it led also to the eradication of some earthworks associated with the later phases of the site's history, features that current CRM practice would favor preserving as examples of the site's evolution. Indeed, the whole concept of reconstruction is now much less acceptable to the heritage community than it was when the Louisbourg project was first proposed and is discouraged in the current Parks Canada CRM policy. Economic considerations aside, such a project would not enjoy the uncritical support today that enabled Louisbourg to rise from the rubble in the 1960s.

The hard reality is that archaeology and reconstruction exist at best in an uneasy symbiosis; the political and economic circumstances that favor a reconstruction provide resources in the form of funding and support services that archaeologists would be unlikely to obtain otherwise. A primary goal of archaeology is the reconstruction of past lifeways, a concept that is, of course, meant to apply to an intellectual exercise rather than to a literal, physical application, although the latter are by no means unknown. The crux of the matter is whether the reconstruction is construed as a three-dimensional model, perhaps to full-scale, or whether, in building upon, and thereby destroying, original remains there is an attempt to pass it off as somehow a restoration of a dilapidated but otherwise extant site. In building upon original remains, Louisbourg risks criticism as an example of the latter approach. Thus the elements of the town and its defenses that lie beyond the current reconstructed area are likely to remain an archaeological site, as are the extensive siege works located in the outlying areas.

Conclusion

Louisbourg's "moment in time" is perhaps less a journey back to the 1740s than it is to the 1960s. The place nevertheless succeeds on a number of levels. It is undeniably a tourist magnet, altering summer visitation patterns to the Maritimes, and transforming the appearance and economy of the modern town of Louisbourg nearby. But it is more. It serves as a vast educational tool, evoking some sense of eighteenth-century French colonial lifestyles and familiarizing visitors with the structures and artifacts of another era. Although purist elements of the heritage community may frown upon reconstructions as a means of preserving the past, the capacity to reach out to a wide public and to depict the past in ways that are both understandable and enjoyable is a powerful force in today's society. And to the visiting scholar, Louisbourg, as a physical manifestation of decades of research, is no less appealing. The artifact collections and the wealth of amassed archaeological and historical documentation make it a rewarding, if underexploited destination. Governments have lavished far greater amounts on programs with far less immediate or long-term benefit economically or culturally.

There may be inconsistencies and flaws that experts in eighteenth-century architecture and material culture could detect, but it would be unfair to characterize Louisbourg as a fraud; certainly there were sustained and extensive efforts to respect the nature of the archaeological data. The real challenge is to continue to move away from the "moment in time" concept and to increase the depth and richness of the interpretative program in a way that more fully respects the complexity of Louisbourg's history in its national context.

References

Baker, Raymond F.
    1978   A Campaign of Amateurs: The Siege of Louisbourg, 1745. *Canadian Historic Sites: Occasional Papers in History and Archaeology* 18: 5–57.

Fowler, Don D.
    1982   Cultural Resources Management. In *Advances in Archaeological Method and Theory*. Vol. 5, edited by Michael B. Schiffer, pp.1–50. Academic Press, New York.

Fry, Bruce W.
    1969   Restoration and Archaeology. *Historical Archaeology* 3: 49–65.

Fry, Bruce W.
    1971   A Rescue Excavation at the Princess Half-Bastion, Fortress of Louisbourg. *Canadian Historic Sites: Occasional Papers in History and Archaeology* 2: 46–54.

Fry, Bruce W.
    1984   An Appearance of Strength: The Fortifications of Louisbourg (2 vols.). *Studies in Archaeology, Architecture and History*. Parks Canada, Ottawa.

Harper, J. R.
    1962.   The Fortress of Louisbourg: A Report of Preliminary Archaeological Investiga-

tions Carried Out in the Summer of 1959 (2 vols.) Manuscript on file, Fortress of Louisbourg.

Harrington, J. C.
1994   From Architrave to Artifact: A Metamorphosis. In *Pioneers in Historical Archaeology: Breaking New Ground,* edited by Stanley South, pp. 1–14. Plenum Press, New York.

Harris, Donald A.
1982   A Summary of the Archaeology of the Townsite of Louisbourg, 1959–1979 (5 vols.). Manuscript on file, Fortress of Louisbourg.

Howard, J. H.
1962   Preliminary Report: The Archaeology of the King's Bastion, 1962. Manuscript on file, Fortress of Louisbourg.

Howard, J. H., P. L. Gall, and K. Lynch
1962   Final Report: The Archaeology of the King's Bastion, 1962. Manuscript on file, Fortress of Louisbourg.

Larrabee, E. M.
1971   Archaeological Research at the Fortress of Louisbourg, 1961–1965. *Canadian Historic Sites: Occasional Papers in History and Archaeology* 2: 8–43.

Lowenthal, David
1985   *The Past Is a Foreign Country.* Cambridge: University Press.

MacLean, Terry
1995   *Louisbourg Heritage: From Ruins to Reconstruction.* University College of Cape Breton Press, Sydney.

Mortimore, G. E
1964   The New Battle of Louisbourg. *The Globe Magazine,* Dec. 5: 16–17. *Globe and Mail,* Toronto.

Rawlyk, G. A.
1967   *Yankees at Louisbourg.* University of Maine Press, Orono, Maine.

Way, Ronald L.
1962   Memorandum on Research: Way to Coleman, 6 March 1962. Manuscript on file, Fortress of Louisbourg.

RODD L. WHEATON ■

Chapter Twelve

Lessons Learned at Bent's Old Fort and Fort Union Trading Post

The reconstruction of Bent's Old Fort, near La Junta, Colorado, and Fort Union Trading Post, near Williston, North Dakota, were each conceived as a means for recapturing the illusion of the "wild and woolly" West of the early nineteenth century. This was the west before metallic gold was discovered in "them thar hills," when furs and buffalo robes were the gold. Each National Historic Site came into the National Park System specifically to illustrate the influence of the far West Indian trade on the upper Missouri River corridor and along the Santa Fe Trail. Thus, historically, the story of these two forts naturally complemented each other while at the same time contrasting, since one was accommodated by steamboats and one by freight wagons.

Fort Union was originally the farthest outpost of the John Jacob Astor American Fur Company consortium, which initiated construction of the fort in 1828 near the mouth of the Yellowstone River on the Missouri. The river connected the fort directly to St. Louis, two thousand miles downstream, while the headwaters of the Missouri and Yellowstone provided access to the trade routes of numerous Indian tribes. Before the 1859 construction of Fort Benton below the Great Falls of Missouri, Fort Union represented the last bastion of civilization on the northern frontier. As such, until Fort Union's demise in 1867, it hosted many notables and their retinues who ventured up the river to see, exploit, and subjugate the West. Astor sold out to Pierre Chouteau, Jr., who proved to be a mighty conglomerate on the Upper Missouri, driving out the competition. At mid-century, Chouteau carried out many improvements to Fort Union to further the corporate image, which included painting the newly enlarged Bourgeois House red, white, and blue. This wooden structure dominated the enceinte of the fort's palisade and was flanked by ranges of dwellings and storerooms. Characteristically, two corner bastions of stone masonry protected the wooden palisade. This fortification style of the upper West, walls surrounding detached structures, was the norm until the advent of military posts with their open planning, and was the product of Anglo-European traditions shipped upriver by steamboat.

On the Santa Fe Trail, Bent's Old Fort represents a different image of the Indian trade. In fact, here trade was subordinate to the mechanics of wagon repair. As Bent's Old Fort former superintendent, Don Hill, has pointed out, it was an 1833 to 1849 "truck stop." It was also built of adobe in the style of the Southwest, inherited from the local Native American and Hispanic cultures of Mexico and New Mexico. The building of this fort, which offered security to commercial enterprise, was thus monolithic, with the interior functions being integrated into the outer walls, leaving the enceinte open for wagons. Though short-lived because of a shift of the Santa Fe Trail route, Bent's Old Fort nevertheless illustrated the entrepreneurship of three individuals. Brothers William and Charles Bent and Ceran St. Vrain found it expedient to capitalize on the overland trail and the cartage between Independence, Missouri, and Santa Fe, New Mexico, while also trading with the local plains tribes who ranged up the Arkansas River system and beyond into the Rocky Mountains. They chose the expedient and indigenous adobe style to meet their immediate needs and capital.

Both forts were destined to be obliterated. In 1868, the U. S. Army found Fort Union unsuitable for a military post and relocated three miles downstream to the confluence of the Yellowstone, where they built Fort Buford. Fort Union was demolished and the wood was recycled as steamboat fuel. All that remained into the twentieth century was forty years of occupational detritus, stone masonry foundations, and demolition debris. Bent's Old Fort was abandoned and partially burned after 1849, only to be rehabilitated in 1861 into a stagecoach station. After 1881, it was finally left to the elements to melt away. Over the subsequent decades, its walls remained until a 1921 Arkansas River flood smoothed the site.

The two sites largely were ignored and ultimately passed into private ownership. In 1926, the local chapter of the Daughters of the American Revolution acquired Bent's Old Fort site; they subsequently donated it to the Colorado Historical Society in 1954. This site was inspected by the National Park Service in 1958 and listed as a National Historic Landmark in 1959. At that time, legislation was introduced in the U.S. Congress to authorize the site as a National Historic Site to be administered by the National Park Service. It came into the system on 3 June 1960. Fort Union Trading Post was nearly forgotten until the president of the Great Northern Railroad began championing the site in the 1920s. Ultimately, the state of North Dakota acquired ten acres of the site and posted an interpretive sign. In 1961, the site was declared a National Historic Landmark. Finally, impetus for consideration as a National Historic Site materialized because the riverbank site was being mined for gravel. In fact, the gravel pit nearest the fort site had nearly destroyed the southwest bastion foundation. Congress authorized the park on 20 June 1966, nearly six years after Bent's Old Fort was authorized.

Archaeology as Background to Reconstructions

The Bent's Old Fort site was excavated partially in 1954 to create an interpretive exhibit utilizing the exposed adobe foundations on stone footings. By the time the Park Service arrived on the scene, most of these remnants had eroded further, with nothing remaining above grade. Acquisition by the National Park Service, from the start, centered on the promise of reconstruction of the fort for interpretative purposes. Toward this end, Bent's Old Fort was excavated in its entirety between September 1963 and July 1966. When this archaeological excavation project was completed, the remaining foundations were left exposed to the weather and continued to erode until Congress provided funds for reconstruction in 1973. The Colorado congressional delegation sponsored the project and it was begun in 1974 with the intent being that it would be Colorado's statehood centennial project, which coincided with the national bicentennial celebration of 1976. Such were the lofty motives of the project, which placated a western state in the face of so much reconstruction efforts taking place on the East Coast which defined most of the country's bicentennial effort. The other, less heralded motive was tourism in the southeast corner of the state of Colorado.

Less immediate interest was generated at Fort Union Trading Post National Historic Site straddling the Montana–North Dakota state line on the Missouri River. This site languished after a 1968 historical study and a four-season archaeological excavation project from 1968 to 1972. In 1978, the new park's first General Management Plan mentioned reconstruction, probably in direct response to the recently completed Bent's Old Fort project. The community of Williston, North Dakota, continued off and on to express an interest in the reconstruction, though the Park Service continued to argue for various alternatives delaying any decision. This impasse was broken in 1979 when Congress, responding to North Dakota's lobbying, asked the National Park Service, once and for all, to come up with a recommendation toward the possibility of reconstruction. The legislation was very specific in asking only if the fort "could be" reconstructed; Congress did not ask if it "should be" reconstructed. Because of the short time frame to reply to Congress, the Rocky Mountain Regional Office of the National Park Service prepared the "Fort Union Reconstruction Analysis" in which it was stated that the Park Service "could" reconstruct Fort Union—partially—based on the available documentation.

In 1984, with the local citizenry looking for a quick economic fix because of a slump in oil and natural gas production, they petitioned the Park Service to reconstruct the flagpole originally located in the center of the enceinte. This project required an immediate archaeological investigation prior to reconstruction, which was required so as to comply with Section 106 of the National Historic Preservation Act of 1966. Thus, at Fort Union the pattern was set with the flagpole reconstruction when Congress authorized reconstruction funding in 1986. Short time frames necessitated archaeology one year in advance of construction that mandated that the project archaeologists provide immediate field information to the project historical architects. This pattern was to repeat itself throughout the Fort Union project, between 1986 and 1991. The Fort Union project differed substantially from the complete archaeological excavation at Bent's Old Fort, over several seasons, which resulted in a published archaeological report that provided the basis, along with the historical documentation, for the preparation of the construction documents several years later for a two-year construction program.

At Bent's Old Fort, Dr. Herbert Dick of Trinidad State Junior College directed the 1954 archaeological excavation that located the site and defined the outline of the fort. This project, on behalf of the Colorado Historical Society, established the existence of the archaeological resource and provided a modicum of site interpretation that had been rudimentarily conducted by the Daughters of the American Revolution after the 1921 Arkansas River flood. This event had been preceded by a long period of neglect when the structure was used as a cattle shed and ultimately salvaged for building materials.

In 1961, with the drafting of the report, "Bent's Old Fort National Historical Site Project," Dr. Dick's 1954 archaeological work played an important role in the decisions to reconstruct at the new park. He was quoted stating that it was his "opinion that the information on Bent's Old Fort is adequate to permit an accurate reconstruction of the post" (Dick 1961: 9). Further it was stated in the text of this report that, "In view of the very complete documentary, pictorial, and archaeological information available as to the dimensions, structural materials, and appearance of Bent's Old Fort ca. 1846, a full scale reconstruction as of that period would be possible." This statement concluded: "Moreover, it is believed that such a reconstruction would be justified under the basic policy statement of the National Park Service on the restoration of historical structures" (Dick 1961: 4). Thus, it was determined that the entire adobe fort eventually would be reconstructed, which led directly to the planning for the next phase of the project that began in 1963 when the National Park Service took over the administration of the historic site.

Park Service archaeologist Jackson "Smokey" W. Moore undertook a three-year project in 1963 to completely excavate the site with the intent to reveal all the archaeological evidence by documenting the remaining in situ fabric for the proposed reconstruction. His intent was to expand on the 1954 excavation project. The excavations were planned to carefully expose the entire site based on scientific methods and fully utilize the most recent historical information. This was being assembled in concert with the archaeological excavations during the same years and involved primarily historian Dwight E. Stinson, Jr. of Bent's Old Fort and architect Charles S. Pope of the Park Service's Western Office of Design and Construction, San Francisco. Stinson and Pope completed Part I of "The Historic Structures Report" for the fort in late 1964 in collaboration with Smokey Moore.

Moore published a monograph in 1973 on the excavations. "Bent's Old Fort, An Archaeological Study" clearly follows the sequence of the excavations, room by

Figure 12.1. Aerial view of Bent's Old Fort archeological excavations looking northwest, 1964. (Photograph: NPS, Bent's Old Fort Collection, Arnold L. Rogers.)

room, with exacting detail drawn from his archaeological notes. The study, issued simultaneously with the preparation of construction documents for the reconstruction, clearly indicated the exceptional amount of information remaining at the site in the 1960s and, indeed, corroborated Dr. Dick's prediction that there was significant information in the archaeological record. Moore's excavations systematically moved through the rows of rooms lining the interior of the fortification's walls and examined every fragment of remaining evidence looking for architectural features such as doors and fireplaces to the depth of original surfaces. Anomalies were carefully revealed that were incorporated into the reconstruction such as storage pits and postholes. Clear evidence of structural alterations and fire damage was recorded as were associate features including drains and structures interpreted as cisterns. All of this information, in the most traditional sense, was documented into Moore's field notes and eventually formed the basis for his book.

Nevertheless, the reconstruction project lagged for nearly seven years until the possibility of realizing reconstruction actually began to become a reality with the completion of the General Master Plan and an Interpretive Study. The site, though, continued to deteriorate as exposed adobe walls eroded beneath concrete caps and applications of Pencapsula, a polyurethane coating believed to be a preservative. Wood shelters failed to stop capillary action within larger sections of adobe wall fragments. The remains of the original walls were simply melting.

The project was revitalized in 1972 when Congress finally authorized funds and the Denver Service Center of the National Park Service advertised for architectural services in anticipation of 1974 construction funds. The Ken R. White Company of Denver was selected to prepare preliminary designs and construction documents. Their final set of construction documents was submitted in October of 1973 for the following construction seasons. While drawing on all the available archaeological data and historical documentation that had been assembled, the construction documents were unique. They were more in the form of very generalized guidance with enough information given for a basic construction contract. As it was anticipated, the selected contractor was an expert in adobe construction and worked out many of the details on site. Several basic premises were incorporated into the reconstruction of Bent's Old Fort. It was determined early on that adobe would be utilized to recapture the spirit of the original building on the original site. However, this necessitated the complete removal of all the remains at the site, and all archaeology within the perimeter of the fort's walls was destroyed in the process of returning the site to its early grades and in sinking new foundations and footings to support the new structure. Initially, a section of the original adobe walls was to be incorporated into the new construction, but this proved unfeasible and a section of wall was simply salvaged for a museum exhibit.

Though the archaeology clearly indicated the adobe wall construction, it was deemed appropriate by the architects to improve on tradition. Concrete footings and foundations were poured and topped with stone masonry coursing to receive the adobe block in several wythes. The core was constructed of reinforced adobe, which unfortunately proved very fluid in wet conditions. This reinforced adobe, which also did not hold up well in compression, tended to slump when wet eventually forcing the facing wythes out at the base and causing the adobe veneers to fall away. Use of metal ties failed between the wythes because there had been no provision for bonding adobe blocks and no realization that the soils would rapidly corrode any metal. Such was also the fate of electrical conduits in walls and radiant heating in earthen floors.

Water was introduced into the wall systems because of the "historic" use of cottonwood logs that, like sponges, soak up water. As cottonwood cures, the grain twists and checks, which acts as a water conduit. This was further complicated by having concrete bond beams, supported on concrete columns, set into the adobe walls. The bond beams were poured around the cottonwood roof vigas, unlike traditional adobe construction where vigas are simply set into the adobe masonry. With the use of concrete, replacement has been a nearly impossible task. Although with good intentions, the architects created a maintenance nightmare that extended

Figure 12.2. Detail of Bent's Old Fort foundations capped with concrete just prior to reconstruction, 1975. (Photograph: NPS, Rodd L. Wheaton.)

through the construction details, the mechanical details, and down to the application of adobe plaster on the wall surfaces.

Initially, it was considered that the structure would be replastered on an annual "interpretative" basis much in the traditional manner of adobe maintenance of the Southwest. However, several weeks before dedication of the fort, in 1976, a horrific rainstorm demonstrated just how vulnerable not only the plaster but also the adobe walls really were. The damage was significant and the cost of repair was equally significant. This disaster began to set the tone for all future maintenance as it was realized that annual replastering was out of the question for the park staff. A long series of quick fixes were instituted that only in the past few years have been reversed slowly by the park's most recent administration.

As ideas such as annual replastering fell by the wayside, other issues arose with the monolithic building. Repairs were continual as the adobe veneers collapsed. All sorts of magic elixirs were conceived, concocted, and tried, to stabilize the adobe as a permanent, "maintenance free" exhibit. All failed. Only with replacement of the historic kind has there been any success. There have been issues of the design and construction of millwork that is just too crude. There are structural problems of hewn beams with half-lap connections being unsupported by columns around the portals. And there are continual water problems: infiltration through the vigas, rising

Figure 12.3. Bent's Old Fort northeast plaza view of interior parapet of corral walls being mud plastered above portal, February 1976. (Photograph: Bent's Old Fort Collection, Gerald Garmen.)

damp, and rising water tables that have filled excavated storage pits under rooms. Roofs have been replaced numerous times to eliminate the combination of built-up roofs and compacted soil that were also the victim of mixed technologies. Finally, there are issues of authenticity. During the reconstruction, many decisions were made based on a desire for a window or a door in a particular location without regard for historicity. To correct these problems, the park staff has relied on the archaeological field notes, as they have no "as built" documents beyond the scant historical records depicting the fort before its demise. This documentation indicated a second floor structure, but little else in specific detailing; it did not define or explain the anomalies which may have been later additions or historical temporary fixes. Much was left to conjecture, but portrayed as "authentic." Nevertheless, the archaeological record has clearly assisted in making informed decisions for repair and interpretation.

At Bent's Old Fort, the archaeological record defined the plan of the building, confirming the pictorial documentation. Archaeology also played a pivotal role in providing examples of hardware and other nonperishable building features. It was used in planning for the furnishing of the rooms that were detailed first by historian Enid Thompson and then by furnishings expert Sarah Olson in the furnishings plan.

Figure 12.4. Bent's Old Fort north gate at interior plaza, 1976. (Photograph: NPS, Rodd L. Wheaton.)

The artifacts provided clues to the lifeways and were used in the late 1990s to reproduce an iron arrow point to be used as a sales item in the trader's store exhibit. Many artifacts are used to interpret the fort, but, as of this writing, most of the collection awaits the construction of a museum structure to interpret the fort's contribution to the fur trade and its role in Santa Fe Trail commerce.

The efforts to rationalize the conjectural aspects of Bent's Old Fort along with the efforts to sustain and maintain the reconstruction played a major role in the

Figure 12.5. Interior of Bent's Old Fort interior plaza, looking south to Arkansas River, prior to reconstruction of fur press, 1976. (Photograph: NPS, Rodd L. Wheaton.)

development of the Fort Union Trading Post project. The Rocky Mountain Region of the National Park Service, which was established in 1974, inherited Bent's Old Fort and all the decisions that had lead to its planning, reconstruction, and mainte-nance. Thus, the regional office was not keen on assuming another such "money pit" and worked initially to thwart the idea that Fort Union should be reconstructed and attempted to explore other ideas as alternatives to a full-scale rebuilding. As early as 1965, the authorizing legislation mentioned development of the site (U.S. Congress 1965, 1966). This may have reflected the 1962 feasibility study regarding Fort Union that suggested reconstruction, but it was qualified with the statement, "However, such treatment [reconstruction] is deemed too costly, and interpretation centered in a modest Visitor Center near the Fort site is recommended. Reconstruc-tion of part of the stockade, and the exhibit of features uncovered during the archae-ological excavations might complete the display" (NPS 1962: 14).

The debate was fueled by the 1967 Fort Union Master Plan that also called for partial reconstruction based on "limitations of our knowledge about the historic post preclude complete authenticity. However, enough of the structural complex will be built on the basis of historical evidence to create a good visual impression, providing the visitors with an exceptionally vivid historical experience" (NPS 1967: 11). The 1978 General Management Plan avoided the reconstruction idea and proposed a large-scale model to be located adjacent to the archaeological site, which would be left undisturbed (NPS 1978: RMP-4, VUP-1). This new twist did not placate the citizens of Williston and North Dakota. They had been given to believe that reconstruction was the promise and that's what they wanted; thus, by 1979 Congress was asking for the definitive statement on reconstruction. The *Fort Union Reconstruction Analysis* brought the controversy to an end by carefully delineating what were historical facts and assumptions and what were archaeological facts and assumptions. For the first time the four earlier seasons of archaeology were carefully analyzed by a team of archaeologists, historical architects, and historians to evaluate the extent of the knowledge and to delineate plans and elevations showing exactly what was known about each structure of the fort. This was the first time that this information had been clearly evaluated and the conclusion was that the fort could, indeed, be partially reconstructed. Congress was so advised by the National Park Service with the publication of the *Analysis*.

Even with this recommendation, it took the citizens of Williston to initiate any activity at the Fort Union site. Their first foray was to ask permission to erect the

Figure 12.6. Archeological excavation of Fort Union Trading Post Bourgeois House, showing stone foundations; taken from flagpole, 1986. (NPS, Midwest Archeological Center, Lincoln, Nebr.)

flagpole in the enceinte at their expense. This project, based on archaeology conducted by the Midwest Archaeological Center in Lincoln, Nebraska, and construction drawings prepared by historical architect Richard Cronenberger of the Rocky Mountain Regional Office, was completed in 1985. As such, the flagpole was a milestone in the movement toward site development and provided impetus for securing a congressional appropriation for the reconstruction of three structural complexes: Bourgeois House, completed in 1986; the palisade and bastions, completed in 1989; and the Indian-Artisan House, completed in 1991. However, to accommodate the reconstruction of the Bourgeois House, it was immediately obvious, because of the short time frame and limited funds, that different project planning was going to have to be effected unlike the management of the Bent's Old Fort reconstruction. Limited funds necessitated the preparation of construction documents as quickly as possible and the task fell to the Historic Preservation Team of the Rocky Mountain Regional Office. It was determined that it would be expedient to contract directly with an architectural firm to begin the drawings based on the existing documentation, which

Figure 12.7.   Aerial view of Fort Union Trading Post looking south to Missouri River showing reconstructed Bourgeois House and archeological excavations of palisade and bastion foundations, 1988. (Photograph: NPS Midwest Archeological Center Collection, Lincoln, Nebr.)

included three circa 1860 stereo-pair photographs of the exterior of the fort, an elevation of the Bourgeois House, and detail of an Indian on the front porch of the Bourgeois House. The existence of photographs was unique to this project and provided irrefutable evidence of scale and detail that was missing in the Bent's Old Fort project, which had to rely exclusively on historic drawings.

Simultaneously, with the architectural construction documents underway, the final archaeological project of the Bourgeois House was undertaken at the same time. The idea of the project archaeologists of the NPS Midwest Archaeological Center was to totally excavate before reconstruction, feed any new information directly into the preparation of construction documents, and recover all data and artifacts from the site, which was slated for obliteration. Because of the *Analysis* report, specific questions could be answered by the archaeology, such as the exact locations of the end elevation doorways to the house. As planned, all the data was immediately incorporated into the construction documents as the archaeologists and architects worked in concert to achieve the goal for construction in 1987. This method of providing site data as quickly as possible had proven satisfactory for the

Figure 12.8. Post-reconstruction view of Fort Union Trading Post looking north with Missouri River in foreground, 1990. (Photograph: Courtesy of Orville C. Loomer, Williston, N. D.)

flagpole and proved on the larger scale that it could work for subsequent Fort Union projects.

Under the direction of William J. Hunt, Jr. of the Midwest Archaeological Center, a massive archaeological project was begun during the field season of 1988 for excavating the bastions and the palisade. Similarly, this project was fed directly into the preparation of construction documents, which, this time, were being prepared by Richard Cronenberger. The archaeology for this Phase II project is believed to be the largest type project ever carried out by the National Park Service because of the number of employees and volunteers working through the summer in advance of the pending reconstruction of the stone masonry bastions and the wooden palisade on its stone foundation. During this season, the archaeology confirmed the parallelogram plan of the palisade, the exact location of bracing, uses of space between the bracing and the exact details of the foundation of the palisade that supported a sill timber, which received the vertical uprights. More important, though, the archaeology clearly demonstrated that the timbers used for the structure were 10 inches by 10 inches, not the previously supposed 12 inches by 12 inches. In theory, this generated a significant cost savings.

Figure 12.9.   Fort Union Trading Post Bourgeois House reconstruction, south facade. (Photograph: NPS, Fort Union Trading Post NHS Collection, Tom Cantarine, Williston, N.D.)

Figure 12.10.   Interior of reconstructed Bourgeois House, Fort Union Trading Post, showing arrangement of new spaces to reflect historical center-hall plan. (Photograph: NPS, Fort Union Trading Post NHS Collection, Tom Cantarine, Williston, N.D.)

Finally, because of the amount of information revealed by the south palisade gate excavation, it was decided to go ahead with a full reconstruction of the log Indian-Artisan House in 1990. This project was intended to provide not only a trade store for interpretation and sales items but also it offered the only opportunity to reconstruct a documented interior that had been recorded by artist Rudolph Kurz in 1851. Careful archaeological investigation revealed that the anomalies of drawing were indeed accurate and the room was successfully re-created in exacting detail within the new log structure with its sod roof.

Meanwhile, Williston and North Dakota citizens were clamoring for more, but it was decided to remain faithful to the concept that only partial reconstruction could be contemplated. In addition, nearly three million artifacts that needed to be catalogued and studied proved to be a further deterrent to any additional excavation. Funds simply did not exist for further work beyond delineating the foundations of other buildings with timbers set on grade. The end result was that the visitors had a major interpretive facility, the local mountain man group had their stage set, and local citizens had a tourist industry handed to them.

Conclusion: What We Have Learned from
Bent's Old Fort and Fort Union

What was learned from the reconstruction of Bent's Old Fort and Fort Union? First, with regard to archaeology, the traditional method of archaeological excavation and report writing worked well as the archaeological work was completed one year in advance of construction with the data being fed directly into construction documents. Post-construction report writing provided confirmation and documentation. At Fort Union, the advantage was that the archaeologist was directly involved with the historical architects and historian to share knowledge and expertise for the completed project. There were no time lags resulting in the need to interpret the archaeological record, and excavation confirmed the historical record such as the accuracy of the 1851 Rudolph Kurz drawings, which were the basis for targeting that date for the reconstruction.

Second, the sequencing of the Fort Union archaeology, where the early excavation data was used for analysis, was invaluable, establishing all the knowns and unknowns for the record. This 1979 *Analysis* report, which utilized all the available historical graphics and photographs, proved to be an invaluable document for determining actual historical conditions and avoiding conjecture. For instance, the rear elevation of the Bourgeois House at Fort Union was unknown. Minimal conjecture led to indicating the possible presence of windows, matching the façade, by the construction of infilled window frames. The nearby kitchen structure was known only by its archaeological footprint, and that it had a gabled roof as indicated in a contemporary drawing. The roof structure was reconstructed and supported on steel columns over the exposed foundation. However, the park visitors, for the most part, did not understand the nuances. The rear windows were believed to be depictions of later alterations and the kitchen was believed to be a picnic shelter behind the Bourgeois House! While interpretive panels have better explained this, the fact remains that the complete reconstruction of Bent's Old Fort, with all of its conjectural flaws, is easier to understand by the layperson and makes a more complete movie set as has been its role on several occasions.

All of this plays a role for the visiting public, for whom the reconstructions are being built in the first place. It is for the visiting public and not necessarily for an elite group of professionals who continually belabor the pros and cons of the whole idea of reconstruction. As has been proven in both of these fort reconstructions, the public enjoys them immensely. The experience of moving through the sculptural adobe qualities of Bent's Old Fort could not be replicated with even a partial reconstruction because of the monographic nature of the original structure. One has an immediate sense of place. Similarly, Fort Union conveys a sense of enclosure and isolation even with the evidence of unreconstructed buildings. No model can convey that presence; no off-site reconstruction can convey the experience of walking on "hallowed" ground.

Third, both reconstructions taught us that we need to plan well in advance for maintenance and proposed use. Bent's Old Fort was a maintenance problem from the start that was only partially considered by the idea of staffing for annual replastering. That never happened and the ephemeral qualities of adobe presented immediate and continual problems particularly where mixed technologies were used in construction and modern functions were planned within period rooms. At Fort Union, we attempted to rectify some of these maintenance considerations. At the wooden structure of the Bourgeois House, this work was facilitated by substituting thickened frame walls for *poteaux en coulisse* log construction. Further consideration was given for interior spaces that were basically unknown. Adaptive use only suggests the original floor plan. Details were carefully considered such as the special consideration given for the placement of fluorescent fixtures and their location within rooms to assure a sense of historicity emanating from the Bourgeois House window sash. Meanwhile, adobe walls melt and timber palisades have a tendency to deteriorate, though at least the original construction of Fort Union lent itself to better long-term preservation by having the sill logs elevated on stone masonry foundations.

The issues of present-day use were resolved by the necessity for office space and exhibit spaces within the reconstructions. The office functions of Bent's Old Fort were moved to the rear rooms of the post; those of Fort Union were located in the Bourgeois House with curatorial storage located to the basement of the Indian-Artisan House. Within this structure, the only documented interior space at Fort Union was reconstructed, where much of the primary living spaces and storage spaces of Bent's Old Fort were fully reconstructed, though with much conjecture, and historically refurnished for interpretation.

In conclusion, the ability to experience refurnished rooms, like the continuing debate over whether to fully reconstruct or to partially reconstruct versus doing nothing at all, remain moot questions best resolved by the park visitors and visiting publics, who wield influence over funding sources. As historic preservation professionals, it is our obligation to provide the best experience through accuracy and interpretation. Bent's Old Fort and Fort Union Trading Post National Historic Sites represent opposite as well as divergent poles in this debate. However, they continue to illustrate the need for thorough archaeology, exhaustive historical research, carefully conceived construction, and meaningful interpretation to present the final product to the public in a manner that conveys the basic fact that reconstructions are not the "real thing."

References

Dick, Herbert
    1961   Bent's Old Fort National Historic Site Project, unpublished manuscript, Department of the Interior, National Park Service, Region Two, Omaha.

NPS (National Park Service)
1962   A Proposed Fort Union Trading Post National Historic Site, Department of the Interior, National Park Service, Midwest Region, Omaha, September 1962.
1967   Master Plan, Fort Union Trading Post National Historic Site, North Dakota-Montana, Department of the Interior, National Park Service, May 1967.
1978   Draft General Management Plan, Fort Union Trading Post National Historic Site, North Dakota-Montana, Department of the Interior, National Park Service, Rocky Mountain Region, Denver, April 1978.

U.S. Congress
1965   Senate Bill, S. 103, page 2, line 8, 6 January 1965.
1966   Public Law 89-458, 89th Congress, H. R. 3957, 20 June 1966.
1985   Public Law 95-625, Section 309.

LYNN A. NEAL ■

Chapter Thirteen

Emergency Ruins Preservation and Restoration at Homolovi Ruins State Park

Ruins reconstruction has a long history in the American Southwest. Jesse Walter Fewkes was one of the earliest proponents of this method of preservation and he conducted immense reconstruction efforts at Cliff Palace and Spruce Tree House in Mesa Verde in the very early 1900s (Fewkes 1909, 1911; Rohn 1977). This paradigm of preservation persists today, as the chapters in this book demonstrate. Stabilization without reconstruction as a method of ruins preservation has a much shorter heritage, starting in the late 1970s, but essentially not catching hold until the late 1980s (Metzger 1986, 1987, 1988a, 1988b; Miles 1988; National Park Service 1985, 1989; Neal 1990; Nordby 1981; Richert and Vivian 1974). This chapter presents a case study that argues for stabilization and preservation-in-place as an alternative to reconstruction, and suggests that, under certain conditions, in-place stabilization without reconstruction is a superior preservation method with regard to cost efficiency, interpretive potential, Native American preference, and long-term conservation effectiveness.

This chapter begins with a description of the project behind the case study, the Homolovi Emergency Ruins Preservation Project, and explains how and why the project occurred. This is followed by a description of the environmental and cultural setting of the project area and project objectives and methods. The chapter concludes with a more general discussion of the preservation efforts at the Homolovi sites and compares the effectiveness of stabilization-without-reconstruction at Homolovi I and III and reconstruction at Homolovi II.

The Project

From August to November 1995, I supervised a program of emergency ruins preservation at sites Homolovi I, II, and III at Homolovi Ruins State Park in Winslow,

Arizona (Neal, Purcell, and Mueller 1996). The work was necessary at I and III due to the severe flooding of the Little Colorado River during the winter of 1993 and again in 1995. A history of flooding at these sites made burial of those portions exposed to floodwater damage the best preservation alternative. Reconstruction of exposed architectural features was not a viable option for a number of reasons. As the direct descendants of the site's original occupants, the Hopi people believe that, in keeping with their traditional beliefs, a policy of preservation-in-place is preferable to reconstruction as a venue for interpretation. This belief is confirmed in the current doctrine of the Hopi Cultural Preservation Office and the Hopi Cultural Resources Advisory Team, as well as in statements to the author and park staff by Hopi visitors to the park. Of equal importance is the lack of direction, funding, and qualified personnel available to conduct preservation maintenance on the already existing stabilized and reconstructed structures.

For this project, the Federal Emergency Management Agency (FEMA) provided the funding for Homolovi I and III. Preservation at Homolovi II, funded by Arizona State Parks, involved exterior and interior treatment on a previously reconstructed masonry kiva located within the site's central plaza.

Environmental and Cultural Setting of the Project Area

Most of the park area is within the Little Colorado River valley and the Painted Desert region of the Colorado Plateau province, mainly north and east of the Little Colorado River. The elevation ranges from nearly 5,200 feet (1585 m) in the east to 4,800 feet (1463 m) on the river. The elevation at Homolovi I is 4,860 feet (1481 m), and the site is on a sandstone mound that rises above the river floodplain on the east side of the river. Homolovi III is also in the floodplain of the Little Colorado River, at an elevation of 4,820 feet (1469 m). The site is on a small rise or dune of wind-deposited sand derived from the sediments of the surrounding floodplain. The site is periodically flooded today, but Adams (1989) notes that the location of the pueblo suggests that this was not the case when it was settled late in the thirteenth century. Currently, the Little Colorado River channel is approximately two hundred meters east of Homolovi III. The Hopi word *Homol'ovi*, translated as "the place of the mounds" or low, rolling hills, best describes the area around Homolovi II. This pueblo was constructed on the western portion of a low, eroding sandstone and conglomerate mesa at an elevation of 4,920 feet (1500 m).

The sites represent contemporaneous Pueblo IV occupations. The vicinity of the Homolovi sites, the central Little Colorado River valley, was occupied by the Winslow branch of the Western Anasazi during the Pueblo IV period (from AD 1275 to 1425). These inhabitants were strongly influenced by the Mogollon people who occupied the Mogollon Rim to the south. The combined tradition of the southern

Anasazi and Mogollon, which characterized the region after AD 1250, is referred to as Western Pueblo rather than Anasazi (Hays, Adams, and Lange 1991: 1).

Project Objectives

As defined for the Homolovi Emergency Ruins Preservation Project, the primary objective of ruins stabilization, more accurately and recently referred to as ruins preservation (defined below), was to arrest or retard deterioration of the identified architectural remains. To accomplish this objective, we undertook initial comprehensive stabilization (Metzger, Matlock, and Reed 1987), followed by recommendations for future maintenance stabilization. Initial comprehensive stabilization involves the overall structural repair of a site, employing construction methods, materials, and techniques that minimize the deterioration of each structure or cultural feature. Such work leaves all of the structures or components of a site in structurally sound condition, while maintaining or preserving the site's appearance, integrity, and scientific value. Following initial comprehensive stabilization, a site requires only monitoring and maintenance. The ultimate goal of this type of stabilization is to preserve the site for future public and professional education and appreciation (Metzger 1986:1).

Ruins preservation more generally is described as the process used to preserve prehistoric and historic sites that are in a "ruined" condition. Most frequently, the methods and techniques of ruins preservation are applied to standing architecture. However, the process is also concerned with curtailing or mitigating factors that have an adverse effect on the integrity and condition of all aspects of a ruined site, including the architecture, all cultural materials and deposits, and the location of the ruin. For Homolovi I and III, site burial was the most productive and efficient means of ruins preservation.

Project Methods

The structural stabilization completed on the kiva at Homolovi II is discussed briefly in the subsequent sections, but the discussion will focus on the work conducted at Homolovi I and III. This emphasis will give the reader an idea of what a ruins preservation project of this scale and type entails, since this project offers an excellent example of a long-term, non-intrusive approach to conservation. The nonintrusive approach is the preferred approach of the author, most ruins preservation specialists, and current management at Arizona State Parks and Homolovi Ruins State Park.

Emergency preservation work at Homolovi I and III involved three broad classes of activities: removal of non-native vegetation and revegetation of native species, documentation, and ruins stabilization. Although the goals were essentially the same at both sites, the methods and degree of repairs differed. Many of the areas that required filling at Homolovi III had been previously excavated and were uncovered or further eroded by the floods. Areas that were filled or repaired at Homolovi I had been exposed and damaged by flooding, not excavation.

Our objective was not to attempt to control or stop the effects of the next possible flood at these sites, but to minimize the effects of everyday erosion caused primarily by wind, rainfall, and subsequent runoff. The recent flooding had accelerated damage from these factors, which had steepened slopes, created erosional gullies, enlarged and extended existing gullies, and scoured surface areas. As a consequence, architectural features and cultural materials had been exposed and severely eroded in some places (figure 13.1).

The Museum of Northern Arizona had conducted earlier preservation work at Homolovi I in 1981 (Dosh 1982), followed by the Cultural Resources Group of Louis Berger and Associates in 1993 (Hohmann 1994). SWCA's efforts included removing vegetation in the floodwater-damaged areas; identifying, mapping, and recording newly exposed features and structures (figure 13.2); stabilizing selected exposed masonry walls (including pretreatment and treatment documentation) (figure 13.3); constructing and repairing retaining walls (figure 13.4); placing a porous soil fabric or geotextile to hold the fill in place and to serve as a horizon marker;

Figure 13.1.   Exposed and eroded masonry wall at Homolovi III. (All figures in chapter 13, courtesy of Lynn A. Neal.)

Figure 13.2. Masonry walls found after removal of large driftwood pile at Homolovi I.

Figure 13.3. Stabilized masonry wall at Homolovi I.

Figure 13.4.   Repaired and expanded retaining walls at Homolovi I.

extensive filling with sterile sand and gravel; contouring and compacting; site cleanup; and finally, revegetating in filled areas. In particular, we completely covered the western and southern room blocks at Homolovi I after they were documented. We also prepared plan maps illustrating the appearance of each site before, during, and after the preservation work. Photographs and slides were taken throughout the project and keyed to site maps for later comparison during monitoring activities.

We carried out the same process at Homolovi III, with the exception of retaining wall construction; instead, we buried nearly the entire pueblo and plaza. Ours were the first preservation efforts at this site, although the Homolovi Research Program, a part of the Research Section of the Arizona State Museum, had excavated portions of the site from 1985 to 1989. Very little of the pueblo had been exposed prior to the excavations and the subsequent flooding. These five seasons of excavation were published as a volume of *Kiva* (vol. 54, no. 3), the journal of the Arizona Archaeological and Historical Society.

Preservation Efforts at Homolovi I and III

Generally, vegetation removal at Homolovi III and I allowed detailed mapping and confirmation of many additional wall segments. Prior to filling, we repaired unstable structural walls with two or more courses exposed, usually by repointing (remortaring and resetting) or replacing stones. At both sites, we contoured the fill to direct drainage away from intact structures and deposits. At Homolovi I, which has a much greater degree of slope, filling and contouring had to be coupled with the repair and addition of basalt riprap walls to further aid in dispersing and slowing runoff (figure 13.5). We used both mechanical and manual methods for filling, contouring, and compacting. The completion of this work created a contoured cap of sterile fill that will protect the underlying ruins by redirecting both storm runoff and channel flow and decreasing the present tendency toward downcutting in the vicinity of the sites.

. We did not conduct any excavations; however, detailed documentation of newly discovered features during the course of the preservation work augmented current archaeological knowledge of these prehistoric sites (Neal, Purcell, and Mueller 1996). Furthermore, the utilization of architectural documentation to systematically evaluate and understand the architectural skills and preferences of the builders is a relatively recent field of study (Metzger 1989). Through proper documentation, the techniques and construction patterns employed by the builders can often be ascertained.

Before beginning the actual preservation repairs, and as a necessary supplement to in-field documentation, we conducted archival research to assess the extent and location of previous archaeological and stabilization work. We also collected

Figure 13.5. Manual filling over geotextile on steep western room block at Homolovi I. Note retaining wall constructed in lower left-hand corner of photograph.

original mortar samples from wall segments that were slated for mortar repairs, and then we collected potential stabilization mortars and compared them with the original mortars for compatibility. All original and selected stabilization mortars were analyzed in the field and also submitted for laboratory analysis.

Preservation Efforts at Kiva 708, Homolovi II

The same procedures were followed during work at Homolovi II. The exposed kiva at Homolovi II consists of a large (10.3 by 7.2 meters), rectangular, subterranean masonry-walled structure with most of its interior features intact. A continuous bench is present along three sides, with a larger bench area and a stone shelf along the southeast wall (figure 13.6). The Homolovi Research Program excavated the kiva during the summer and fall of 1993, and it was subsequently reconstructed from 1993 to 1994 (Hohmann 1994). Since this feature is subsurface, was not backfilled, and is otherwise uncovered, additional maintenance repairs were warranted. We documented the kiva's current condition, completed some mortar repairs on walls and features, added fill to the kiva floor and benches, added fill to the structure's exterior

Figure 13.6.   Bench area and stone shelf along southeast wall of kiva at Homolovi II, before repairs.

(contouring it to direct runoff away from the kiva), reseeded around the exterior, and eventually removed a wood-slatted opening in the reconstructed roof of the ventilator tunnel (figure 13.7). This opening had been designed to provide an interpretive *cut-away* view of the tunnel's roof construction. However, this is an excellent example of a situation where reconstruction failed to meet its initial objectives. The reconstruction did not reflect the true native construction, it was not being interpreted, and it was creating impacts to the intact bench and interior tunnel walls.

Summary and Conclusion

We used an abundance of materials to complete the preservation work at the three pueblos: a total of fifty-six eighteen-wheeler loads of fill, three eighteen-wheeler loads of riprap, one dump-truck load of gravel, and enough soil fabric to cover two-thirds of a football field. Thirteen structures received treatment, totaling 27 linear meters of wall segments. In completing these structural repairs, we used 103 liters of unamended mortar, 19 liters of amended mortar, and forty replacement stones. This is a logistics-, labor-, and time-intensive process. The fieldwork took approximately three months to complete, with an average crew size of four to five people.

Figure 13.7. Final overview of kiva at Homolovi II, after repairs completed, but before removal of wood-slatted, bermed opening in roof of ventilator tunnel.

A front-end loader was the main mechanical device used for moving the materials onto the sites; we moved materials manually to more remote task areas. The reward of this type of preservation is that it requires little subsequent maintenance, especially since most stabilized structures were buried. We recommended that the sites be officially monitored for signs of erosion at least twice a year, particularly after heavy rains, to see if the repairs are holding. If this monitoring schedule is adhered to by park staff, and they perform necessary maintenance repairs on a cyclical basis, the long-term result is cost-effective preservation-in-place. Nearly a year after completion of the fieldwork, I conducted a session of monitoring and minor maintenance at the three ruins. This provided the necessary baseline guidelines and training to enable park personnel to carry out the maintenance aspects of the park's future preservation needs.

In addition to the low level of maintenance, burial as a means of preservation at Homolovi was the best alternative for several other reasons. On the whole, exposed stabilized and reconstructed structures have not worked at Homolovi. Due to the open and unprotected environment, the poor quality of some previous stabilization work, the lack of preservation funding and personnel to document and maintain the developed features, and the lack of on-site interpretive materials, signage, and staff, the Homolovi example starkly illustrates the problems of on-site reconstruction, which unjustifiably sacrifices intact architecture. In many cases, such intrusive on-site work interpretively skews and devalues the resource's authenticity.

Since completion of the preservation work at Homolovi in 1995, the repairs at all three sites are faring relatively well, considering the environmental conditions in the region and lack of attention to maintaining the repairs. When maintenance needs go unattended, the results can be quite detrimental to the resource, particularly those site areas and structures left exposed to the elements. I went back to do more repairs in late 1999, following a January 1998 earthquake in the area that had reportedly damaged the kiva at Homolovi II. I generally found the kiva to be in stable condition but in immediate need of several maintenance repairs; it was obvious that maintenance had not been done as recommended. Cracks reported by the park's risk management consultants, two of three existing pre-earthquake, required only minor repair. Of more concern, however, were the somewhat alarming condition of the once-intact deflector on the kiva's floor and the overall lack of maintenance of the structure. Along with reconstructing the deflector, repointing of interior mortar joints in all walls was done, fill on the benches was re-contoured, fifteen stones were reset (mostly capstones that had been kicked out of place), and the hidden protective cover over the ventilator tunnel was replaced. In summary, it seemed that the southeast bench area, in particular, had suffered damage more likely related to visitor access into the structure by way of jumping onto the broad bench than by the earthquake.

The contrasting results at Homolovi I and III and Homolovi II highlight the opportunities and limitations of preservation at parks such as Homolovi. This ruins preservation project offered a positive example of the efficacy of protecting a site by burial and erosion control as compared to the weaknesses of constant repair to opened exhibits and possible mitigation for the effects of continued natural and human impacts to these sites. At Homolovi, site burial is the obvious preservation choice to avoid resource loss or costly mitigation of features that would potentially be left unmaintained and uninterpreted. Furthermore, documentation prior to burial makes archaeological information accessible.

As an important ancestral site of the Hopi people, they typically prefer protection by burial to letting the sites of Homolovi fall into disrepair or losing them entirely. Burial also allows the sites to be left relatively unaltered and available for further investigation in the future. Generally, sites that we as archaeologists and resource managers are not prepared to protect, manage, and properly mitigate and interpret should not be developed for the public. The lack of direction, funding, and qualified personnel to interpret and conduct maintenance on stabilizations or reconstructions was therefore a significant factor in deciding the appropriate course of action for preserving the Homolovi sites. Additionally, reconstruction versus stabilization of exposed architectural features was not a viable option since the indigenous descendants prefer preservation-in-place to on-site reconstruction. In closing, the Homolovi example illustrates that we must make the commitment to actively develop and carry out cultural resource management plans that take into account claimant tribal views and needs and include preservation methods, trained personnel, and sources of funding for conducting and insuring long-term ruins preservation.

References

Adams, E. C.
    1989   Homolovi III: A Pueblo Hamlet in the Middle Little Colorado River Valley. In *The Homolovi Research Program: Investigations into the Prehistory of the Middle Little Colorado River Valley. Kiva* 54(3): 217–230.

Dosh, S. G.
    1982   The Emergency Protection of Homolovi I Ruin. Manuscript on file, Museum of Northern Arizona, Flagstaff, Arizona.

Fewkes, J. W.
    1909   Antiquities of the Mesa Verde National Park, Spruce Tree House. *Bureau of American Ethnology Bulletin* 41, Washington, D.C.
    1911   Antiquities of the Mesa Verde National Park, Cliff Palace. *Bureau of American Ethnology Bulletin* 51, Washington, D.C.

Hays, K. A., E. C. Adams, and R. C. Lange
    1991   Regional Prehistory and Research. In *Homolovi II: Archaeology of an Ancestral Hopi Village, Arizona,* edited by E. C. Adams and K. A. Hays, pp. 1–9. Anthropological Papers of the University of Arizona No. 55, Tucson, Arizona.

Hohmann, J. W.
1994   *Limited Stabilization and Backfilling Activities at Three Ruins Located within Homolovi Ruins State Park, Winslow, Arizona.* Cultural Resources Group Research Report No. 15. Louis Berger and Associates, Phoenix, Arizona.

Metzger, T. R.
1986   Chapter 1: Introduction. In *The Structural Stabilization of Nine Prehistoric Ruins in Wupatki National Monument, Northeastern Arizona: Report of the 1985 Field Season,* compiled by S. M. Chandler and J. K. Gaunt (p. 1). Nickens and Associates Ruins Stabilization Report No. 24, Montrose, Colorado.
1987   Ruins Stabilization Doesn't Have to Be a Dirty Word. *ASCA Report* 14(1): 3–8.
1988a Preservation/Archaeological Research Needs for Ruins Preservation Projects. Division of Conservation, Southwest Cultural Resources Center, National Park Service, Santa Fe, New Mexico.
1988b *Ruins Stabilization Report, Technical Series No. 53: Ruins Stabilization—A Handbook.* Prepared for Rocky Mountain Region, National Park Service, Denver, Colorado.
1989   Project Work Plan, Fiscal Year 1989, Wupatki National Monument, Stabilization of Eleven Prehistoric Sites. Manuscript on file, Division of Conservation, Southwest Cultural Resources Center, National Park Service, Santa Fe, New Mexico.

Metzger, T. R., G. M. Matlock, and A. D. Reed
1987   *Prehistoric Ruins Stabilization Plan, Canyonlands National Park, Utah.* Nickens and Associates Ruins Stabilization Report No. 17, Montrose, Colorado.

Miles, Judy
1987   Guidelines for Handling Archaeological Documentation. Draft manuscript on file, Division of Conservation, Southwest Cultural Resources Center, National Park Service, Santa Fe, New Mexico.

National Park Service
1985   *Cultural Resource Management Guidelines NPS-28.* Washington, D.C.
1987   Chapter 5. In *National Park Service Management Policies Manual.* Washington, D.C.

Neal, L. A.
1987   Filling the Void between Academics and Bureaucracy: My Internship Experience at Wupatki National Monument. Manuscript on file, Department of Anthropology, Northern Arizona University, Flagstaff, Arizona.

Neal, L. A., D. E. Purcell, and N. K. Mueller
1996   *Emergency Ruins Preservation at Homolovi I, II, and III, Homolovi Ruins State Park, Winslow, Arizona.* SWCA Environmental Consultants, SWCA Archaeological Report No. 96–22, Flagstaff, Arizona.

Nordby, L. V.
1981   *Non-destructive Archeology at Sliding Rock Ruin: An Experiment in the Methodology of the Conservation Ethic.* Division of Conservation, Southwest Cultural Resources Center, National Park Service, Santa Fe, New Mexico.

Richert, R. V. S., and R. G. Vivian
  1974 *Ruins Stabilization in the Southwestern United States*. National Park Service, Publications in Archaeology No. 10, Washington, D.C.

Rohn, A.
  1977 *Cultural Change and Continuity on Chapin Mesa*. The Regents Press of Kansas, Lawrence.

PART III

Virtual Reconstructions

KAREN A. BRUSH ■

Chapter Fourteen

Modeling Amarna
Computer Reconstructions of an Egyptian Palace

Physical reconstructions of archaeological features can offer insights into the technology of their creation and the practicality of their use. They are also expensive,
potentially destructive of the archaeological record, and difficult to modify when
theories change. They may also create an indelible visual impression of but one
interpretation of the past. Scale models are less likely to permanently color the viewer's interpretation of the past, but they are also difficult to modify and can offer only
limited perspectives of a feature.

Computer generated reconstructions of archaeological sites present many of
the same problems as more concrete reconstructions. The ability to incorporate photographic materials from a site into such models, creating animated "walk-
throughs" of these models, can leave one feeling as though one has actually visited
the past: a past which is constantly being reinterpreted and is thus unlikely to ever
be "correct." But computer models have one great advantage over their material
counterparts, namely, they are readily altered. This makes them the ideal medium
for exploring alternative reconstruction hypotheses and presenting these hypotheses
to the public. Such models may also be viewed from virtually any perspective, creating almost the same "realistic" illusion of the past as on-site reconstructions. This
chapter presents an ongoing series of computer models illustrating alternative reconstructions of the North Palace at Amarna, Egypt (figure 14.1).

In the fifth year of his reign, sometime around 1350 BC, the Egyptian pharaoh
Akhenaten decided to construct a new capital city called Akhetaten "the Horizon of
the Aten," halfway between Memphis and Thebes in the area of modern day Tell
el'Amarna. Amarna offers a unique vision of the past. Akhenaten specifically chose
a site for his city that had not been previously inhabited. The city was built and
flourished in the remaining twelve years of his reign, before being rapidly abandoned after his death. Until their discovery at the end of the nineteenth century, the
ruins lay undisturbed by further habitation or construction.

Archaeological excavations of the city at el'Amarna proceeded continuously

Figure 14.1.   Inside the computer model of the North Palace at Amarna. (All figures in chapter 14, courtesy of Karen A. Brush.)

from the late 1800s until 1935. In 1979, the Egypt Exploration Society began an investigation of the site that continues today under direction of Barry J. Kemp, reader in Egyptology, University of Cambridge. For some years now, the author has been engaged in the construction of a number of alternative computer models of this palace. These models allow Dr. Kemp to visually explore alternative structural models of the palace with relative ease. Eventually, still images from these models will be used as illustrative materials in the museum currently being planned for the site (figure 14.2).

The North Palace at Amarna is a rectangular building compound which lies facing the river in an isolated position along the Royal processional road between the pharaoh's principal residence in the North Riverside Palace and the Northern Suburb of the city proper. The mud-brick walls of this palace are fragile and have been badly damaged since their initial excavation in the 1920s, in part because the bricks are rich in manure and thus make excellent fertilizer for the fields of modern Amarna. To the tourist they present a bewildering monochromatic maze that is difficult to interpret. In this, the tourist is not alone. The North Palace at Amarna is a somewhat mysterious building and archaeologists are still trying to understand all of its functions.

The isolation of the palace, its position along the Great Royal Road, and a number of inscriptions of the name of one of the royal women overwritten by that

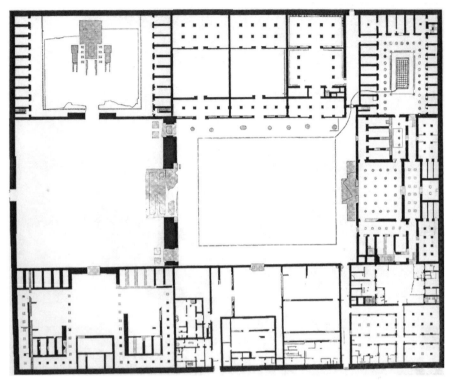

Figure 14.2. Floorplan of the North Palace at Amarna.

of the Princess Meritaten, eldest daughter and heiress of Akhenaten, suggest that the structure was a self-contained harem-palace for a major queen and her household. Such palaces are documented both from texts and from the site of Medinet el-Ghurab (Kemp 1991: 279).

The North Palace contains several distinct sections arranged around a central forecourt and garden court. The function of many of these sections is unclear. At the northwest corner lay an open-air altar for the Aten cult, and at the eastern end there was clearly a reception hall. There was also a stable with stone troughs and hitching stones, which, from the carvings of ibex and antelope on the troughs, may have been a zoo of sorts. In the southeast corner of the palace, there may have stood a vineyard (Whittemore 1926) and in the northeast corner there lies a small garden court surrounded by rooms from which fragments of bright paintings survive (Whittemore 1926) (figure 14.3).

The most famous of these is the "green room," in which was preserved perhaps the finest example of Egyptian art: the bird life in the swamps' mural recorded in drawings by Charles Wilkinson and in facsimile by Nina and Norman de Garis Davies. This mural, which depicts doves and kingfishers amidst a marsh of lotus and

Figure 14.3.   Computer reconstruction of the Green Room, Garden Court.

water lilies, originally ran all the way around the room. Breaking the design are numerous small niches framed in dark blue paint. The function of the odd little niches, painted to look like windows, which interrupt this frieze, is uncertain though it has been suggested that they were nesting places for birds and that this entire court served as an aviary (Whittemore 1926). Fragments of a scene of men feeding and herding geese were recorded from the south end of this court, suggesting that birds were an important part of the court's overall decorative scheme regardless of its function.

The presence of a hypothetical zoo and aviary suggest to some that this palace was related to the nature-habitats found at the outskirts of Amarna and closely associated with the royal women. There is, however, no direct evidence to support the interpretation of the Garden Court as an aviary. Another interpretation is that this court was a residence for members of the court, possibly the women, given its protected position at the back of the palace and its proximity to the reception halls.

One of the significant questions about the court is whether it consisted only of a single story with staircases leading onto a flat roof or whether it had a partial second story with more spacious living quarters than were available on the first floor. Unfortunately, the court was excavated in the 1920s and the fill removed so that direct evidence for a second story may never be found.

The work entailed in constructing a basic model of the Garden Court from the excavated plans was quite straightforward and took about a week to complete. Copies of this model could then easily be modified to reflect hypothetical numbers of stories, wall heights, colors, numbers, and positions of doors and windows, creating a series of alternative reconstructions. By bringing the investigators' theories to life, these models help to clarify potential flaws in hypotheses and can suggest avenues for future research (figures 14.4 and 14.5).

Plans are currently underway to build a museum at the site of El Amarna to aid visitors in interpreting the remains. However, interpretation of the ruins, especially those of the North Palace, is far from complete. Indeed, like most archaeological research, it is likely that new interpretations of its features will be discussed in perpetuity. Yet the visitor to the site understandably wishes to know "what it looked like" and indeed they need to have some idea of what it looked like to understand what they are looking at. The impression that the North Palace was a dark brown structure with rough brick walls and dirt floors set in the middle of a dusty plain is as misleading as any well-researched reconstruction could possibly be.

This was a building with white gypsum floors, brightly painted walls, and courtyards filled with vegetation and possibly pools of water. Its walls were high enough to provide shade in the morning and evening. Its hallways bustled with life. The countryside around it was cultivated as it no longer is today. To leave the visitor to the site without some inkling of all of this, to allow them to reach their own misinterpretation of the site based on a maze of soil discolorations and knee-high walls, is not consistent with the educational goals of archaeology (figure 14.6).

Figure 14.4.   One-story reconstruction of the Garden Court.

Figure 14.5. Two-story reconstruction of the Garden Court.

Figure 14.6. The Garden Court with papyrus plants. The papyrus and bird image is a photograph of a wall mural from Amarna that has been texture-mapped onto a clear panel placed inside the model.

One of the biggest questions facing the interpreter is how photo-realistic reconstructions of a site should be. If an image is too realistic, it may permanently color visitors views of the past and make it more difficult for them to accept changing hypotheses. On the other hand, too simplistic a model, or none at all, may have the same effect as indicated by the number of people who mentally picture the Athenian Parthenon as a white building. Fortunately, a single computer model can be used to generate everything from a simple hidden-line drawing to a fully-textured image complete with shadows set in a photographic background (figure 14.7).

The simplest three-dimensional (3D) models have a cartoon-like appearance. Initially each modeled object has a single color and when fully rendered looks a bit like plastic. Three-dimensional cartoons emphasize in their very simplicity the hypothetical nature of a reconstruction. They are also very useful for illustrating different aspects of a site, such as building phases or the nature of preservation. Such cartoon images are also swiftly rendered and it does not take eternity or a vast bank account to create a walk-through animation using these images.

Texture-mapping is the technique whereby a photograph or a painted image is "mapped" onto the surface of a 3D object, thus giving its surface a more complex appearance. A model may be completely mapped or maps may be applied only to selected portions. Each texture map takes time to render and the higher the resolution and clarity of the map the longer it takes. This is why extensive use of good texture maps is seldom seen in animations (figure 14.8).

Animated tours or walk-throughs of computer models have captured the public imagination and are increasingly present in museum displays and on TV. However,

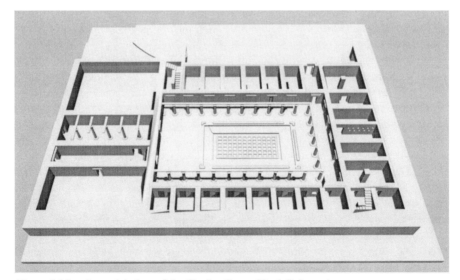

Figure 14.7. An aerial view of the Garden Court, North Palace, Amarna.

Figure 14.8. A hypothetical reconstruction of an eastern room in the Garden Court. The mural fragment on the wall and the small chest are both examples of texture-mapped images.

high-resolution full-screen images take time (as much as half an hour on a small computer) to render and a minimum animation speed is ten frames per second. This is why so many animations seen in museums today move incredibly rapidly, fill only part of a screen, and are of fairly low-resolution with jagged edges and simple cartoon colors.

To produce a high-resolution walk-through of any duration requires a very powerful computer and hence a great deal of money. Still images of computer models can be as effective and are both less expensive than animations and easier to present. At a remote location such as Amarna, video machines or computer kiosks would be almost impossible to maintain. It should also be noted that, in the case of computer kiosks, very few visitors to an exhibit can see the screen at one time unless a larger secondary screen is provided to show others what the terminal operator is doing. Observation suggests that children tend to wait anxiously in line at such terminals, looking neither right nor left, until their parents have seen the exhibit and tug them away into another room. While having such displays in exhibits may be necessary in order to attract public attention, they are not necessarily the best use of computer imagery or an institution's funds (figure 14.9).

The danger of creating too vivid an impression of a hypothetical past increases with the increasing photo-realism of the computer-generated images. For this rea-

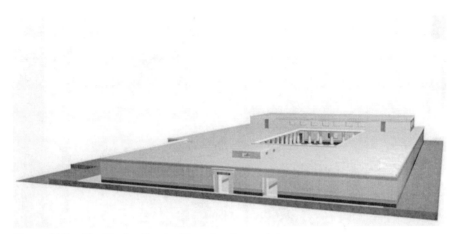

Figure 14.9. The Garden Court with roof and second story.

son, as well as for considerations of time and cost, many exhibitors may opt to keep such models as simple as possible. Another alternative is to take advantage of the flexibility of computer models to present several different versions of the past, each perhaps as realistic as the next. Used in this way, computer models can help visitors to not only envision the possibilities of the past but also to understand more clearly that archaeology is not wholly an empirical science and that the past can never be completely recovered nor entirely understood.

How and if one chooses to reconstruct a site may be partially determined by costs. Computer models can be outrageously expensive but they certainly do not have to be. If you want to link your theodolite to your computer and accurately model each brick and artifact in loving detail and then do a ten-minute high-resolution walk-through, and you want it all done quickly, you are looking at a very powerful machine and a considerable amount of money. But if you have humbler aims, the costs can be quite reasonable. You can purchase the software you need for as little as a thousand dollars and a reasonable graphics computer and monitor with lots of RAM (random-access memory) for another four thousand (these prices should drop with time). Then all you need is someone with basic computer skills and some time. The learning curves for most 3D modeling programs are decreasing and architectural forms are some of the simplest forms to generate (figure 14.10).

I am personally in favor of archaeological reconstructions because they were what first interested me in archaeology and history as a child. While I recognize the dangers inherent in presenting too plausible an image of an incompletely understood past, I believe it is possible to explain to the public that reconstructions are essentially hypotheses and not facts. One way to do this is to present alternative reconstructive hypotheses, and, for this, the readily changeable computer model is ideal.

Figure 14.10.   Garden Court with people (the author and a man from a wall mural).

References

Kemp, B. J.
    1991   Egypt in Microcosm: The City of El-Amarna. In *Ancient Egypt: Anatomy of a
            Civilization*, pp. 261–317. Routledge, New York.

Whittemore, T.
    1926   The excavations at El-'Amarnah, season 1924–1925. *Journal of Egyptian
            Archaeology* 12: 3–12.

Suggested Reading

Aldred, C.
    1982   El-'Amarna. In *Excavating in Egypt: The Egypt Exploration Society 1882–
            1982*, edited by T. G. H. James, pp. 89–106. British Museum Publications, Uni-
            versity of Chicago Press, Chicago.

Jones, M.
    1983   Preliminary Report on the El-'Amarna Expedition, 1981–1982. Appendix 1:
            The North City. *Journal of Egyptian Archaeology* 69:15–21.

Kemp, B. J.
　1984–1989　Amarna Reports, Vols. 1–5, London. EES Occasional Publications 2, edited by A. J. Spencer, Egypt Exploration Society, London.

Newton, F. G.
　1924　Excavations at El-'Amarnah, 1923–1924. *Journal of Egyptian Archaeology* 10: 294–298.
　1929　The Mural Painting of El-'Amarnah. Memorial Volume, Egypt Exploration Society, London.

Pendlebury, J. D. S.
　1931　Preliminary Report of Excavations at Tell el-'Amarnah, 1931–1932. *Journal of Egyptian Archaeology* 17: 240–243.
　1932　Preliminary Report of Excavations at Tell el-'Amarnah, 1931–1932. *Journal of Egyptian Archaeology* 18: 143–145.

Petrie, W. M. F.
　1894　*Tell el Amarna*. Methuen and Co., London.

ROBERT DANIELS-DWYER ■

Chapter Fifteen

Beyond the Artist's Impression
From Photo-Realism to Integrated Reconstruction in Buildings Archaeology

The presentation of models that have been colored and lewdly dressed with the allurement of painting is the mark of no architect intent on conveying the facts: rather it is that of a conceited one, striving to attract and seduce the eye of the beholder.

—Leon Battista Alberti 1988: 33

Traditionally, reconstructions in buildings archaeology are based upon the concept of the artist's impression: a fully fleshed presentation of the building "as it was." In fact, of course, this image is produced after discussion with archaeologists, who have themselves labored over their site data, to produce their professional interpretation. The image is, however, alienated from the data: Once it is produced, it is not possible to work back from the image to the data. Because of this, there must always exist ethical concerns about the ability of the audience to assess the validity of the reconstruction.

Developments in computer graphics in the 1980s made it possible to use Computer Aided Design (CAD) and Computer Aided Engineering (CAE) software to produce computer reconstructions in British archaeology. The benefits of this technology have been seen in the use of multiple reconstruction images, leading to photo-realistic images and walk-through animations; we are now on the verge of interactive virtual reality reconstruction. This technology has only increased the ethical dilemma, as we have a psychological presupposition to trust computer images as being "scientific," and so more "true."

While archaeological reconstruction modeling has been concerned with photo-realism, the construction industry has worked toward developing an integrated construction process to increase efficiency. This approach can be of benefit to archaeology, as I argue below. Such integrated reconstruction models can, first of all, link archaeological observation to the theory underlying the reconstruction. Second, the model can deal with more than the appearance of the building.

The Tyranny of the Artist's Reconstruction

Traditional reconstructions in buildings archaeology are based upon the concept of the artist's impression: a fully finished presentation of the building "as it was." Between the reconstruction and the data stand the interpretations of the archaeologists, and these interpretations are not made explicit. It is for this reason, I suggest, that we often feel uneasy about reconstructions; we see them as "bread and circuses" for popular consumption, rather than as a part of scholarly discourse. Ian Hodder (1989: 273) has criticized site reports as being stripped of their context, as presenting the data and conclusions of an "experiment" without the methodology. Reconstruction drawings take this one stage further, and present only the conclusion.

The artist's reconstruction is both constrained and creative. It is constrained because only one possible interpretation can be presented, and because it is only possible to present a single view of the reconstruction thesis. Another view requires a fresh drawing, which means expense. This problem can be overcome by the use of a three-dimensional plastic model, but this is usually at the expense of detail. It is creative because the artist is able to choose the view of the reconstruction with which the archaeologist is most confident and conceal or sketch areas that are not clear. A reconstruction can still be valid when it incorporates areas of ignorance. It is unethical, however, to fail to admit this limitation to the reconstruction thesis.

The artist's reconstruction is perceived subconsciously as authoritative, while at the same time we are not able to assess it, and we often suspect that it attempts to carry off a partial understanding as a complete one. It is for this reason that ethical concerns with reconstruction arise.

Because reconstructions have traditionally been drawn, we are also strongly inclined to think of reconstructions as being necessarily visual. In fact, any reconstruction must incorporate ideas about such things as individual structural elements, construction materials, structural properties, cultural influences, and phasing. These cannot be presented in a conventional reconstruction, but become possible with computer reconstructions; in fact, questions that could be discreetly avoided in conventional reconstructions must be directly and explicitly addressed in a computer reconstruction.

British archaeology has been concerned in the main with reproducing the traditional reconstruction in a more advanced way with computers: a *quantitative* development. I argue that it is possible to use computer modeling to achieve a *qualitative* development in archaeological reconstruction.

An Introduction to Modeling Software

Research in the computer modeling of buildings has, of course, been carried out primarily in the construction industry. Two types of software have been involved:

Computer Aided Design and Computer Aided Engineering (Woodwark 1986; Hoffman and Rossignac 1996). During the 1980s, these two types of software have gradually converged in many areas of their functionality. Rather than drawing a sharp line between CAD and CAE, it is now often more useful to discuss software in terms of its features, such as solid modeling and photo-realism.

CAD was originally intended to replace the use of paper drawings. Such drawings were drawn in two dimensions, with entities such as points, lines, and circles. Each of these entities was independently defined, its location recorded to millimeter accuracy, or greater. In the mid-1980s, CAD packages were developed with which three-dimensional drawings could be produced. It became possible to join together the plans and the elevations in a design for the first time, to produce a complete model of the project. Three-dimensional design was encouraged by the Royal Institute of Chartered Surveyors, as it enabled a complete design description (Atkin, Gill, and Newton 1987: 35). Such three-dimensional models were produced using "surfaces" rather than simply extending the use of two-dimensional lines into three dimensions; this made visualization much simpler and more effective.

CAE was developed to answer questions about physical properties of designs. As such, the software worked from the outset in three dimensions. Rather than using lines or surfaces, CAE worked with solids, as these best represented real-world objects, and they could readily provide information about, for example, volume or mass.

Although solid models were a more true representation of reality because of this, and were popular in principle with architects and surveyors (Atkin, Gill and Newton 1987: 34; Crosley 1988: 120), they were also much more cumbersome to use. Data were entered through batches of command lines, rather than the graphical user interfaces (GUI) of the CAD systems, which received data through digitizing tablets, light pens, and mice, and displayed the results immediately on the screen. The sophisticated solid modelers of CAE packages also require far greater memory and processor power to run. However, since 1990, simple solid modelers have been integrated into some professional CAD packages.

Photo–Realistic Reconstruction Modeling

Computer graphics research in the 1980s made it possible to move beyond simply coloring-in surfaces or the faces, to represent features such as texture and lighting, and to attempt to make the image appear as real as a photograph—photo-realism. Work on advanced data visualization was carried out in CAE as well as CAD (Burridge, Collins, Galton, Halbert, Heywood, Latham, Phippen, Quarendon, Reilly, Ricketts, Simmons, Todd, Walter, and Woodwark 1989). IBM's interest in CAE visualization had a direct affect on the development of computer modeling in British archaeology.

It is possible to divide the development of reconstruction models in British archaeology into two separate traditions: CAE development-led projects and small-scale CAD projects (Chapman 1990; Reilly 1992).

The major reconstruction projects in this country have been carried out using CAE solid modelers. The earliest was a solid model of the Roman Temple Precinct at Bath, England, followed by the Legionary Baths at Caerleon, Wales, in 1985, both produced by John Woodwark and Adrian Bowyer of the School of Engineering at the University of Bath. In 1986, Woodwark joined IBM's research center near Winchester, Hampshire, and worked on the WINSOM solid modeler, used to produce an animated tour of the Saxon Minster at Winchester. These projects were motivated by a desire to test the data visualization properties of CAE software on a challenging data set (Chapman 1990).

Beginning in 1988, North Cheshire College Computer-Aided Engineering Centre used the data provided by Lancaster University Archaeology Unit in its work on Furness Abbey, Cumbria, England, as the basis of a project investigating the applications of CAE (DeLooze and Wood 1991). This project did make some use of the ability of solid modelers to provide data on the physical properties of the reconstruction (Wood and Chapman 1992: 143).

CAE projects have, on the whole, been marked by the selection of buildings that contain a large amount of repetition of elements in a relatively simple design. This is because once a structural element has been defined, it can be copied and re-used as many times as necessary, at very little extra effort.

Although these CAE-based projects appear to have been of more benefit to the engineers than to the archaeologists, they did provide the archaeologists with access to technology and expertise that would not otherwise have been possible. Where archaeologists have not had this technical support, there has been piecemeal use of surface modelers, since the very end of the 1980s. They have mainly used CAD packages. Two early projects are worthy of mention in tracing the historical development of reconstruction modeling.

Papoudos, then at the University of Oxford, was part of an excavation project at Toumba Thessaloniki, Greece, which recorded all site data using AutoCAD, and then produced a reconstruction model. This was a considerable investment of resources. They spent £10,000 on computer equipment over six years, with a total project budget of only £12,000 a year (Kotsakis, Andreou, Vargas and Papoudas 1995). This project was a rare example of real field data being used to produce a reconstruction.

Gill Chapman used GCAL, a non-CAD surface modeler, to produce a simplified reconstruction of Langcliffe Quarry Limekiln, near Settle in North Yorkshire, as part of her M.Sc. at Teesside Polytechnic, England (Chapman 1990). This was to test her thesis that the most beneficial use of three-dimensional modeling in archaeology was not photo-realism, but to give an overall impression of the way in which space was utilized. This could be done cheaply and simply with a surface modeler, without the major technical support of the CAE projects of the 1980s.

Although three-dimensional models are produced using CAD in British archaeology, they are primarily the result of photogrammetric surveys of standing buildings, as part of cultural resource management projects, rather than as reconstructions. Very few reconstruction models have been produced.

Almost all of the archaeological reconstruction work carried out has been concerned with visualization. That is to say, it has continued the traditional idea that "the reconstruction" is a reconstruction of how something appeared. This is because of the research interests of the software engineers in the CAE projects, and of the archaeologists. The archaeologists at first wanted "pretty pictures" to present their sites. Increasingly, there is interest in using computers to produce simple visualizations of reconstruction hypotheses, in order to see how spaces fitted together within a site. However, in order to re-create the atmosphere of the reconstructed building, a degree of photo-realism may be necessary in some cases, for example, to see how light is distributed; this is affected by factors such as the decoration of the rooms and the presence of smoke. Advances in computer data processing power make it possible to test out such hypotheses, altering scene parameters, while maintaining a high level of photo-realism. This is the proposed purpose of the INSITE project at the University of Bristol, England (Chalmers, Stoddart, Belcher, and Day 1996). It will eventually be possible to produce images rapidly enough to allow for interactive, "virtual reality" reconstructions.

Integrated Reconstruction Modeling

Integrated Modeling in the Construction Industry

Visualization, although an important part of the design process, has not been the only development in modeling software. Each entity within a CAD or CAE model is individually fully defined. If CAE entities, and groups of CAD entities, are used to represent meaningful real-world objects, they become what I have described as "structural models" (Daniels 1997). That is to say, they model the structure of a building rather than simply its appearance. It is then possible to attach real-world properties to these objects. As the number of parties in the construction process using computers increased (architects, quantity surveyors, engineers, contractors, accountants), there was increasing duplication of data, and so integration was recommended (Atkin, Gill, and Newton 1987, p. 46). Once a suitable common data format is established, it should be possible to share a common structural model, with each party attaching its own data to the entities in the model. These data could in turn be linked to external databases of general information. This leads to "intelligent" drawings, where entities know what they are and can tell you what their properties are, by reference to these databases.

In recent years, object-oriented techniques have begun to be introduced into modeling software. Whereas surface models had no real meaning outside geometry, and solid models gave us volume and mass, objects attempt to model real-world objects more closely. "It is the purpose of object-oriented packages to bring CAD into the real world" (Spöhrer and O'Halloran 1996: 8). Objects contain within themselves their data, and a definition of how they will interact with the outside world. A wall object not only knows that it is a wall, as in an intelligent drawing, but knows also that it cannot coexist in the same space as a door. If a door is inserted, the wall can redefine itself, to leave a space for the door. Just as solids give greater integrity to the data in a drawing than groups of surfaces, so objects give greater integrity to the data than intelligent entities.

Integrated modeling can bring together a large amount of information relating to archaeological reconstructions, to bring about a qualitative change in the nature of such reconstructions.

Linking Reconstruction and Data

Because each entity in a reconstruction is independently defined, it is possible to have more than one spatial entity in the same space. We can put entities onto different "layers" (which can be thought of as sheets of drafting film). This makes it possible to control the presentation of spatial information on the screen, to help the user. It is therefore possible to have in the model not only the final reconstruction but also the original field data on which this observation is based.

The importance of keeping the field data separate from any interpretation or reconstruction has been stressed by Steve Nickerson (1996): "on the computer, it is necessary to draw a line the length that it is and if, after drawing the four walls of a room to their measured lengths they do not join perfectly, as they never will, the filleting [joining up at the corners] of these lines to make a clean corner constitutes an untruth on the part of the draughtsman as to the state of the building." From this initial recording of field data is produced a model of the building as it is, with, for example, Nickerson's lines filleted. After this comes the reconstruction model.

Because each element in a computer model is explicitly defined, its creators cannot avoid problematic areas, but must confront them. David Clarke (1972: 3) wrote, "Model definition is a route to the explicit theory which essentially defines a vigorous discipline." That Clarke was talking about mathematical models is not relevant: Reconstruction models are also the application of theory to data. When we must deal with archaeological data explicitly to produce a reconstruction, we become aware of the limitations of that data. Those working on WINSOM considered these limitations to be deficiencies (Burridge et al. 1989: 562). In fact, the limitations in archaeological data are an essential part of their nature, and these limitations can be built into the model. As it is possible to attach data to any entity, it is possible to attach a degree of confidence that each part of the reconstruction is correct. It is also possible to declare explicitly why we believe a part of the reconstruction to be the way that it is. Thus, we are able to move one stage closer to linking the reconstruction to the data.

The reconstruction images used for illustrations are derived directly from the reconstruction data, which are explicitly defined: There is no further interpretative intervention by an artist. This does not mean that the illustration image cannot be selected to present the reconstruction hypothesis in the best light. This is a well-known ruse in data visualization (Gershon 1993). What it means is that, as far as possible, we have made the reconstruction process explicit, and have made it possible for the reconstruction to be assessed.

Reconstructing Beyond Appearances

As mentioned above, archaeologists have been taken up with producing a reconstruction that accurately portrays the appearance of a building. As I have also said, the elements of a building have more properties than their appearance. An integrated model is able to handle these extra dimensions of the reconstruction. I have advocated elsewhere that solid modelers be the standard modeler used for producing structural models because they provide better representations of real-world objects than surface modelers, as they possess physical properties (Daniels 1997). It is therefore possible to ask engineering questions about these reconstructions, which may, in some cases, affect their feasibility. My own research is related to the economics of construction of Roman housing, using case studies in Ostia and Pompeii. Entities in the reconstruction models have information about their building material, which in turn is linked to information about sourcing, and the cost of extracting, working, and building with those materials.

As well as physical properties, integrated models may be useful for archaeological questions about the cultural perception of the building. Huang (1995: 200) has pointed out, in a design context, that computers can visualize data other than as photo-realistic images. We experience materials not only in a visual way but also in aural, olfactory, and tactile ways, and our experience of materials is shaped in part by our memories and thoughts. To this, I would add our cultural background. So reconstruction models can not only deal with substantive issues, such as engineering and construction costing, but also, potentially, with the way in which these buildings operate at an individual level of perception, issues which we might describe as "post-processual." These are sometimes subjective statements by the archaeologist, but they are also explicit statements. If we are to make subjective statements, then it is better that we make it explicit what our personal opinion is, so that others are better able to recognize it and assess it.

Finally, an integrated model can include full details of all stratigraphy and recovered environmental data and artifacts from excavations. In this way, the integrated model becomes a representation of the full site archive, and theories derived from the model will have the same authority as those derived from a more traditional archive.

Using the Reconstruction Data

Having added these extra dimensions to our model, integrating all possible information about it, there are two questions to be addressed. The first is, how is the data to be presented to the user? The second is, how much control can the user be given over the integrated reconstruction database?

Data can, of course, be presented in text form for each entity, to give a precise, complete description of that entity. Such an approach is necessary for detailed analysis, for example, for quantitative construction calculations. It is not, however, the best way to gain an overall impression of the data. It is in simplifying data that we are often best able to detect patterns within it; the human mind is best able to interpret data that are presented through shape, color, and even movement, rather than as text or numbers.

Data visualization is a long-established branch of computer graphics, allowing scientists and mathematicians to gain access to complex information, primarily through the use of color. In many cases, colors have cultural associations with abstract concepts, which can be used in the data visualization (Thorell and Smith 1990). We could thus produce an image of our reconstruction that draws attention to its most expensive elements, or to elements that suggest tradition by their style.

How much control can the user be given over access to the reconstruction data? There is no reason for the user to be presented only with completed reconstruction images. The user can now be empowered to go back to the original field data, and to work through the reconstruction from there. The degree to which this is possible depends only on the power of the user interface that is provided. While a public display copy of the model may only be able to produce different views of the reconstruction, a full research copy may allow users to produce their own reconstruction from the available data; if some data are sensitive, then access to them can be controlled. The archaeologists lose their authority to be the sole interpreters of the site. To use the computer model would give a similar power to reinterpret as access to a traditional site archive.

Conclusion

I have argued here that through advances in computer technology, it is possible to integrate fully our archaeological data, uniting together all our data about the building or site with our interpretative theories. Once this is done, the reconstruction becomes something not separate from "proper archaeology," but another element in the professional interpretation.

It should be stressed that what is being advocated here is the application of developments in construction software to archaeology. The techniques outlined do exist in the construction industry, but many are still at the development stage, or an early stage of use. We should be aware of what is developing, but not fear that unless we act at once, we shall be left behind. Computers can provide real solutions to problems, but we should recognize that different levels of the problem require different levels of computer involvement. To use a powerful technique on a simple problem may only result in spending unnecessary time and money for results that a simple technique could have produced equally well. To produce an integrated archaeological model would be a time-consuming business, and should only be undertaken where the complexity of the data is such that the time taken will be worth while because of greater effectiveness and efficiency at the interpretation stage.

References

Alberti L.
    1988   *On the Art of Building: In Ten Books*. Translated by J. Rykwert, N. Leach, and R. Taverner. (First published in Latin in 1450.) MIT, Cambridge, Mass.

Atkin B., M. Gill, and A. R. Newton
    1987   *CAD Techniques: Opportunities for Chartered Quantity Surveyors*. Royal Institute of Chartered Surveyors, London.

Burridge, J., B. Collins, B. Galton, A. Halbert, T. Heywood, W. Latham, P. Phippen, P. Quarendon, P. Reilly, M. Ricketts, J. Simmons, S. Todd, A. Walter, and J. Woodwark.
    1989   The WINSOM Solid Modeller and Its Application to Data Visualization. *IBM Systems Journal* 28(4): 548–568.

Chalmers, A., S. Stoddart, M. Belcher, and M. Day
    1996   *INSITE: An Interactive Photo-Realistic Visualization System for Archaeological Sites*. www.bris.ac.uk/Depts/Archaeology/html/insit2.htm.

Chapman, G.
    1990   3D Computer Visualization of Archaeological Data: With Particular Reference to Reconstruction Modelling. Unpublished Master's dissertation, Teesside Polytechnic, School of Computing and Mathematics: Division of Postgraduate Studies and CAD, Middlesborough.

Clarke, D., ed.
    1972   *Models in Archaeology*. Methuen, London.

Crosley, M.
    1988   *The Architect's Guide to Computer-Aided Design*. Wiley, New York.

Daniels, R.
    1997   The Need for the Solid Modelling of Structure in the Archaeology of Buildings. *Internet Archaeology* 2: 2. 3.

DeLooze, K., and J. Wood
    1991   Furness Abbey Survey Project: The Applications of Computer Graphics and

Data Visualization to Reconstruction Modelling of an Historic Monument. In *Computer Applications and Quantitative Methods in Archaeology 1990*, edited by K. Lockyear, S. Rahtz, (pp. 141–148). British Archaeological Reports, Oxford.

Gershon N. (Chair)
1993   How to Lie and Confuse with Visualization. In *Computer Graphics Proceedings. Siggraph* 93, pp. 387–388. Association for Computer Machinery, New York.

Hodder, I.
1989   Writing Archaeology: Site Reports in Context. *Antiquity* 63: 268–274.

Hoffmann, C., and J. Rossignac
1996   A Road Map to Solid Modeling. *IEEE Transactions on Visualization and Computer Graphics* 2(1): 3–10.

Huang, J.
1995   Interactive Material Visualization System in Architectural Design. In *Visualization and Intelligent Design in Engineering and Architecture II*, edited by S. Hernández and C. Brebbia, pp.100–206. Computational Mechanics Publications, Southampton.

Kotsakis, K., S. Andreou, A. Vargas, and D. Papoudas
1995   Reconstructing a Bronze Age Site with CAD. In *Computer Applications and Quantitative Methods in Archaeology 1994*, edited by J. Hugget and N. Ryan, pp. 181–187. Tempus Reparatum, Oxford.

Nickerson, S.
1996   *Object Oriented Recording: Comments on Digital Extant Recording in the Field.* http://www.nickerson.icomos.org/steve/oor.txt.

Reilly, P.
1992   Three-Dimensional Modelling and Primary Archaeological Data. In *Archaeology and the Information Age: A Global Perspective*, edited by P. Reilly and S. Rahtz, pp. 147–173. Routledge, London.

Spöhrer, R., and J. O'Halloran
1996   Subject: Object. *Architech* 1(1): 8–9.

Thorell, L., and W. Smith
1990   *Color: Using Computer Color Effectively: An Illustrated Reference.* Hewlett Packard/Prentice Hall, Englewood Cliffs, N. J.

Wood, J., and G. Chapman
1992   Three-Dimensional Computer Visualization of Historic Buildings—With Particular Reference to Reconstruction Modelling. In *Archaeology and the Information Age: A Global Perspective*, edited by P. Reilly and S. Rahtz, pp. 147–173. Routledge, London.

Woodwark, J.
1986.   *Computing Shape.* Butterworths, London.

PART IV

The Future of Reconstruction

VERGIL E. NOBLE ■

Chapter 16

The Value of Reconstructions
An Archaeological Perspective

The good critic is he who narrates the adventures of his soul among masterpieces.

—Anatole France

Most of my professional life in archaeology has been occupied with the mission of historic site reconstruction, and so I welcomed the opportunity to serve as a discussant in the 1997 symposium from which this volume ultimately originates. In fact, the eighteenth-century milling site at the Straits of Mackinac in northern Michigan—where I first dulled the blade of a trowel in 1973—arose from the forest floor some ten years later and is now one of several popular reconstructed historic sites associated with the more familiar Fort Michilimackinac. Little did I suspect as I embarked on this career, however, that I would spend much of my next twenty-five years involved with similar applied undertakings.

In 1974, I worked on Michigan State University's excavations at the site of Fort Ouiatenon near Lafayette, Indiana, which ran six years with the generous support of a county historical society bent on raising another eighteenth-century fur-trading site from obscurity to modern tourist attraction. A crew member in that first season, I eventually spent a total of five hot summers on the site, directing the 1977–1979 field research as my doctoral research project. Our sponsors did not realize at the outset, however, that the cost to undertake a reconstruction of the French trading post ultimately would prove beyond their means, or that the archaeological evidence from which they hoped to build could be so ambiguous. Attaining their goal would not be cheap, nor would the path to reconstruction be clear-cut, and so it eludes them still.

Of course, we at the university had tried from the very start to underscore the point that their primary source of inspiration, Fort Michilimackinac, initially was reconstructed with state funding at 1950s prices and largely with convict labor. Further, its favorable location in a well-established resort area, literally in the shadow of the Mackinac Bridge and a major interstate highway, helped generate the steady revenue required to support expansion of the research and reconstruction programs in later years. Nearly five hundred million vehicles now cross that bridge each year, and most weary travelers enjoy the opportunity to stretch their legs at the convenient attraction. Indeed, a partial site reconstruction was already generating gate receipts before the start of Michigan State's 1959 archaeological investigations under the direction of Moreau Maxwell and a young field assistant from the University of Michigan named Lewis Binford (Maxwell and Binford 1961). A reconstructed Fort Ouiatenon, however well done, was not likely to draw visitors to this cornfield on the Wabash River floodplain in numbers anything like those that applied at the Straits of Mackinac.

An even more important point we tried to make, from our direct knowledge, was that certain aspects of the Fort Michilimackinac reconstruction initially had gone forward without the firm support of archaeological field data. After all, Michilimackinac was occupied actively and intensively for a long period of time—about three-quarters of a century, leaving much of the archaeological record a confusing jumble of superimposed features and partial remains, often difficult to recognize and interpret. As we suspected, the same was true of Fort Ouiatenon; this was a recurring annoyance for our sponsors and for ourselves.

My connections with site reconstruction continued to be strong after leaving graduate school. While serving as director of the Midwestern Archeological Research Center at Illinois State University, in the mid-1980s, I administered research to enhance the partial reconstruction at Fort de Chartres III, situated on the banks of the Mississippi River not far below St. Louis. Subsequently, while with the National Park Service, I have worked frequently within the confines of a reconstructed fur-trade depot at Grand Portage National Monument on the north shore of Lake Superior. I also directed a three-year archaeological study between Cleveland and Akron, Ohio, contributing to the reconstruction (or, more accurately, the adaptive reuse) of the Ohio and Erie Canal towpath, which now serves as a multiple-use trail in Cuyahoga Valley National Park. Furthermore, I have returned on several other occasions to the Cuyahoga Valley to excavate around historic structures undergoing restoration near the canal.

In fact, most of my archaeological fieldwork performed over the last fifteen years has been associated with the restoration of extant nineteenth-century buildings, including several presidential homes in the Midwest. I consider such efforts relevant to this discussion because attempts to return a historic structure to the appearance it had during a particular period usually entails the demolition of non-historic elements, the search for physical evidence of removed or obscured historic elements, and the retrieval of other potentially significant information that is encountered in the process. Such activities are the closest in my own background to the stabilization of prehistoric ruins or the preservation efforts at Ironbridge Gorge and, of course, the restoration of George Washington's Mt. Vernon.

Those experiences, and others like them, have collectively shaped my basic philosophy on site reconstruction, which has evolved from one that was rather idealistic and abstract to one that today is more pragmatic and grounded in reality. Despite having assumed a more liberal stance toward archaeological site reconstruction in recent years, however, I still hold dearly to one fundamental principle analogous to a basic tenet of the physician's Hippocratic Oath: "First, do no harm."

By that I mean to say that it is incumbent upon us all to exercise due caution so as not to destroy a site with true archaeological integrity, albeit an imperfect record, without ample justification. Archaeology performed simply for the purpose of erecting something that is doubtless much further removed from reality, as an approximation of past conditions, is a lamentable expenditure of financial and cultural resources. We must make clear to the sponsors and advocates of site reconstructions that archaeology is, in fact, a destructive process and that we must not exploit the finite cultural resources contained in a site immoderately and without compelling reasons. Only rarely can total excavation of a site be justified, even if considerable time and money are available to support such a goal. Rather a conscious effort should made to preserve parts of any site we choose to reconstruct when alternatives to excavation exist.

Equally crucial, in my view, is the need for excavation programs associated with site reconstruction to be pursuant of broader research problems, and not simply driven by the specific needs of planners. Of course, any archaeologist involved with mission-oriented research, as Swannack (1975) called it, must make a sincere attempt to satisfy the sponsors who finance the work. But the same basic data required for reconstruction planning can, and should, be put to scientific uses beyond the bare requirements of historical accuracy in reconstruction (cf. Noble 1979; South 1977). In fact, it is quite probable that any increase of general knowledge so obtained at an archaeological site would provide ample grist for public interpretation once the reconstruction was accomplished.

By the same token, as professional archaeologists, we must be sure to apprise our sponsors of the distinct limitations that are inherent to this discipline. Not everything reconstruction planners might want to know can be learned through excavation. If we are not clear on this key point, needless excavation is apt to be undertaken with frustration and disappointment the likely result.

Those who would reconstruct sites must also take pains not to mislead visitors with anachronistic elements that are designed to "look old," but for which there is no reasonable basis to include them in the historic scene. For example, I would much prefer to see tastefully compatible, but clearly modern, street lighting when it is required for visitor safety in a restored historic neighborhood, rather than ersatz gaslights on a street that had no lighting at all during the interpreted period. On the other hand, the illusion of a scene largely unblemished by the modern world can be reasonably established through the clever concealment of necessary amenities in "period" trappings. A weathered wooden barrel, for example, might readily serve as a trash receptacle without unduly compromising the historic scene.

Thus, my concerns are, first, for the tangible cultural resources that survive in the ground and, second, for the intangible impressions that might be formed in the minds of site visitors. Nevertheless, the ideals I still embrace are now tempered by additional practical and pragmatic factors, not the least of which is the indisputable fact that site reconstruction is a way to make our collective efforts in archaeology better understood and more relevant to the public. My ideals are also moderated by the fact that most tourists are not seeking authenticity or an education when they visit a reconstructed archaeological site. To the contrary, as Edward Bruner (1994) found in his study of a popular Illinois attraction, most visitors are simply after a pleasant diversion and are perhaps drawn by some ill-defined need to reaffirm how good our lives are today in comparison with those of yesteryear.

Now there are several general points that I think we can draw from the chapters in this volume as a collective. First, a reconstruction is no more than a means toward a larger purpose. It is a product based on research efforts that are or should be coordinated and interdisciplinary; it is a product usually effected with the benefit of modern materials in science and technology; and it is a product that often employs intuition and imagination on the part of its creators. But a reconstruction is not an end in itself, nor is it capable of presenting the entire story of the site, the environs, or the times on its own. The reconstruction must be used in concert with other interpretative methods in order to serve some desired outcome.

And what is that larger purpose? The answer usually heard is that reconstructions are created to educate the public about the past, which is surely a worthy goal. But as so many of the contributors to this volume have indicated, the true driving forces behind site reconstruction are ultimately economic, political, or social, and simple entertainment of site visitors is often deemed more important than education as long as it gets them through the front gate. Even when education is indeed a prime element of the intended outcome, whatever story is chosen for the telling is apt to be crafted specifically to satisfy the needs of a hidden agenda. This is done by emphasizing a particular point of view or interpretation of events, rather than by attending to some altruistic notion of impartially representing the past.

One other important point we must acknowledge at the outset is that any site we might reconstruct was doubtless part of a more extensive, complex, and ever-changing system. A reconstructed site, especially one frozen in time by an unchanging built environment, is inherently limited in what it can tell the average visitor who might spend no more than an hour or two engaged with it. An important quality is lost, I think, when we seek to portray the dynamic as static. Innovative approaches to interpretation can overcome some of those limitations, but it is the rare case where such efforts actually have been made.

Fortunately, this volume is blessed with many good and widely varied examples of site reconstruction for our consideration. Having stated my background with regard to the issues, as well as my biases, I will now offer specific commentary that, of necessity, is much too brief to do justice to the authors. My hope is to point out one or two things in each contribution that I found to be of particular interest and worthy of note.

Commentary on the Chapters in This Book

I found Don Linebaugh's chapter on the checkered career of Roland Robbins interesting in many respects. Though I admit that I had never heard of Robbins before reading this chapter, his situation is all too familiar to me. Indeed, the poor fellow could have been the hapless model for a paper I published in the pages of *Historical Archaeology*, wherein I described the dysfunctional futility that all too often has been known to surround site reconstruction efforts (Noble 1996).

The review of his bitter experiences starkly personalizes the conflicting values with which one must contend as an archaeologist caught up in the often upside-down world of mission-oriented research. Robbins's situation was not unusual for its time, of course, and though we have made great strides since then, the many problems he encountered have not entirely vanished from the scene in this more enlightened age of collaborative effort. Robbins himself was unusual, however, in tendering a principled resignation when faced with what he considered intolerable circumstances, and I thank Linebaugh for bringing the lessons of this life to our attention.

The reconstruction of Colonial Williamsburg represents one of the earliest and most ambitious collaborations between field archaeologists and planners ever undertaken, and it is interesting to see by Marley Brown and Edward Chappell's lights how notions of historical authenticity at the site have changed since its beginnings. Still at the vanguard of attempts at full-scale site reconstruction, the foundation has, in recent years, also introduced innovative ruins-like partial reconstructions at the site of Wolstenholm Town.

Well known and widely respected for his meticulous field methods, former head of archaeology Ivor Noël Hume perhaps was too demanding in his early admonition to avoid the "slippery path" of speculation, which he argued will lead away from historical accuracy toward fantasy. We must acknowledge that a great deal of archaeology is necessarily based on little more than informed speculation, drawn as it is from incomplete facts, and that such interpretations of the data are hardly fantastic if they are consistent with a broader framework of knowledge. Especially when dealing with historic-period sites, so familiar to Noël Hume, we are not groping blindly in the dark, dependent entirely upon material remains to keep us on the right path. To the contrary, we can infer a great deal about colonial life at any given site in North America from the cumulative research efforts at contemporary sites and from other lines of evidence, even if documentary records relating to a subject site do not survive. In other words, at this stage we should have a pretty good idea of what is possible, what is probable, and what is neither possible nor probable in a particular historic scene.

Speculation of a type perhaps more acceptable to strict reconstructionists also can play an important role in site interpretive efforts, as the authors point out, by raising questions about the past, not necessarily as it was but as it might have been. Using archaeology and history to pose alternative theories of past events, especially when the record is silent or ambiguous, engages the visitor in thought processes that practitioners in both fields employ as the means toward discovery. Moreover, to imply that the study of a reconstructed site has left no unanswered questions would misrepresent the manner in which our knowledge tends to progress, as it is so often the case that new data raise more questions than they answer.

Barry Mackintosh's overview of National Park Service policy and description of actual case studies was especially interesting to me, not only because I learned much about my own agency from it but also because development of the modern discipline of historical archaeology is intimately associated with early NPS reconstruction efforts. My own research interests and academic roots trace back to places like Jamestown in the 1950s, where agency archaeologists J. C. Harrington and John L. Cotter, among others, parlayed the search for structural foundations and authentic examples of building hardware into a new field of study. Indeed, historical archaeology has grown and diversified immensely over the past fifty years, expanding its scope on a global scale, but it is still commonly connected with heritage tourism and reconstruction.

Mackintosh ably chronicles the evolution of National Park Service policy and describes the conflicts inherent to reconstruction. Of course, the need to excavate and thereby destroy archaeological deposits in order to create an on-site reconstruction is merely an extreme case of the more general conflict between resource preservation and visitor use in our national park areas. Park managers, guided by policy, are continuously called upon to balance those interests. As he points out, however, policy can be and often is liberally interpreted to suit desired ends. Law is something altogether different. In addition to the Historic Sites Act of 1935, which explicitly provides a justification for reconstruction, planners and managers must also attend to the National Historic Preservation Act of 1966, as amended, which establishes a process for review of all federally sanctioned undertakings that may affect cultural resources. Although the so-called Section 106 process does not guarantee that preservation interests will always prevail, it at least ensures that the public and professionals outside the agency will have an opportunity to provide input during the planning stages.

The controversy surrounding reconstruction of the blacksmith shop at Mt. Vernon, as Esther White describes it, underscores one of my earlier points about the problems that inevitably arise from attempts to interpret a designated historic period at reconstructed sites. The early decision to present Mt. Vernon as it appeared in the last year of George Washington's life, so defined the desired cultural landscape as to justify the elimination of later historic elements, such as the icehouse, not associated with that particular time. A terrible preservation dilemma arises when significance is defined so narrowly, which can be ameliorated in treatment plans only by the systematic recordation of unwanted features before their removal.

Of course, at sites occupied over long periods of time, it is almost always necessary to limit what is physically represented to the public; otherwise, the pastiche of unrelated structural components from different periods will leave visitors bewildered by implying association where there is none. That does not preclude, however, the prospect of interpreting the broader context in a variety of other ways. Elaborating on aspects of the full history of an interpreted site, with such devices as brochures, wayside panels, exhibits, and even the oral narratives of guides, can give visitors an impression of site complexity without unduly intruding on the primary interpretive mission.

White's concluding point about depicting utilitarian aspects of life at Mt. Vernon, in stark contrast with the trappings of an elegant plantation, is an important one. Just as there is misrepresentation in a pristine, reconstructed past of well-kept lawns and spotless privies, it would not be an accurate depiction of a working plantation if only the life of the gentleman planter were on display. The lives of many, including slaves, contributed to the workings of Mt. Vernon, and their stories can enrich the public's understanding of Washington and his times. It is essential that visitors to such sites also be made aware of the less attractive aspects of our historic past, including mundane features we now find unfamiliar, and common practices we now find abhorrent.

Harold Mytum claims that the reconstruction of an Iron Age fort at Castell Henllys is unique in Britain, and that may in fact be a modest appraisal, for I know of nothing else quite like it anywhere. As he is quick to acknowledge in his overview, one may readily mark both strengths and weaknesses in the approach that has been taken at the site. In my view, however, the strengths far outweigh whatever weaknesses are noted.

Archaeological data have formed the basis for certain reconstructions at Castell Henllys, but they have not constrained experimentation in the construction of others there. Some structural details are conjectural, whereas reconstructions accomplished with reductions in scale are outright misleading. Even those departures from past reality, however, can be shown to serve a purpose in offering selected groups a fuller site experience.

What is more remarkable about this site, to my mind, is the very important part it now plays in contemporary Welsh culture. Flawed or not, the fact that the reconstructed site makes visible a glorious Celtic heritage as it was—or simply as it might have been—before its eclipse under the shadow of English dominion is no trifling matter. Indeed, the social uplift and empowerment of dominated groups through such linkages is precisely what contemporary critical theorists have told us should be the ultimate purpose of doing archaeology in our modern world (Leone et al. 1987). The site's appeal to those embracing New Age metaphysics also shows that a reconstructed site can attract an unexpected audience and achieve an even broader significance than planners intended.

As Peter Fowler and Susan Mills acknowledge in the subtitle of their chapter, Bede's World is a creation (a "modern simulacrum," as they later call it) rather than a reconstruction. Elements of this simulated seventh-century village are derived largely from what archaeologists have learned from medieval sites elsewhere and from surviving records relating to the Venerable Bede and his times. Like all of the cases reported in this volume, much of the end product is the result of professional judgments drawn from incomplete and often conflicting evidence. The rest is essentially speculation and experimentation in search of a fuller understanding of life in the Middle Ages. As such, Bede's World is as much a research project as it is a product of research.

Bede's World stands out, however, for its holistic emphasis on the cultural landscape; even the term "world" underscores the fact that the village was not an isolated place in time, but part of a larger system. Many reconstructed heritage sites focus on the built environment and fail to address in any meaningful way the surrounding environs that also surely would have reflected a human presence. British archaeologists have long been interested in the study of cultural landscapes, and there is much we can learn from their pioneering research in the United Kingdom.

Marion Blockley's exposition on Ironbridge Gorge stands out in sharp contrast with the others in this volume, as that sprawling World Heritage Site comprises practically all of the site treatment alternatives imaginable. This owes, in large part, to the fact that Ironbridge Gorge was still a vibrant community when the preservation efforts began, and it is still occupied by real people living out their day-to-day lives, rather than reenactors. The effort here was not simply a matter of rendering the invisible cultural heritage once again visible, though that surely was an aspect of the program. Indeed, the real successes at Ironbridge seem to be where the least efforts were taken in ruins stabilization, structural rehabilitation, and adaptive reuse.

I am not troubled in the least by the in-filled windows still present on some historic structures, nor by the many telephone and electrical wires strung above the busy streets. Most anyone can filter out such obvious additions to the scene, whereas it is difficult for even the period expert to conjure a corrected mental picture of the sanitized reconstructions that have been attempted. Blockley also points out, however, that intensive visitor use can be detrimental in areas where archaeological contexts still survive—a concern that should be heeded at many sites open to the public.

The case of the reconstructed Byzantine village house at Qasrin, which Ann Killebrew ably examines, illustrates practically the entire range of troubling consequences associated with reconstruction and poses interesting parallels with the blacksmith shop at Mt. Vernon. While the effort can be praised for its attempt to depict daily life, in contrast with the usual emphasis on monumental architecture, the decision to focus interpretation entirely on one of several periods at this multicomponent site robs visitors of the ability to comprehend its full meaning. Moreover, that limitation is clearly intended to advance political claims of Jewish sovereignty.

Characterizing the interpretive program's exclusion of data unrelated to that mission as a "misuse" of the past, however, seems an overly harsh indictment. At least the data were collected responsibly at Qasrin, if not used in the interpretation. In every depiction of the past, the interpreter winnows the facts and repeatedly makes conscious choices about which facts to emphasize. This is true of historians, biographers, film directors, and even archaeologists. The past is always viewed through a lens that obscures as much as it reveals, and it is constantly reinterpreted in light of new cultural realities. As academics, we might wish for complete and objective truth in all depictions of the past, but we must accept the fact that selective use of the past can serve many equally legitimate purposes apart from the intrinsic value of accumulated knowledge.

Ron Williamson's review of reconstruction efforts in eastern Canada reveals a fundamental shift of emphasis from one that championed the dominant European heritage and discouraged divisive themes to one that now includes native points of view and controversial challenges to traditional interpretations of the past. No doubt, this reflects the Canadian government's raised awareness of a broader social history enriched by other voices. But it also reflects the increasing inclusion of native peoples in the design and execution of site reconstructions, as well as the fact that some tribal governments are now undertaking their own heritage tourism programs. The result is a more balanced representation of Canadian history and one that has new relevance to native peoples, as demonstrated by their increased visitation at many reconstructed sites.

Lingering questions and heated debates about the aboveground appearance of certain longhouse types may enthrall academics, but they need not unduly inhibit the designs of reconstructions. After all, unless there should exist written accounts of those who actually saw the structures at a particular site, in most cases an archaeologist will at best be able to determine only the footprint of a longhouse or, if one is extremely fortunate, special activity areas with a structure. Designs that are not fully supported by hard data, however, should be based on at least sound interpretations.

Fort Loudon in Tennessee shares much in common with other sites described in this volume—and with several eighteenth-century French sites in my own experience farther north. Here an entire site was threatened by a public works project, and the only viable solution for mitigating the inundation of Fort Loudon was near-total excavation. What the land managers in charge did not have to do, of course, was to build up the location with fill and reconstruct the fort at a much higher elevation. That was a choice for which they deserve commendation.

Joe Distretti and Carl Kuttruff disclose that the initial decision to reconstruct was based on many factors other than education, which by now should be almost axiomatic. They also point out that the reconstruction is both imperfect and incomplete, as all such attempts must be, but its acknowledged artifice in at least one sense is shown to be a distinct advantage. The authors tacitly concede that a totally accurate reconstruction of the fort environment would be self-defeating, as sensibilities of modern visitors would likely be offended by the squalor. With that I must totally agree, for most people today would not even enter most early historic environments if the sites were accurate in every detail, and those who did would hardly be inclined to stay long once inside the compound. Occasional reenactments and demonstration activities hosted at the site of Fort Loudon, however, represent a reasonable attempt to re-create the former ambiance on a much smaller scale.

The reconstruction at Louisbourg, as I know from personal experience, is one of the most impressive historic sites in North America. I have probably visited scores of historic sites in the past thirty years, often while at a conference or traveling cross-country, but Louisbourg is the only one I recall seeing as a specific destination. Of course, the site is not really on the way to anywhere, so the fact that so many visitors come to see it each year is clear evidence of the potential impact heritage tourism may have on local economies.

Bruce Fry describes the economic and political motivations behind the reconstruction of Louisbourg, as well as the common problems one may encounter when implementing any reconstruction. The problems at Louisbourg were enormous, in proportion with the grand scale of this ambitious project, but some could have been avoided had planners not been so obsessively devoted to authenticity. The use of "typical" structural elements in the absence of hard evidence is a perfectly reasonable approach to reconstruction, and there is no justification for making costly changes after the fact—even in light of new archaeological evidence—when they will not affect the visitor experience. Indeed, many of the changes made at considerable expense were so minor that not even the most discerning eye would have noticed the difference.

The sites of Bent's Old Fort and Fort Union Trading Post, like the Fortress of Louisbourg, are not readily accessible as tourist attractions and were reconstructed in the interest of advancing a political and economic agenda. Unlike Louisbourg, however, these two units of the U.S. National Park System have languished in quiet obscurity with relatively low visitation (barely fifty thousand recreational visits per year between the two of them). Although there was considerable local support for both developments, neither reconstruction could have been attempted without federal backing. Fortunately, the government is not in the business of showing a profit, for gate receipts alone would never be sufficient to staff and maintain the sites.

Interestingly, Wheaton makes the point that planners failed to consider the cost and difficulty of maintaining the sites properly. In one sense, of course, structural deterioration adds an "authentic" look to historic sites, most of which were in constant disrepair while in actual use. Common sense, of course, demands that the places should be kept up, but replacement materials need not match adjacent elements exactly—thereby homogenizing the scene.

He also points to the advantage of having the project archaeologist directly involved with the historical architects and historians who were involved with planning the reconstruction at Fort Union. Although the immediacy of information exchange certainly facilitated the undertaking and advanced the pace of reconstruction, there is more to archaeology than providing data for an accurate replication of the fort's perimeter and structures within it. As in the case of Louisbourg, the Fort Union site yielded an enormous artifact assemblage, which is still undergoing study nearly a decade after completion of excavations. Fortunately, National Park Service administrators have continued to support post-field analysis even though the restoration effort that generated the data was finished long ago. But when the primary reports are all written, there will still be the continuing expense of periodic conservation treatment and perpetual curation of the collections. That is another mainte-nance cost that planners almost never take into account when reconstruction projects are contemplated.

Lynn Neal offers a compelling alternative argument for preservation in place under certain circumstances. In this interesting case from Arizona, one of several sets of stabilized prehistoric ruins in a state park environment were threatened with destruction by flooding. Unlike the situation at Fort Loudon, where inundation would be complete and virtually irreversible, here the rising waters would be more confined and their overall impact less severe. Accordingly, the affected ruins simply were buried to save them from further deterioration.

Even though one of several important park features is now obscured from pub-lic view, it still survives and could be reclaimed. I found it refreshing to see that preservation of an intact archaeological context won out over the more typical atti-tude that American know-how can overcome any natural problem and that the least-cost solution prevailed. An engineered solution is still an option for some other day, perhaps, but for now the ruins are protected until such time as more drastic measures are warranted.

As an aside, I was particularly struck by Neal's almost passing remark on con-currence of the Hopi people in this preservation effort. It is worth noting that their attitude differs markedly with another taken by at least one tribal group in northern Wisconsin that was presented with a plan to preserve some rock art in a National Park Service unit of my acquaintance. Though the petroglyph is considered a sacred site, the tribal elders insisted that it be left alone, saying they understood that nothing lasts forever and that our misplaced good intentions would only compromise its cul-tural significance. Indeed, they argued that our proposal, if implemented, would be far worse than the site vandalism it was meant to mitigate, since those defacing the petroglyph were acting out of mere thoughtlessness—their point being, of course, that anthropologists and cultural resource professionals should know better than ignorant vandals.

The virtual reality of computer reconstructions opens exciting new interpreta-tive possibilities for archaeological sites of all types and conditions. Applications using data from the site of Amarna, as described by Karen Brush, show the potential advantages of using our modern technological innovations for better understanding the human past. Indeed, the flexibility of computer simulations permits almost limit-less options in site representation, ranging from the most basic to the most elaborate of theoretical constructs.

Although the Amarna example is still in its formative stages, computer-gener-ated drawings hold great promise for scholars and for site visitors. As a research tool, graphic representations such as these offer a powerful portal through which the archaeologist can examine the past. Further, in combination with more traditional approaches to archaeological site interpretation, computer images and interactive programs have the potential to provide an increasingly sophisticated public new ways to appreciate the results of that research.

The contribution by Robert Daniels-Dwyer on photo-realism is an interesting elaboration of techniques explored in Karen Brush's chapter on Amarna. The interactive use of virtual-reality reconstructions may have particular appeal to younger minds nurtured on video games, potentially exciting them to delve more deeply into the past. At the same time, Daniels-Dwyer acknowledges the ethical concerns we must consider, when the average person interprets computers as scientific producers of "truth" and may not be able to assess the validity of visual interpretations.

That dilemma notwithstanding, 3-D computer simulations can be powerful tools for recording archaeological data and for subsequent analytical manipulation. New software developments designed for architects and builders provide a means to visualize data never before available to the archaeologist, and the implications for future research are as great as those promised by early statistical applications that were permitted by room-sized "high-speed" computers introduced in the 1960s. The fact that machines capable of even more sophisticated applications can now be held in the palm of one's hand shows how far we have come and suggests how far we may yet go.

Conclusion

The 1997 symposium that inspired this volume posed a simple question: "To reconstruct or not to reconstruct." But there is no easy answer to that question, nor do I think the proposition should be put as a choice between mutually exclusive alternatives. As we have seen from the diverse examples published here, site reconstructions may be simple or elaborate, partial or total, physical or electronic, on-site or off-site. In other words, a reconstruction need not be all or nothing. In fact, the optimum representation probably lies somewhere between the extremes and employs a wide variety of media.

A reconstruction need not be painstakingly true to the historic reality in order to be "authentic" or successful in achieving the kinds of linkages with the past that are desired by most visitors. Indeed, since there is hardly any real prospect of creating a full-blown, historically accurate reconstruction, no matter how exhaustive the research, there is little point in setting such an ambitious yet ultimately futile goal. At all times we must keep our eyes on what we want to accomplish and what can realistically be achieved.

I will conclude by saying that any archaeological site open to the public should have qualities that can stir imaginations and inspire emotional connections to the past. Further, it seems to me that the quality that can do that best is *visibility*. Pictures and artifacts on exhibit do much to convey information about the past, to be sure. Even witnessing a distant natural phenomenon like the Hale-Bopp comet, which so fascinated the world at the time of our symposium, has the power to take one's imagination back 4,200 years at a glimpse. But what can compare with actually entering a cultural environment that might have been familiar to our remote ancestors? Though we live in a time when our perceptions are jaded by common miracles and hyperbole, when it seems that nothing can surprise us, the sights, sounds, and smells of an earlier time may do just that.

I think everyone can agree that, in the best of all possible worlds, site reconstruction should be supported by sound archaeological research and that site reconstruction, in turn, can do much to promote public support for archaeology. That does not mean, however, that archaeologists hold all the answers to design questions, nor that reconstruction designers dare not extrapolate beyond information derived from archaeological research at the site. They should instead be free to fill in the gaps with what is known from other sites and the historical record. Our duty, as archaeologists involved with such undertakings, is to know the limitations of our own methods, work within them, and provide the best data we can—always mindful of the fact that the archaeological resources are finite and should not be expended needlessly.

Make no mistake about it, site reconstruction is here to stay, and heritage tourism is a growth industry the world over. Further, let us not be fooled into thinking that the fundamental question of whether to reconstruct a site will be asked of an archaeologist. More likely, it will be a politician or a banker who answers that one. In fact, the archaeologist is likely to be one of the last members attached to a reconstruction planning team.

Instead, it seems to me that we must each ask of ourselves whether we want to be a party to such enterprises. We do have the option, after all, to do other things with our careers. But if the answer to that question is "yes," those who choose to participate must make a commitment to practice good science, act ethically, work responsibly with others in the planning, counsel wisely, and take every reasonable measure to make the reconstruction the best it can be.

Moreover, we need to recognize that there are other equally legitimate points of view that sometimes are at odds with the archaeologist's most favored position. Doubtless there will be times when one must compromise on an issue, and there may even be those times when planners simply refuse to hear the project archaeologist on a point of fact or interpretation. One must then determine, with due respect paid to our professional standards, how much is tolerable for the greater good.

The answer to that question will be harder than the first, for all of us involved with reconstructions experience our moments of doubt. Some, like Roland Robbins, may decide that the better course is to withdraw quietly, whereas others will stay in hopes of making incremental progress and thereby improve the final results. None of us works in isolation, and so that decision should not be simply one of personal choice. Rather, we must all look to the larger archaeological community for guidance in the practice of our profession.

In these times, archaeology cannot advance as a viable pursuit without public support; today's professional emphasis on public education and outreach activities is ample testimony to that realization. Therefore, it should be no surprise that the archaeological community sees much to be gained through the continued development of sites for tourism, at least in principle. Unfortunately, for too long the horror tales of site reconstruction, few though they might be, are what have captured our attention.

This book represents an important contribution to the archaeological literature if it does nothing more than disabuse the more negative perceptions of site reconstruction. Among these contributions are real success stories worthy of our notice. We should learn from their good works and strive to do better still.

References

Bruner, Edward M.
　　1994　Abraham Lincoln as Authentic Reproduction: A Critique of Postmodernism. *American Anthropologist* 96(2): 397–415.

Leone, Mark P., Parker B. Potter, Jr., and Paul A. Shackel
　　1987　Toward a Critical Archaeology. *Current Anthropology* 28(3): 283–302.

Maxwell, Moreau S., and Lewis H. [sic] Binford
　　1961　Excavation at Fort Michilimackinac, Mackinac [sic] City, Michigan, 1959 Season. *Publications of The Museum, Michigan State University, Cultural Series* 1(1). East Lansing.

Noble, Vergil E.
　　1979　On Planning and Preservation. *Historical Archaeology* 13:120–122.
　　1996　Yesterday, Today, and Tomorrow: A Plea for Change in the Practice of Historical Archaeology. *Historical Archaeology* 30(2): 74–84.

South, Stanley
　　1977　*Method and Theory in Historical Archaeology.* Academic Press, New York.

Swannack, J. D.
　　1975　Mission-oriented Agencies: Means and Ends of Historic Sites Archaeology. *Historical Archaeology* 9: 81–82.

Index

About the Contributors

MARION BLOCKLEY lives in the Ironbridge Gorge World Heritage Site and was, until recently, director of the Ironbridge Institute, a postgraduate center for teaching and research, jointly managed by the University of Birmingham and the Ironbridge Gorge Museum Trust. She is currently director of an inner-city community trust, undertaking the conservation and restoration of a Humphry Repton landscaped park, funded by the Heritage Lottery Fund.

MARLEY R. BROWN III is the director of archaeological research at Colonial Williamsburg and research professor of anthropology and history at the College of William and Mary. Brown received his bachelor's and doctoral degrees in anthropology from Brown University. In 2003, he celebrated his twentieth anniversary as head of Colonial Williamsburg's archaeological research program. Before coming to Williamsburg, Brown served on the faculties of Franklin Pierce College, Brown University, and Sonoma State University. He also spent two years with the National Park Service in their San Francisco regional office. He has been interested in issues relating to archaeology and reconstruction within the outdoor living history context since the late 1960s, when he worked at Plimoth Plantation's archaeological laboratory under the direction of the late James Deetz.

KAREN A. BRUSH's doctoral research was in early medieval European archaeology (Cambridge University, United Kingdom) and she also has degrees in anthropology, geology, and geophysics. She currently serves on the board of directors for The Explorers Club, a nonprofit organization dedicated to promoting scientific exploration worldwide. She became interested in archaeological reconstructions because they were what first attracted her to archaeology and history as a child. She believes that changeable computer models are ideal for public presentation because they allow the public to understand reconstructions as alternative reconstructive hypotheses of an incompletely understood past rather than as facts.

EDWARD A. CHAPPELL is director of architectural research at Colonial Williamsburg, where he has responsibility for historic preservation, the interpretation of buildings, and restoration. He studied history and architecture at the College of William and Mary and the University of Virginia, and he has worked as a historical archaeologist in England and for the Virginia Department of Historic Resources.

ROBERT DANIELS-DWYER, after reading archaeology and anthropology at Cambridge, graduated from the University of Southampton with a M.Sc. in archaeological computing and from the University of Reading with a Ph.D. in the economics of private construction in Roman Italy. He has worked as standing buildings officer for two University of Reading projects, the Insula of the Paintings at Ostia, and the House of Amarantus at Pompeii, and he has developed three-dimensional recording and reconstruction models for these structures. Since 1998, he has worked in information management, and he is currently data quality architect at Yell, the international directories company.

JOE P. DISTRETTI is originally from the western part of Tennessee. He spent two tours with the U.S. Marines in Vietnam and then, after his discharge, attended the University of Tennessee, Knoxville. After graduate studies at UT, he joined the Tennessee State Parks System and was assigned to the nascent Fort Loudoun project in 1981. It was at this time that he and Kuttruff completed plans for the reconstruction of the fort and its environs. He continued in that position for sixteen years until he was transferred to another state park. He has taught at the University of Tennessee, Knoxville, and at Cleveland State Community College, Cleveland, Tennessee. He has served as a humanities scholar in several local historical society projects and with the East Tennessee Historical Society. His interest in colonial and military history has led to several published articles. Joe retired from the state park service in 2001. He and his wife Sharon currently reside in Muscle Shoals, Alabama, where he is activity involved in historical research.

PETER J. FOWLER (M.A., PH.D., F.S.A., F.R.HIST.S.) was secretary to the Royal Commission on Historical Monuments (England) and professor of archaeology at the University of Newcastle upon Tyne. He now lives in London and Lozére, France, writing and working as a consultant, in particular for ICOMOS/UNESCO in Paris on World Heritage matters. He is currently completing a ten-year study of the landscape archaeology of the Causses in Languedoc.

BRUCE W. FRY, after studying archaeology at the University of Cardiff, Wales, joined the Historic Sites branch of Parks Canada to work on the Fortress of Louisbourg reconstruction project. His research on the fortifications and further studies in France on the evolution of French fortifications formed the basis for a doctoral thesis. He later worked for Parks Canada as a research manager in Quebec and in Ottawa, retiring after more than thirty years to live once more in Cape Breton, close to the Fortress of Louisbourg. He taught a course in historical archaeology at the University College of Cape Breton for several years and still gives occasional lectures and tours on the fortifications and siege sites around the fortress.

JOHN H. JAMESON, JR. is a senior archaeologist with the National Park Service's Southeast Archaeological Center in Tallahassee, Florida. His twenty-plus years of federal service have encompassed a broad range of projects involving archaeological fieldwork and cultural resource management in several regions of the United States and overseas. A recognized leader in public archaeology, he is a key player in the development of training courses for park rangers and archaeologists in the effective interpretation of archaeological resources. His very first experience in the field in archaeology was as an assistant to Stanley South at Ninety Six National Historic Site in South Carolina, where a notable example of an effective reconstruction from archaeological evidence was carried out. Jameson is the originator and coordinator of the Center's Public Interpretation Initiative, a long-term public outreach program, international in scope, that has involved numerous government-sponsored symposia, training workshops, seminars, website development, and publications on the topic of public education and interpretation of cultural resources. He was the compiler/ editor of a major work on the public interpretation of archaeology, entitled *Presenting Archaeology to the Public: Digging for Truths* (AltaMira Press, 1997). His career focus on increasing public access, appreciation, and inspiration from archaeology is exemplified by his leading role in the production of *Ancient Muses: Archaeology and the Arts* (University of Alabama Press, 2003) that seeks to make archaeology "come alive" for public audiences by personalizing and demystifying the research process.

ANN E. KILLEBREW's involvement in presenting archaeological sites to the public occurred by "accident." While pursuing her Ph.D. degree in archaeology at the Hebrew University of Jerusalem, she became involved in the excavations at ancient Qasrin. Directing excavations at this major tourist site in the 1980s forced her to address the relationship between archaeology and the public on a daily basis, an experience she describes in this volume. During the past decade, her interest in public archaeology broadened to include heritage education programs. From 1998 to 2002, she coordinated and designed several heritage courses at the Ename Center for Public Archaeology and Heritage Presentation (Belgium). She currently serves as one of the principal coordinators in a joint Israeli-Palestinian heritage program entitled "Recognizing and Preserving the Common Heritage of Israel and the Palestinian National Authority" funded by the U.S. Department of State.

CARL KUTTRUFF received his B.A. in geography and anthropology at Louisiana State University in 1965, and the M.A. and Ph.D. degrees from Southern Illinois University in 1970 and 1974. His professional experience includes university teaching, extensive fieldwork, and other types of research on prehistoric and historic archaeological sites, as well as studies of museum and archival collections. His survey, excavation, and other research work on prehistoric cultures ranges from the Archaic period through the late prehistoric period, and his historic period research covers a broad range of sites and topics that span the time from the mid-eighteenth century through the 1940s. He has had a long-standing research interest in military sites including forts, fortifications, and battlefields, and he has done extensive archival and field research on military sites of the French and Indian War (Fort Loudoun), the Revolutionary War, the Civil War, early-twentieth-century seacoast defenses, and World War II. He has done research in Illinois, Missouri, Tennessee, Arkansas, Alabama, Mississippi, Louisiana, Texas, South Carolina, and New York, as well as Mexico, Poland, the Philippine Islands, the Marshall Islands, and Wake Island. He is currently an adjunct professor in human ecology at Louisiana State University and a consulting archaeologist.

DONALD W. LINEBAUGH is the director of the Program for Archaeological Research (PAR) and an assistant professor of anthropology at the University of Kentucky. The PAR conducts archaeological, architectural, and historical research for government and private organizations on a grant and contractual basis. Prior to joining the faculty at Kentucky in 1997, he served for nine years as the co-director of the Center for Archaeological Research and as adjunct assistant professor of anthropology at the College of William and Mary. Don was named to the faculty of the Historic Preservation Program in the University of Kentucky's College of Architecture in 2001. He is the current editor of *Kentucky Archaeology*, the newsletter of the Kentucky Organization of Professional Archaeologists, and features editor for the *VAN - Vernacular Architecture Newsletter*. His research interests are broad and include a range of topics: the development of urban centers; the history of archaeology and historic preservation; historic landscapes and the natural and cultural environment; seventeenth- and eighteenth-century plantations in the Tidewater Chesapeake; archaeological excavation and preservation of industrial and craft/trade sites; ethnicity, particularly the interaction of German and English cultures in the Valley of Virginia and into Kentucky; and, most recently, New England town studies. He is finishing a book project based on his dissertation work on archaeologist Roland Robbins, titled *The Man Who Found Thoreau: Roland Wells Robbins and the Search for New England's Buried Past*.

BARRY MACKINTOSH is a former bureau historian for the National Park Service in Washington, D.C. Before coming to Washington in 1970 as an assistant to NPS chief historian Robert Utley, he served as park historian at two parks with controversial reconstructions, Fort Caroline National Memorial in Florida and Booker T. Washington National Monument in Virginia. With current chief historian, Dwight Pitcaithley, he has been an outspoken critic of inauthentic reconstructions.

SUSAN MILLS studied English and related literature at the University of York and Anglo-Saxon and Viking Studies at the University of Durham. She has excavated on Roman and early medieval sites in northern England, Scotland, Orkney, and Shetland. For several years, she was a medieval pottery researcher in the Department of Archaeology, University of Durham. In 1986, she became curator of the Bede Monastery Museum in Jarrow. She worked there throughout its period of major development, as the museum evolved into Bede's World, with a striking new museum and an experimental early medieval farm and landscape. In November 1999, she became the museum and heritage officer for Clackmannanshire Council in central Scotland. She is based in Alloa, where she is in the process of establishing a new museum, archives, and local history center for Clackmannanshire, a county which has suffered considerable economic decline in recent years with the loss of its core textile and brewing industries. Beyond a purely educational mission, the goals of the new center are to facilitate heritage tourism as well as a stronger infrastructure and sense of civic pride.

HAROLD MYTUM is reader in the Department of Archaeology at the University of York, England. He has directed excavations and been involved with reconstructions at Castell Henllys Iron Age fort site for over two decades, and is currently writing a monograph on the project. Research interests include western Britain and Ireland from later prehistory to modern times and historical archaeology (particularly burials and memorial monuments), as well as experimental archaeology and public interpretation.

LYNN A. NEAL has been a practicing archaeologist in the private and public sectors for fifteen years. She currently serves as director of the Cultural Resources Program for EnviroSystems Management, Inc., in Flagstaff, Arizona. Neal received her master of arts degree in applied archaeology from Northern Arizona University in 1990. Under the applied program, Neal was trained as a ruins preservationist through a National Park Service internship, and has since conducted dozens of hands-on preservation projects and presented workshops for the public and private sectors to provide a better understanding of the cultural resource compliance process and as a means of educating developers about historic preservation alternatives. She has also been actively involved in refining methodologies related to long-term monitoring and preservation planning and has served as a preservation consultant to the National Park Service, Arizona State Parks, and private landowners and developers. Ms. Neal has directed numerous projects throughout Arizona, southern Utah, southeast Nevada, and New Mexico. She has also worked in southern California, southwest Colorado, Guam, and Saipan, and has done underwater archaeology in Jamaica and at Glen Canyon National Recreation Area.

VERGIL E. NOBLE has thirty years of experience in historical archaeology of the midwestern United States, with particular emphasis on the eighteenth-century French fur trade in the upper Great Lakes and Mississippi River valley. He received a doctorate in anthropology from Michigan State University in 1983. Much of his archaeological fieldwork has been associated with projects related to reconstruction of colonial fortifications and, more recently, the restoration of extant historic structures, including several presidential homes. Noble has been an archaeologist with the National Park Service since 1987 and currently coordinates the external technical assistance program for archaeological National Historic Landmark properties in the thirteen-state Midwest Region. He is a past president of the Society for Historical Archaeology.

DWIGHT PITCAITHLEY has worked in the National Park Service since 1976, rising to the position of chief historian in 1995. Much of his work focuses on encouraging the National Park Service to act as fertile environment for interdisciplinary cooperation in the humanities and between the humanities and the natural sciences as they address their central responsibilities: to preserve, research, and educate. He is an adjunct professor at George Mason University and is active in many historical societies, serving on the editorial board for the publication *The Public Historian,* and as president for the National Council on Public History. He has published numerous notable articles including: "Historic Sites: What Can Be Learned by Them," "The American Civil War and the Preservation of Memory," and "The Future of the NPS History Program." Throughout his career, he has been an outspoken critic of unauthenticated reconstructions.

RODD L. WHEATON is the assistant regional director, Cultural Resources and Partnerships, for the Intermountain Region of the National Park Service. He holds a bachelor's degree in architecture from the University of Idaho and a master of architectural history degree from the University of Virginia. Upon graduation, he worked for architect Orin M. Bullock, Jr., FAIA, in Baltimore, Maryland, before joining the National Park Service in 1972 as a historical architect for the Historic American Buildings Survey in Washington, D.C. From Washington, Mr. Wheaton relocated to Denver, Colorado, in 1974 to join the cultural resource staff of the newly formed Rocky Mountain Region, as the regional historical architect. That position, and various manifestations as branch chief and division chief, involved the reconstructions of Bent's Old Fort and Fort Union Trading Post. At Bent's Old Fort, Mr. Wheaton was involved primarily in maintenance concerns for preserving the reconstruction's integrity. For Fort Union Trading Post, Mr. Wheaton was the project director for the region and provided oversight on all aspects of the reconstruction including the archaeology that was conducted by the Midwest Archaeological Center. In 1995, Mr. Wheaton assumed the position of assistant regional director for the newly formed Intermountain Region that includes eight states from Texas to Montana.

ESTHER C. WHITE has been the on the archaeological staff at Mount Vernon, George and Martha Washington's Potomac River plantation, since 1989, directing the archaeological research since 1994. Mount Vernon's archaeologists are currently excavating a 1797 whiskey distillery, in preparation of an anticipated reconstruction where the process of creating spirits in the eighteenth century is interpreted. A native of Greensboro, North Carolina, Ms. White graduated from the University of North Carolina at Chapel Hill with a B.A. in history and anthropology, and holds an M.A. in historical archaeology from the College of William and Mary.

RONALD F. WILLIAMSON received his Ph.D. in anthropology from McGill University and is senior partner and chief archaeologist with Archaeological Services, Inc., the largest archaeological consulting firm in Ontario, Canada. The corporation provides a variety of archaeological consulting and heritage planning services. Dr. Williamson has directed hundreds of archaeological consulting projects over the past twenty years, including more than a dozen archaeological master planning studies for Ontario municipalities. In addition to many scholarly books and articles, he has cowritten a number of popular accounts of the pre-contact archaeology of southern Ontario. He is an adjunct professor in the Department of Anthropology at the University of Toronto and is an associate member of the graduate faculty. He is also a former president of the Canadian Association of Professional Heritage Consultants, a national organization dedicated to furthering the cause of heritage resource conservation and excellence in heritage consultation.